T0076054

Get the eBook FREE!

(PDF, ePub, Kindle, and liveBook all included)

We believe that once you buy a book from us, you should be
able to read it in any format we have available. To get electronic
versions of this book at no additional cost to you, purchase and
then register this book at the Manning website.

Go to https://www.manning.com/freebook and follow the
instructions to complete your pBook registration.

That's it!
Thanks from Manning!

Cloud Observability
in Action

MICHAEL HAUSENBLAS

MANNING
SHELTER ISLAND

For online information and ordering of this and other Manning books, please visit
www.manning.com. The publisher offers discounts on this book when ordered in quantity.
For more information, please contact

Special Sales Department
Manning Publications Co.
20 Baldwin Road
PO Box 761
Shelter Island, NY 11964
Email: orders@manning.com

 Manning Publications Co.
20 Baldwin Road
PO Box 761
Shelter Island, NY 11964

Development editor: Ian Hough
Technical editor: Jamie Riedesel
Review editor: Aleks Dragosavljević
Production editor: Deirdre Blanchfield-Hiam
Copy editor: Christian Berk
Proofreader: Katie Tennant
Technical proofreader: Ernest Gabriel Bossi Carranza
Typesetter: Dennis Dalinnik
Cover designer: Marija Tudor

ISBN: 9781633439597
Printed in the United States of America

To my family: my wife Anneliese; our kids Iannis, Ranya, Saphira;
as well as Snoopy the dog and Charles the cat

brief contents

contents

preface

We truly live in exciting times! The rise of cloud-native technologies, starting some 10 years ago with Docker and Kubernetes, and the availability of cloud offerings that enable you to run large-scale applications based on a microservices architecture have changed the way we write and operate software.

I had the luck and pleasure of being part of that journey, starting in the container space in 2015 and then working in the Kubernetes space until 2021. There was one aspect of cloud native that stood out to me: given the dynamics of containers and function-as-a-service, if you don't have insights into what's going on in your system and aren't able to ask ad hoc questions about the state and trends, you're effectively driving a car blindfolded. When I changed teams in AWS to focus on observability, Open-Telemetry had just been formed, and the space was quickly developing. Now, at the time of publication, it's fair to say that observability has gone mainstream.

One thing that I only realized in hindsight was that what drew me to the observability space, besides the open source nature of the ecosystem around the Cloud Native Computing Foundation (CNCF) project, was the fact that observability is essentially an application area of data engineering. It's about generating, collecting, storing, and querying data, based on pipelines. Why do I point this out? Before I got into the world of containers, I spent more than a decade in data engineering, first in applied research and then in a start-up, where I got to apply the lessons learned, back in the "big data" days.

When the opportunity came to share what I had learned in the past 20 years, both in the data engineering and cloud-native spaces, in the context of providing a hands-on guide for observability, it was clear to me that this is the right time and place. The basic idea was to cover the entire observability space, from where the data is generated to how it is collected and processed to how it is consumed by humans and software—all with the goal of understanding observability's underlying principles and methods, using open source software for demonstration so that anyone interested in the topic can try it out themselves, without having to worry about costs.

I hope this book serves as a reference and guide on your journey to introducing observability in your organization. It will have served its purpose if it helps you create solutions that enable your team to benefit from cloud-native offerings, without flying blind.

acknowledgments

Writing a book is a long-term commitment, usually a year or longer. While this is not my first book, and I was able to apply lessons learned from the past experiences, it goes without saying that the outcome is something I didn't achieve on my own, as a number of people helped shape and improve this book.

To start, I'd like to thank my family, who supported and motivated me the entire time! Next, I'd like to say a big thank you to Ian Hough, my editor at Manning, for all your guidance (and patience). While I spent most of the time with Ian, there are several folks at Manning who helped make this book a reality, and I am grateful for everything you did: Malena Selic, Marina Matesic, Ivan Martinović, Rebecca Rinehart, Stjepan Jurekovic, Ana Romac, Susan Honeywell, Mike Stephens, and Marjan Bace. I also thank my project editor, Deirdre Blanchfield-Hiam; my copy editor, Christian Berk; my proofreader, Katie Tennant; and my technical proofreader, Ernest Gabriel Bossi Carranza.

My stellar tech editor, Jamie Riedesel, deserves a huge shout-out! Jamie is a staff engineer at Dropbox with over twenty years of experience in IT. She influenced and shaped this book significantly, providing guidance on how to explain things, feedback on technical aspects, and motivation to try even harder. Thank you. But I'd also like to thank a number of folks who provided feedback on various chapters, sharing valuable insights: Frederic Branczyk, Matthias Loibl, Kit Merker; and Manning reviewers Adrian Buturuga, Alessandro Campeis, Bhavin Thaker, Bobby Lin, Borko Djurkovic, Chris Haggstrom, Clifford Thurber, Doyle Turner, Ernesto Bossi, Fernando Bernardino, Filipe Teixeira, Ganesh Swaminathan, Ian Bartholomew, Ioannis Atsonios, Jakub

Warczarek, Jan Krueger, Jorge Ezequiel Bo, Juan Luis, Ken Finnigan, Kent Spill er, Kosmas Chatzimichalis, Maciej Drozdzowski, Madhav Ayyagari, Michael Bright, Michele Di Pede, Miguel Montalvo, Onofrei George, Pablo Chacin, Rahul Modpur, Rui Liu, Sander Zegveld, Sanjeev Jaiswal, Satadru Roy, Sebastian Czech, Stefan Turalski, Stephen Muss, Vivek Dhami, and Wesley Rolnick.

Finally, thanks go to my awesome colleagues at AWS for their support and feedback as well as the open source communities of which I've been a part, especially in the context of CNCF. It has been an honor and a pleasure.

about this book

Observability is the capability to continuously generate and discover actionable insights based on signals from the (cloud-native) system under observation, with the goal of influencing the system. We approach the topic from a return-on-investment perspective: we look at costs and benefits, from the sources to telemetry (including agents) to the signal destinations (backends), including time series data stores, such as Prometheus, and frontends, such as Grafana.

Throughout the book, I use open source tooling, including, but not limited to, OpenTelemetry (collector), Prometheus, Loki, Jaeger, and Grafana to demonstrate the different concepts and enable you to experiment with them without any costs, other than your time.

Who should read this book

The book focuses primarily on developers, DevOps/site reliability engineers (SREs), who are working with cloud-native applications. It is meant for anyone interested in running cloud-native applications, be that in Kubernetes or using function-as-a-service offerings, such as AWS Lambda.

Also, I believe that if you are a release manager, an IT architect, a security and network engineer, a tech lead, or a product manager in the cloud-native space, you can benefit from the book. The book can be used with any public cloud (I use AWS for several demonstrations, purely for the sake of familiarity) as well as with any cloud-native setup on-prem (e.g., Kubernetes in the data center).

How this book is organized

The book has 11 chapters and an appendix with the following content:

- Chapter 1 provides you with an end-to-end example and defines the terminology, from sources to agents to destinations. It also discusses use cases, roles, and challenges in the context of observability.
- Chapter 2 discusses different telemetry signal types (logs, metrics, and traces), when to use which signal, how to collect signals, and the associated costs and benefits.
- Chapter 3 covers signal sources, where telemetry is generated. We discuss the types of sources that exist and when to select which source, how you can gain actionable insights from selecting the right sources for a task, and how to deal with instrumenting code you own, including supply chain aspects.
- Chapter 4 discusses different telemetry agents from log routers to OpenTelemetry. You will learn how to select and use agents, with an emphasis on what OpenTelemetry brings to the table for unified telemetry management.
- Chapter 5 focuses on backend destinations for telemetry signals, acting as the source of truth. You will learn to use and select backends for logs, metrics, and traces, with deep dives into time series databases, like Prometheus, and column-oriented datastores, such as ClickHouse.
- Chapter 6 discusses observability frontends as the place where you consume the telemetry signals. You will learn about pure frontends and all-in-ones as well as how to go about selecting them.
- Chapter 7 covers an aspect of cloud-native solutions called *cloud operations*, including how to detect when something is not working the way that it should; react to abnormal behavior; and learn from previous mistakes. You will also learn about alerting, usage, and cost tracking.
- Chapter 8 dives deep on distributed tracing and how it can help you understand and troubleshoot microservices.
- Chapter 9 dives deep into observability for developers, covering continuous profiling and developer productivity tooling.
- Chapter 10 discusses service level objectives, showing you how to use them to address the question of how satisfied the consumer of a service is.
- Chapter 11 dives deep into signal correlation, addressing the challenge of a single telemetry signal type usually not being able to answer all of your observability questions and what you can do to address this challenge.
- The appendix walks you through a complete end-to-end example, using OpenTelemetry, Prometheus, Jaeger, and Grafana.

Chapters 2 through 6 provide the conceptual foundation, so if you're entirely new to the observability space, I'd recommend working through those first. Chapters 7 through

11 focus on certain operational or development-related aspects of observability, capturing best practices, and you can read them out of order, if you prefer to do so.

About the code

This book contains many examples of source code both in numbered listings and in line with normal text. In both cases, source code is formatted in a `fixed-width font` `like this` to separate it from ordinary text.

In many cases, the original source code has been reformatted; we've added line breaks and reworked indentation to accommodate the available page space in the book. In rare cases, even this was not enough, and listings include line-continuation markers (➥). Additionally, comments in the source code have often been removed from the listings when the code is described in the text. Code annotations accompany many of the listings, highlighting important concepts.

You can get executable snippets of code from the liveBook (online) version of this book at https://livebook.manning.com/book/cloud-observability-in-action. The complete code for the examples in the book is available for download from the Manning website at https://www.manning.com/books/cloud-observability-in-action, and from GitHub at https://github.com/mhausenblas/o11y-in-action.cloud/tree/main/code.

liveBook discussion forum

Purchase of *Cloud Observability in Action* includes free access to liveBook, Manning's online reading platform. Using liveBook's exclusive discussion features, you can attach comments to the book globally or to specific sections or paragraphs. It's a snap to make notes for yourself, ask and answer technical questions, and receive help from the author and other users. To access the forum, go to https://livebook.manning.com/book/cloud-observability-in-action/discussion. You can also learn more about Manning's forums and the rules of conduct at https://livebook.manning.com/discussion.

Manning's commitment to our readers is to provide a venue where a meaningful dialogue between individual readers and between readers and the author can take place. It is not a commitment to any specific amount of participation on the part of the author, whose contribution to the forum remains voluntary (and unpaid). We suggest you try asking him some challenging questions lest his interest stray! The forum and the archives of previous discussions will be accessible from the publisher's website as long as the book is in print.

Online resources

If you want to dive deeper into certain topics, check out the following online resources:

- The further reading section of the book (https://o11y-in-action.cloud/further-reading/), which lists articles, books, and tooling

- "Return on Investment Driven Observability" (https://arxiv.org/abs/2303.13402), a short article I published that discusses challenges that arise when rolling out observability in organizations and how you can, grounded in return on investment (ROI) analysis, address said challenges
- The OpenTelemetry blog (https://opentelemetry.io/blog/)

about the author

Michael Hausenblas works in the Amazon Web Services (AWS) open source observability service team, where he leads the OpenTelemetry activities. He has more than 20 years of experience in data engineering and cloud-native systems. Before AWS, Michael worked at Red Hat on Kubernetes, Mesosphere (now D2iQ) on Mesos and Kubernetes, MapR (now part of HPE) as chief data engineer, and spent more than a decade in applied research in the symbolic AI space.

about the cover illustration

The figure on the cover of *Cloud Observability in Action* is "Cauchoise," or "Woman from the Caux," taken from a collection by Jacques Grasset de Saint-Sauveur, published in 1797. Each illustration is finely drawn and colored by hand.

In those days, it was easy to identify where people lived and what their trade or station in life was just by their dress. Manning celebrates the inventiveness and initiative of the computer business with book covers based on the rich diversity of regional culture centuries ago, brought back to life by pictures from collections such as this one.

End-to-end observability

In cloud-native environments, such as public cloud offerings like AWS or on-premises infrastructure (e.g., a Kubernetes cluster), one typically deals with many moving parts. These parts range from the infrastructure layer, including compute (e.g., VMs or containers) and databases, to the application code you own.

Depending on your role and the environment, you may be responsible for any number of the pieces in the puzzle. Let's have a look at a concrete example: consider a serverless Kubernetes environment in a cloud provider. In this case, both the Kubernetes control plane and the data plane (the worker nodes) are managed for you, which means you can focus on your application code in terms of operations.

No matter what part you're responsible for, you want to know what's going on so that you can react to and, ideally, even proactively manage situations such as a sudden usage spike (because the marketing department launched a 25%-off campaign without telling you) or due to a third-party integration failing and impacting your application. The scope of components you own or can directly influence determines what you should be focusing on in terms of observability.

The bottom line is that you don't want to fly blind. What exactly this means in the context of cloud-native systems is what we will explore in this chapter in a hands-on manner. While it's important to see things in action, as we progress, we will also try to capture the gist of the concepts via more formal means, including definitions.

This book assumes you are familiar with cloud-native environments. In general, you would expect to find microservice architectures, a large number of relatively short-lived components working together to provide the functionality. This includes cloud provider services (I'm using AWS to demonstrate the ideas here); container technologies, including Docker and Kubernetes; and function-as-a-service (FaaS) offerings, especially AWS Lambda. In case you want to read up, here are some suggestions:

- *Kubernetes in Action, Second Edition*, by Marko Lukša (Manning, 2020)
- *AWS Lambda in Action* by Danilo Poccia (Manning, 2016)

Further, I recommend *Software Telemetry* by Jamie Riedesel (Manning, 2021), which is complementary to this book and provides useful deep dives into certain observability aspects we won't dive into in detail in this book.

In this book, we focus on cloud-native environments. We mainly use open source observability tooling so that you can try out everything without licensing costs. However, it is important to understand that while we use open source tooling to show the concepts in action, they are universally applicable. That is, in a professional environment, you should always consider offloading parts or all of the tooling to the managed offerings your cloud provider of choice has or, equally, the offerings of observability vendors such as Datadog, Splunk, New Relic, Honeycomb, or Dynatrace. Before we get into cloud-native environments and what observability means in that context, let's step back a bit and look at it from a conceptual level.

1.1   What is observability?

What is observability, and why should you care? When we say *observability*, we mean trying to understand the internal system state via measuring data available to the outside. Typically, we do this to act upon it.

Before we get to a more formal definition of observability, let's review a few core concepts we will be using throughout the book:

- *System*—Short for *system under observation* (SUO). This is the cloud-native platform (and applications running on it) you care about and are responsible for.
- *Signals*—Information observable from the outside of a system. There are different signal types (the most common are logs, metrics, and traces), and they are generated by sources. Chapter 2 covers the signal types in detail.

- *Sources*—Part of the infrastructure and application layer, such as a microservice, a device, a database, a message queue, or the operating system. They typically must be instrumented to emit signals. We will discuss sources in chapter 3.
- *Agents*—Responsible for signal collection, processing, and routing. Chapter 4 is dedicated to agents and their usage.
- *Destinations*—Where you consume signals, for different reasons and use cases. These include visualizations (e.g., dashboards), alerting, long-term storage (for regulatory purposes), and analytics (finding new usages for an app). We will dive deep into backend and frontend destinations in chapters 5 and 6, respectively.
- *Telemetry*—The process of collecting signals from sources, routing or preprocessing via agents, and ingestion to destinations.

Figure 1.1 provides you with a visual depiction of observability. The motivation is to gather signals from a system represented by a collection of sources via agents to destinations for consumption by either a human or an app, with the goal of understanding and influencing the system.

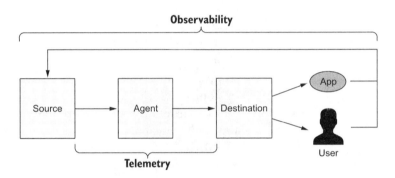

Figure 1.1   Observability overview

Observability represents, in essence, a feedback loop. A human user might, for example, restart a service based on the gathered information. In the case of an app, this could be a cluster autoscaler that adds worker nodes based on the system utilization measured.

The most important aspect of observability is to provide actionable insights. Simply displaying an error message in a log line or having a dashboard with fancy graphics is not sufficient.

DEFINITION   *Observability* is the capability to continuously generate and discover actionable insights based on signals from the system under observation, with the goal of influencing the system.

The field of observability is growing and covering more and more domains, including developer observability (which we will cover in chapter 9) and data observability.

But how do you know what signals are relevant, and how do you make the most out of them? Before we get to this topic, let's first step back a bit to set the scene, have a look at common observability use cases, and define roles and tasks.

1.2 *Observability use cases*

Observability is a means to an end. In other words, when you have a certain challenge or task at hand you want to address, observability supports you in achieving said task faster or managing said challenge more effectively. Let's have a look at common use cases now and see what kind of requirements arise from them:

- *Understanding the impact of code changes*—As a developer, you often add a new feature or fix bugs in your code base. How do you understand the impact of these code changes? What are the relevant data points you need to assess the (potentially negative) effects, such as slower execution or more resource usage?
- *Understanding third-party dependencies*—As a developer, you may use things that are outside of your control—for example, external APIs (payment, location services, etc.). How do you know they are available, healthy, and performing as they should?
- *Measuring user experience (UX)*—As a developer, site reliability engineer (SRE), or operator, you want to make sure your app or service is responsive and reliable. How and where do you measure this?
- *Tracking health and performance*—As an operator, you want to be able to understand the health of your service or app, which can include the overall uptime, the response time distribution, and the parties impacted by a partial or full outage (e.g., paying customers, free-tier users, or canary accounts).
- *Blast radius exploration*—Just like health and UX, on a more fundamental level, you may wish to understand the blast radius for any of your direct apps or services and the underlying platform (e.g., a deployment running in a Kubernetes cluster). How can you tell whether an error is in your app or in the Kubernetes data plane or underlying VM?
- *Optimizing a service*—As a developer, you want to carry out optimizations, including performance, resource usage, costs, and response time of your service. How can you measure these?
- *Increasing developer productivity*—As a service owner or engineering manager, you're interested in your developers being productive. Now, a set of big screens and a comfy gaming chair sure help with that, as well as a no-meeting Monday, Tuesday, and Friday. But how can you measure developer productivity around the code produced from a long-term (maintenance) perspective?
- *Auditing access and tracking compliance*—As an operator, you want to keep track of who has access to different services and customer data, for example. How does your system capture both permissions and access, automatically allow you to alert on unauthorized access, and provide you with an audit trail in case of inspection (for regulatory purposes, let's say)?

This was just a very concise and compressed taste of potential observability use cases. If you would like to learn more about observability use cases, signals, and methods, I strongly encourage you to peruse the "Observability Whitepaper" (which I had the pleasure of contributing to; http://mng.bz/ EQJO) by the Cloud Native Computing Foundation's Technical Advisory Group for Observability or, more informally, *CNCF TAG o11y.* (The term *o11y* refers to *observability*).

> ### Observability vs. monitoring
> Is *observability* just a new buzzword for *monitoring*, or are these distinct concepts that relate to each other? When monitoring, you're looking at the health of a system (e.g., your platform or a particular service). Observability is conceptually broader; while health is still relevant, it also considers changes in your system, such as what the impact of a code change is or what external dependencies contribute to (for example, the p90 of the response time of one of your services). Marketing terms aside, you can think of monitoring as shorthand for *system health and performance-related observability*, and that's how I will treat it in this book.

With some use cases under our belts, let's move on to different roles within an organization. We'll discuss their goals and tasks to more fully appreciate and understand how observability can assist different people on your team and in the wider organization.

1.3 Roles and goals

Nowadays, building products is a team sport. Except in the case of a small tool, a variety of different job functions or roles typically work together to realize a software-based offering. The different roles involved in the software creation and operation process focus on different tasks along the application life cycle:

- *Developers*—Developers write code, test and document it, and make artifacts, such as a container image, a binary, or a script (for interpreted languages, such as Python), available for deployment. Observability can help to more quickly iterate (finding bugs via logs and traces), optimize runtime behavior (identifying slow code paths via traces), and support operations (via metrics and logs).
- *Release and test engineers*—A release engineer can own CI and/or CD pipelines and needs visibility into build, test, and deploy processes. In this context, some organizations have a dedicated tester (or QA tester) role that has similar requirements as those for release engineers.
- *DevOps roles*—Some teams have DevOps roles, which are partially responsible for code, often own operations (are on call), and establish and enforce good practices. Similar considerations as with developers apply concerning observability, and in addition, metrics are typically useful for either dashboards or alerts. One notable DevOps role is an SRE, who coaches developers or supports other DevOps roles, helping them to meet certain operational goals (we will come back to that in the last chapter on SLOs and SLIs).

- *Infrastructure and platform operations*—In environments that are not cloud native, these are usually called *system administrators* or *sysadmins*. They own the platform (IaaS or containers) and provide (self-service) access to the platform to developers and DevOps roles. They are usually interested in low-level signals, such as utilization of resources and cost-related signals.
- *Nonengineering roles*—A product owner is often called a *product (or project) manager* and owns a feature, a service, or an entire application, depending on the scope and size. These roles usually focus on end user–facing indicators as well as performance and usability. Another nontechnical role is that of a business stakeholder. They represent the part of the organization that specifies the requirements and usually focuses on financial indicators, such as usage, revenue, or units sold. For this role, technical indicators are usually irrelevant. Table 1.1 shows example observability flows across the roles discussed in this section.

Table 1.1 Example flows per role

Role	Example flow
Developer	Uses traces to figure out which microservice along the request path is slow
Developer	Uses continuous profiling to speed up the hot path of a microservice
DevOps	Receives an alert about a component being down and then uses metrics plotted in a dashboard to understand the alert in context
DevOps	Uses metrics to narrow down components causing high latency; then jumps to traces to drill into a specific request path; and then looks at logs of one microservice, serving on that request path for details (correlation)
SRE	Tracks goals and their fulfillment, advising developers via dashboards
Platform operator	Uses a cluster-level dashboard to track autoscaling over time
Release engineer	Uses a dashboard to monitor the build progress of a microservice artifact (e.g., a container image) to, for example, prevent performance regressions
Product manager	Uses a CD dashboard to monitor deployment progress of microservices
Business stakeholder	Uses a dashboard to track weekly revenue and SLA violations

Let's now have a look at a concrete example of a cloud-native system, the signal sources, and telemetry.

1.4   *Example microservices app*

We will be using Weaveworks's microservices application, Sock Shop (https://microservices-demo.github.io/), to explore observability. Figure 1.2 shows its overall architecture. The Sock Shop example app is a simple demo app built using different languages and frameworks (Spring Boot, Go kit, and Node.js) and is packaged using Open Container Initiative–compliant container images. This makes it widely usable from container orchestrators, such as Kubernetes, Docker Compose, and ECS, as well as in FaaSs, such as AWS Lambda. We will show the example app running in Kubernetes.

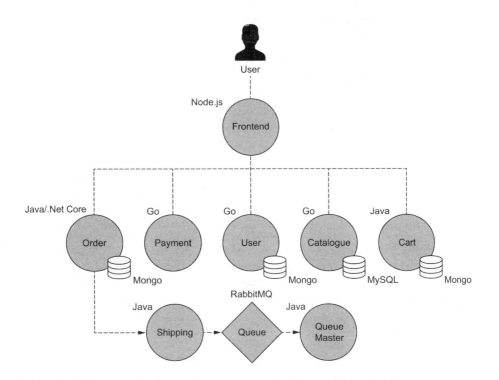

Figure 1.2　The example microservices app we use for observability exploration

> **TIP**　Throughout the book, you will find me using a didactical device to explain concepts along the boundaries of logs, metrics, and traces. This is purely to structure the content and make it easier for you to learn and find information. The practical reality is much messier, since projects and products have the tendency to expand their scopes; therefore, a clear-cut explanation, such as "This thing is for logs" or "Use XYZ for metrics," is in most cases not applicable in the real world.

To set up the example microservices app, you need a Kubernetes cluster. Then, follow the steps in the following listing.

Listing 1.1　Local observability

Clones the example app repo and changes into the directory where the Kubernetes deployment YAML docs are located

```
$ git clone https://github.com/microservices-demo/microservices-demo.git && \
    cd microservices-demo/deploy/kubernetes/

$ kubectl create namespace sock-shop
```

Creates a Kubernetes namespace that acts as a logical home for our app

```
$ kubectl apply -f complete-demo.yaml

$ kubectl -n sock-shop port-forward svc/front-end 8888:80
```

Creates all necessary Kubernetes resources (deployments, services, etc.) that together make up the app; if you want to keep an eye on it, waiting until all resources are ready, you can (in a different terminal session) use the watch kubectl -n sock-shop get deploy,pod,svc command.

Once all pods are ready, you can make the frontend accessible on your local machine using the port-forward command.

If you successfully set up the Sock Shop app, you can access the entry point (the front-end service) in your browser. Head over to http://localhost:8888, and you should see something akin to what is depicted in figure 1.3.

Next, you want to generate some traffic, so log in (in the right-hand upper corner) with the username user and the password password, and then add some items to your shopping cart. Now, what about observability? Let's have a look at a concrete example end to end.

The Sock Shop example app emits various signals. Let's take a closer look at two signal types, logs and metrics, to explore what exactly is emitted and what would be necessary to introduce observability for a given role.

In terms of the logs signal type, Sock Shop services emit a variety of logs. One example, looking at the orders service, is as follows (output edited to fit):

```
$ kubectl logs deploy/orders
2021-10-25 14:33:10.649  INFO [bootstrap,,,] 7 --- [           main] s.c.a.
AnnotationConfigApplicationContext : Refreshing org.springframework.context.
annotation.AnnotationConfigApplicationContext@51521cc1: startup date
[Mon Oct 25 14:33:10 GMT 2021]; root of context hierarchy
2021-10-25 14:33:16.838  INFO [bootstrap,,,] 7 --- [           main] tratio
Delegate$BeanPostProcessorChecker : Bean 'configurationPropertiesRebinderAu
toConfiguration' of type [class org.springframework.cloud.autoconfigure.Con
figurationPropertiesRebinderAutoConfiguration$$EnhancerBySpringCGLIB$$b894f
39] is not eligible for getting processed by all BeanPostProcessors (for ex
ample: not eligible for auto-proxying)
...
```

In this case, the source is the orders service, and the signal type is logs.

> **NOTE** Nearly everyone uses logs (in contrast to metrics or even traces), yet there is much less standardization and interoperability going on in this signal type compared to others. While OpenTelemetry is, at the time of publication, stable for traces and almost stable for metrics, we're still working in the community to achieve a similar level of coverage for logs.

To make the logs actionable, for a developer to fix a bug, for example, we would need the following:

- An agent (like Fluent Bit) to route the logs to a destination
- A destination, such as OpenSearch or CloudWatch

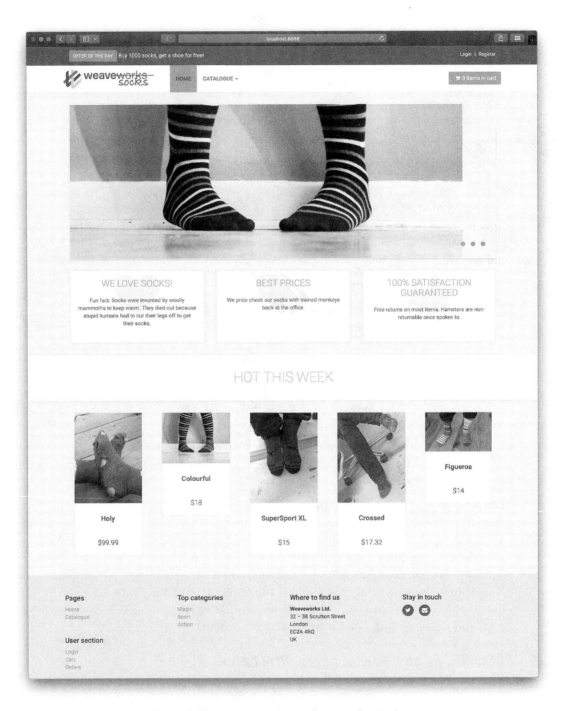

Figure 1.3   Screenshot of the Sock Shop example microservices app frontend

The services also expose metrics in the Prometheus exposition format (e.g., looking at the `front-end` service we forwarded to the local machine earlier). The following output is edited to fit:

```
$ curl localhost:8888/metrics
# HELP process_cpu_user_seconds_total Total user CPU time spent in seconds.
# TYPE process_cpu_user_seconds_total counter
process_cpu_user_seconds_total 156.37216999999978
...
```

In this case, the source is the `front-end` service, and the signal type is metrics.

Note

When talking with customers, I notice that many are facing the same challenge: feeling the need to collect and retain all metrics because "we might need them." Try to prune as much as possible on ingest and check if metrics that land in destinations are actually used. These are some questions you can ask yourself about whether collecting a particular metric is necessary:

- Is that metric used in an alert? Is it used in a dashboard?
- Can you think of a use case where you could derive insights from the metric? Would an aggregate be sufficient?
- Would a trace be a better choice here?

To make the metrics actionable, for an SRE to assess indicators, for example, we would need the following:

- An agent (e.g., Prometheus or OpenTelemetry collector) to scrape the metrics
- A destination, such as Prometheus or, for long-term storage and federation, Cortex or Thanos

For now, we will not consider traces, since they require a little bit more setup (both from the telemetry side and the destination), but in a nutshell, you can think of traces as providing an overview of the execution across services, including the duration and status of the service that successfully handled the request.

We've had an initial exposure to logs and metrics now. Before we go deeper into cloud observability throughout the rest of this book, let's finish this chapter by looking at the challenges you will need to keep in mind when dealing with cloud-native systems and how observability can help to address them.

1.5   *Challenges and how observability helps*

Cloud-native environments and the apps running on them face several challenges. In this subsection, we discuss the most pressing of these and show how observability can help.

In general (ignoring the details of the packaging and scheduling, such as a Kubernetes pod versus a Lambda function), cloud-native systems have the following characteristics:

- *They are distributed in nature.* Most of the communication is not in process—and maybe not even on the same machine (e.g., using inter-process communication [IPC] mechanisms)—but takes place via the network.
- *Due to the distributed nature, not only the* what *but also the* where *is crucial.* Think of a number of microservices along the request path serving a specific user. You want to be able to understand what's going on end to end and also be able to drill down into each of the services.
- *The volatility of the services is higher compared to a monolith running on, say, a VM.* Pods (and, with it, their IP addresses) come and go, new versions of a Lambda function might be pushed out every hour, and so on.

Let's now look at how observability can help address the challenges found in and with cloud-native systems. With cloud native systems, you don't want to fly blind; having an automated way to collect all relevant signals and use them as input for decisions—that is, actionable insight—is the ideal.

1.5.1 *Return on investment*

To understand the right level of investment (i.e., time and money) into observability, you need to know about the costs first:

- *Instrumentation costs*—These include developers' time, which is an ongoing cost.
- *Signal retention*—These costs (e.g., log storage) can be one-off but usually fall under the pay-as-you-go model.
- *Overhead of agents and instrumentation*—This manifests in compute and memory resource usage on top of what the service itself uses. Costs should be in the low single-digit range of CPU and RAM utilization. For example, the AWS Open-Telemetry Collector (http://mng.bz/N2J1) provides a report on the footprint across different signal types.
- *Network usage*—Costs of this type, such as egress traffic, may be a significant cost driver for observability solutions.

The return on the investment into observability is harder to calculate. Determining your return depends mainly on how clear the goals are. We will discuss the goals of different roles shortly. For example, you can measure the mean time to recovery (MTTR; https://www.atlassian.com/incident-management/kpis/common-metrics) for a given service before and after instrumentation. But there are also many human-related factors (e.g., on-call stress or work–life balance) that count toward the gain. You can read more about the topic in "Return on Investment Driven Observability" (https://arxiv .org/abs/2303.13402), a short paper I published on the topic.

1.5.2   *Signal correlation*

Different signal types are usually good for different tasks. Also, a single signal type is typically unable to answer all the questions you might have. We will discuss signal correlation in detail in chapter 11; however, I'd like to provide you with a quick motivational example here.

Let's say you are on call and get paged (in the middle of the night). You fire up your laptop and look at a Grafana dashboard linked in the alert you received. From the dashboard, which, say, plots Prometheus metrics, you can gather that certain services in your microservices app have an increased error rate in the past 20 minutes. You have a hunch that this may be related to the recent upgrade of a service. You use the trace ID from an exemplar (http://mng.bz/D4Jw) embedded in the Prometheus metrics as an entry point to have a closer look at the involved services, using the distributed tracing tool Jaeger. In Jaeger, you see the traces duration distribution and error codes and drill down into the logs of the service to verify your hypothesis.

In this scenario, you correlated the different signal types (metric to traces to logs) and were able to confirm your hypothesis quickly and effectively. A simple form of correlation is a time-based one, which is something you get in many frontends, such as Grafana, without additional effort out of the box. This means you use a time period to query different backends to manually find signals that tell you the whole story.

1.5.3   *Portability*

Avoid lock-in by choosing open standards and open source. This ensures you can use the same mechanisms and tooling in different environments (e.g., cloud providers or on-premises infrastructure) without having to change much of your setup. For example, if you instrument your applications using OpenTelemetry, then you can switch from one destination to another without having to change your application or agents.

Summary

- Cloud-native systems, such as Kubernetes, produce a large volume of telemetry signals.
- Sources of telemetry signals can be your code, APIs (e.g., an AWS service), a database, and so on.
- The term *telemetry* refers to the process of collecting signals from sources, processing them via agents, and ingesting them into observability destinations, where they can be consumed by humans and machines.
- In general, *observability* means getting actionable insights from signals to understand and influence the system under observation.
- There are many use cases for observability, from reducing MTTR to cost optimizations to increasing developer productivity.
- Observability is relevant to different roles (developers, DevOps, nontechnical roles, etc.) to perform their typical tasks.

- We had a look at a concrete example setup of a cloud-native app (a container-ized microservices app in Kubernetes), its signals, and what observability could mean in this context.
- Challenges of cloud-native systems include their distributed nature and the volatility of the involved components.
- Observability can help address the challenges found in cloud-native systems by allowing you not to fly blind.
- It is important to understand the costs and return on investment of observability.
- Signal correlation is important, as it enables you to combine different signal types to answer all questions you may have about a system.

Signal types

In the context of observability, signals play a central role: this is the intel we're basing our decisions on. On a high level, we can differentiate between signals numerical in nature (e.g., the number of service invocations) and signals that carry textual payload that requires human interpretation (e.g., a log line).

As discussed in chapter 1, the system under observation, or just *system* (e.g., a Kubernetes application or a serverless app based on Lambda functions), emits signals from various sources. You, as a human, or equally a piece of software, then use these signals to understand the system and make decisions to influence it. There is a one-to-many relation between the system and sources. Your system typically involves compute, storage, and network, each of these representing a signal source. We will cover the sources in detail in chapter 3.

In terms of signals (and sources), we can differentiate between two cases:

- Sources, such as code, that you own and can instrument yourself (that is, decide where and what kind of signals to emit).
- Sources you don't own, meaning any signals will be predefined. Your task is limited to selecting which signals to consume, in this case. This might be due to several reasons:
  - Code that is a dependency of your code (library, package, module, etc.).
  - The component's source code is not available (e.g., a binary file).
  - The component only offers a (networked) API. Any managed service from your cloud provider of choice falls into this category.

No matter whether you own the code and can decide what signal types to emit or are working with a component you don't own, at some point in time, you want to collect the signals and send them to a central place for processing and storage. This is the telemetry part.

With observability, you want to take an approach driven by return on investment (ROI). In other words, you not only need to understand the different signals available but also the costs of each signal type and what they enable you to do.

In this chapter, we will review the most common signal types, examine how to instrument and collect each, and discuss the costs and benefits of doing so.

2.1 Reference example

While there are several signals to consider, in practice, the three most commonly used are logs, metrics, and traces. In this chapter, we will use a running reference example, a simple Go program called the `echo` service, exposing an HTTP interface, to see the three common signal types in action.

Change to the `ch02/base/` directory, where you find the `main.go` program shown in listing 2.1. As we progress, we will instrument our reference example with different signals with the goal to consume and interact with the signals using open source tooling, including Grafana, Prometheus, and Jaeger.

Listing 2.1 Example Go program to be instrumented

```
package main

import (
    "fmt"
    "log"
    "math/rand"
    "net/http"
    "time"
)

func handleEcho(w http.ResponseWriter, r *http.Request) {
    message := r.URL.Query().Get("message")
    if rand.Intn(100) > 90 {
```

> Retrieves the payload to echo from the query parameter message, with the result of being able to interact with the service by issuing an HTTP GET to /echo?message

> Simulates a 10% error case

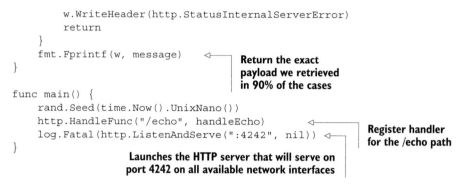

```
            w.WriteHeader(http.StatusInternalServerError)
            return
        }
        fmt.Fprintf(w, message)          ◁─┐  Return the exact
    }                                       │  payload we retrieved
                                            │  in 90% of the cases
func main() {
    rand.Seed(time.Now().UnixNano())
    http.HandleFunc("/echo", handleEcho)     ◁─┐  Register handler
    log.Fatal(http.ListenAndServe(":4242", nil))  ◁─┤  for the /echo path
}
      Launches the HTTP server that will serve on
      port 4242 on all available network interfaces
```

First, let's build the echo service, as shown in the following listing.

Listing 2.2   Building our example Go program

```
$ go build -o echosvc .     ◁─┐  Builds the executable, which is then available
                               │  in the current directory as ./echosvc
```

Now, you can run the service with ./echosvc in the same directory. To invoke it via its HTTP API, you would use the following code (in a separate terminal session):

```
$ curl localhost:4242/echo?message=test

test
```

By default, I will use Grafana as the destination, since it allows us to visualize and interact with a wide array of data sources in a uniform manner. This is will allow you to reproduce everything for free with open source. Now that we've laid out our reference example, let's talk about a way to assess the costs of instrumentation, before we move to the instrument itself.

> **Tip**
>
> To see the signals going forward, in Grafana, you will need to put some load onto the echo service. One option is to do something like the following directly from the shell (calling the endpoint every second):
>
> ```
> while true ; do curl -s -o
> /dev/null localhost:4242/echo ; sleep 1 ; done
> ```
>
> Alternatively, you can use something more fancy, such as a full-blown testing tool like Salvo (https://github.com/tarekziade/salvo) or even K6 (https://k6.io/docs/testing-guides/api-load-testing/).

2.2 *Assessing instrumentation costs*

To assess the costs of instrumentation per signal type, we will use a simple measure: the *business logic to instrumentation* (B2I) ratio.

> ### The B2I ratio
>
> To calculate the B2I ratio, determine the number of lines of code (LOC) before adding an instrumentation (adding code for emitting signals for a signal type), and then determine the LOC after the instrumentation. The B2I ratio is then
>
> ```
> B2I = LOC_AFTER_INSTRUMENTATION/LOC_BEFORE_INSTRUMENTATION
> ```
>
> In an ideal world, the B2I ratio would be 1, representing zero instrumentation costs in the code. However, in reality, the more LOC you dedicate to instrumentation, the higher the B2I ratio is. For example, if your code has 3800 LOC and you added 400 LOC for instrumentation (say, to emit logs and metrics), then you'd end up with a B2I ratio of 1.105, from (3800 + 400) / 3800.

There are two things worth mentioning concerning B2I:

- It's up to you to decide whether to consider telemetry libraries such as an Open-Telemetry SDK (https://opentelemetry.io/docs/instrumentation/) in your B2I ratio calculation. From a pragmatic point of view, focusing on your own code (excluding these dependencies) might make the most sense. This is what I will do in the remainder of the chapter.
- The B2I ratio is a simple measure and should by no means serve as an indicator of how well your code is instrumented or tell you if your code is *over-instrumented.* Goodhart's law (see Strathern and Marilyn, 1997, "Improving Ratings: Audit in the British University System," *European Review,* John Wiley & Sons) states that when a measure becomes a target, it ceases to be a good measure—this applies here. Use the B2I ratio as a rough guide in a regression validation, rather than an absolute North star.

With the theory and overview out of the way, let's now review the three basic signal types: logs, metrics, and traces. In the remainder of the chapter, we will do the following for each signal type:

1 Define the signal characteristics and semantics.
2 Discuss how to instrument our example `echo` service.
3 Set up the telemetry to collect and route the signal.
4 Analyze costs (in terms of resource usage and efforts) and benefits of the signal.
5 Explain how the respective signal can contribute to an observability solution.

2.3   *Logs*

Let's begin by focusing on logs. Logs are signals with a textual payload that capture an event. An *event* is an umbrella term for anything of interest that happens in the code, be it on the happy path (a completed upload) or unexpected or erroneous behavior ("failed to store items in shopping basket").

Logs are timestamped and should be structured, ideally including some context (e.g., labels) that can be used for correlation with other signals. Usually, humans consume logs, either directly, by searching for an event, or indirectly, via correlation.

NOTE There are many ways to refer to a single log event, including log lines, log items, log entries, and perhaps others I have not come across yet. To keep things simple, we will consistently use the term *event* here, but these terms are, by and large, interchangeable.

In the context of logs, we usually differentiate between *levels*, which can represent the nature of a log event. Different programming languages, libraries, and frameworks have, over time, established conventions; however, the following are some common semantics:

- Fine-grained logs events that are relevant for developing or fixing a bug (DEBUG)
- Production-type log events, including the following:
  - Expected behavior (usually INFO)
  - Unexpected behavior, such as WARNING or ERROR

There are several log standards and formats available, including line-oriented formats, such as syslog RFC 5424 (https://tools.ietf.org/html/rfc5424) and the Apache common log format (CLF; http://mng.bz/lWg8); JSON log formats (supported by most modern libraries); and binary formats, such as the journal file format (http://mng .bz/Bmw8), found in the context of systemd. To learn more, check out Graylog's Logs Format Guide (http://mng.bz/d1nO). Some good practices in the context of logs include the following:

- Consider what to log, with the goal of providing actionable insights (context is king).
- Log to stdout rather than to a fixed location, such as a file. This enables log agents to collect and route your log events. See also the entry in the 12-factor methodology (https://12factor.net/logs) for some background.
- Use labels to enhance the value of a log event. For example, you can use the component name or type, the kind of source, or the type of operation as labels to aid filtering for events.

TIP If you're wondering how you can "future proof" your strategies around logs, I recommend reading Ben Sigelman's (cofounder of Lightstep, known for his work on OpenTelemetry, Google Dapper, and Monarch) 2001 Twitter thread, "Why Tracing Might Replace (Almost) All Logging" (http://mng.bz/ rWzD), in which he argues that in cloud-native systems, tracing will replace logging for the brunt of the workload via instrumentation about the transactions themselves (as opposed to logging about infrastructure or other resources). This makes sense, at least for a large number of use cases for logs in a transactional setup, and I want to encourage you to consider this kind of thinking and apply it to your environment, if you're in a position to do so. Naturally, many environments are more on the brown field than green field end of the spectrum, so it can be difficult or take a lot of time and energy to establish this tracing-centered (as opposed to logs-centered) approach.

2.3.1 Instrumentation

Let's now see logs in action. For this, we instrument our `echo` service so that it emits log events. The following listing shows our `echo` service instrumented with logs.

Listing 2.3 Example Go program, instrumented to emit structured logs

```go
package main

import (
    "fmt"
    "math/rand"
    "net/http"
    "time"

    log "github.com/sirupsen/logrus"
)

func handleEcho(w http.ResponseWriter, r *http.Request) {
    message := r.URL.Query().Get("message")
    log.WithFields(log.Fields{
        "service": "echo",
    }).Info("Got input ", message)
    if rand.Intn(100) > 90 {
        log.WithFields(log.Fields{
            "service": "echo",
        }).Error("Something really bad happened :(")
        w.WriteHeader(500)
        return
    }
    fmt.Fprintf(w, message)
}

func main() {
    rand.Seed(time.Now().UnixNano())
    log.SetFormatter(&log.JSONFormatter{})
    http.HandleFunc("/echo", handleEcho)
    log.Fatal(http.ListenAndServe(":4242", nil))
}
```

No matter what, always emit an **INFO** log line here that confirms the input value we got via the query parameter message. Note the "service": "echo" in the line above (and again in the error case below): this provides a context for the event, allowing you to pinpoint the service.

Emit an **ERROR** log line in error case.

Configure the logger to emit log lines formatted in JSON. Also, note that the logger we're using here, logrus (https://github.com/Sirupsen/ logrus), defaults to output to stderr, something we have to consider when we consume the logs, later.

To build the service, you also need to define its dependencies via a file called `go.mod` (shown in the following listing).

Listing 2.4 Example Go program dependencies file `go.mod`

```
module collyia/ch2/logs

go 1.20

require github.com/sirupsen/logrus v1.8.1
```

Now, to pull in the echo service dependencies, run the following command:

```
$ go mod vendor
```

Complete the build by executing go build, as explained in listing 2.2.

2.3.2 *Telemetry*

We are now in the position to execute the echo service locally and send the log events it emits during its execution to certain destinations, such as to the screen and into a file:

```
$ ./echosvc 2>&1 | \
  tee echo.log
```

> **Execute the echosvc and redirect its stderr output to stdout.**

> **Use the tee command to show the log lines on the terminal, at the same time appending the log lines to a file called echo.log. We will use this file as an input to ship to a destination in the next step.**

Next, we will use some open source tools, provided by Grafana Labs, to route and collect the logs. We capture the logs of our echo service with Promtail (http://mng .bz/V1J0) and ship them to Loki (https://grafana.com/docs/loki/latest/) as a destination (as a data source in Grafana). Using Grafana as the frontend, you can then view and query the logs as you desire.

To set up our log scenario, use the Docker Compose manifest file shown in the following listing. It launches everything needed, from the destination to the frontend.

Listing 2.5 Using docker-compose.yaml to stand up Promtail, Loki, and Grafana

```yaml
version: "3.5"
networks:
  loki:
services:
  loki:
    image: grafana/loki:2.4.0
    ports:
      - "3100:3100"
    command: -config.file=/etc/loki/local-config.yaml
    networks:
      - loki
  promtail:
    image: grafana/promtail:2.4.0
    volumes:
      - ./promtail-config.yaml:/etc/promtail/config.yml
      - ./echo.log:/var/log/echo.log
    command: -config.file=/etc/promtail/config.yml
    networks:
      - loki
  grafana:
    image: grafana/grafana:latest
    ports:
      - "3000:3000"
    networks:
      - loki
```

> **Defines the location of the Promtail config file. We map the host local file promtail-config.yaml into the container to /etc/promtail/config.yml, where Promtail expects to find it.**

> **Maps the host local file echo.log (which our echo services logs to) into the container to /var/log/echo.log. We will use that in listing 2.6 to define the log processing and routing pipeline.**

TIP While using Docker Compose to develop locally or test apps is certainly handy, for a production setup, Kubernetes is much more useful. For example, you can install the Promtail, Loki, and Grafana stack via Helm charts or using Tanka (https://tanka.dev/).

Now that we have set up the framework for launching the logs destination (Loki), the telemetry agent (Promtail), and the frontend (Grafana) via our Docker Compose file (listing 2.5) we need one more thing in place: configuring Promtail, our log router/ingester. The Docker Compose manifest references (in line 15) this Promtail configuration file, which we call promtail-config.yaml, as shown in the following listing.

Listing 2.6 Promtail configuration file promtail-config.yaml

```
server:
  http_listen_port: 9080
  grpc_listen_port: 0

positions:
  filename: /tmp/positions.yaml

clients:
  - url: http://loki:3100/loki/api/v1/push

scrape_configs:
- job_name: app
  static_configs:
  - targets:
      - localhost
    labels:
      job: echosvc
      __path__: /var/log/echo.log
  pipeline_stages:
  - json:
      expressions:
        level: level
        payload: msg
        timestamp: time
        service: service
  - labels:
      level:
      service:
```

This defines the input for Promtail. Here, we tell it to ingest logs from a file called /var/log/echo.log (which we mounted from the host via a volume in line 16 of the Docker Compose manifest).

This is the first part of the Promtail pipeline (http://mng.bz/x48e). It maps the input JSON fields that our echo service emits (e.g., service or level, the right-hand side here, the values) to labels we want to filter for in Loki; for example, service or level (the same names here, but you can, and often must, normalize keys, and that's a good place to do this).

Here, we define the labels we want to index or expose.

Assuming you stored the content of listing 2.5 in a file called docker-compose.yaml, it's straightforward to bring up the stack using the following code:

```
$ docker-compose -f docker-compose.yaml up
Creating network "logs_loki" with the default driver
Pulling loki (grafana/loki:2.4.0)...
2.4.0: Pulling from grafana/loki
...
Status: Downloaded newer image for grafana/promtail:2.4.0
Creating logs_loki_1    ... done
```

```
Creating logs_promtail_1 ... done
Creating logs_grafana_1  ... done
Attaching to logs_loki_1, logs_grafana_1, logs_promtail_1
...
```

Now, you can head over to http://localhost:3000/ in your browser to log into Grafana. Use the following defaults (be sure to skip the password change request after you enter the credentials):

- Username: `admin`
- Password: `admin`

Next, configure the Loki data source as shown in figure 2.1 (note that the screenshot has been edited so that it focuses on the relevant parts; in reality, you would see many more options on this screen). The only config you need to set in this step is the data source URL, which is `http://loki:3100`, thanks to our Docker Compose setup.

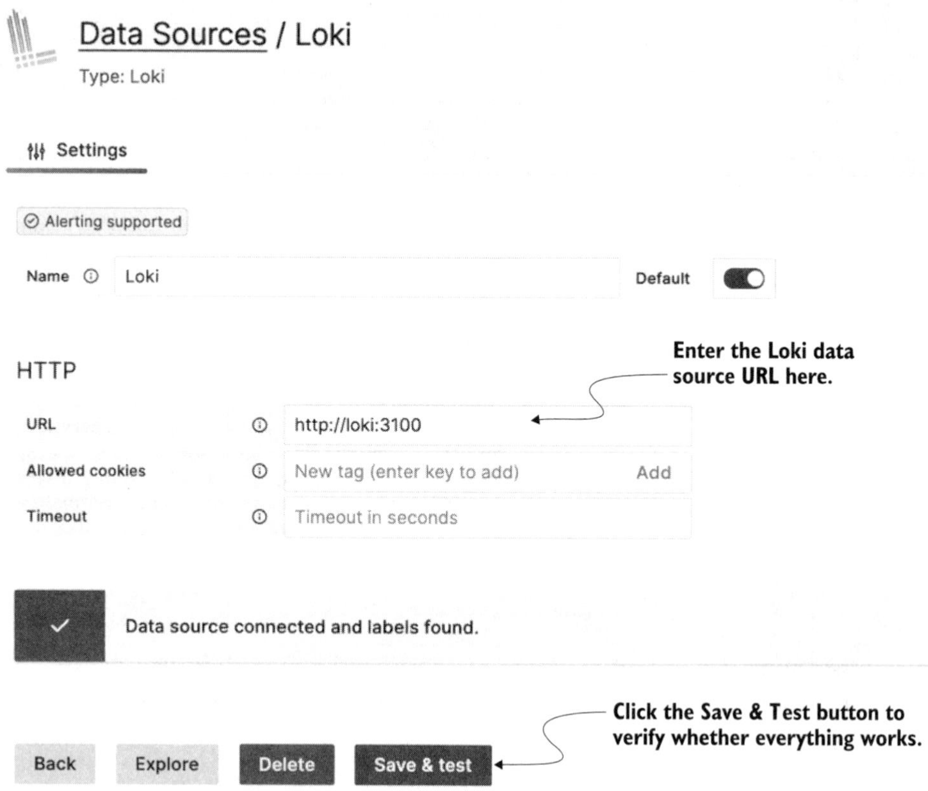

Figure 2.1   Adding and configuring the Loki data source in Grafana

Now, you can head over to the Explore tab, which looks like a compass, in the left-hand menu. Select Loki as the data source (if it is not already set as the default), and under the Labels filter, select `service` as the label from the dropdown box and `echo` as the value. If you then select a certain time range, you should see something akin to what is shown in figure 2.2.

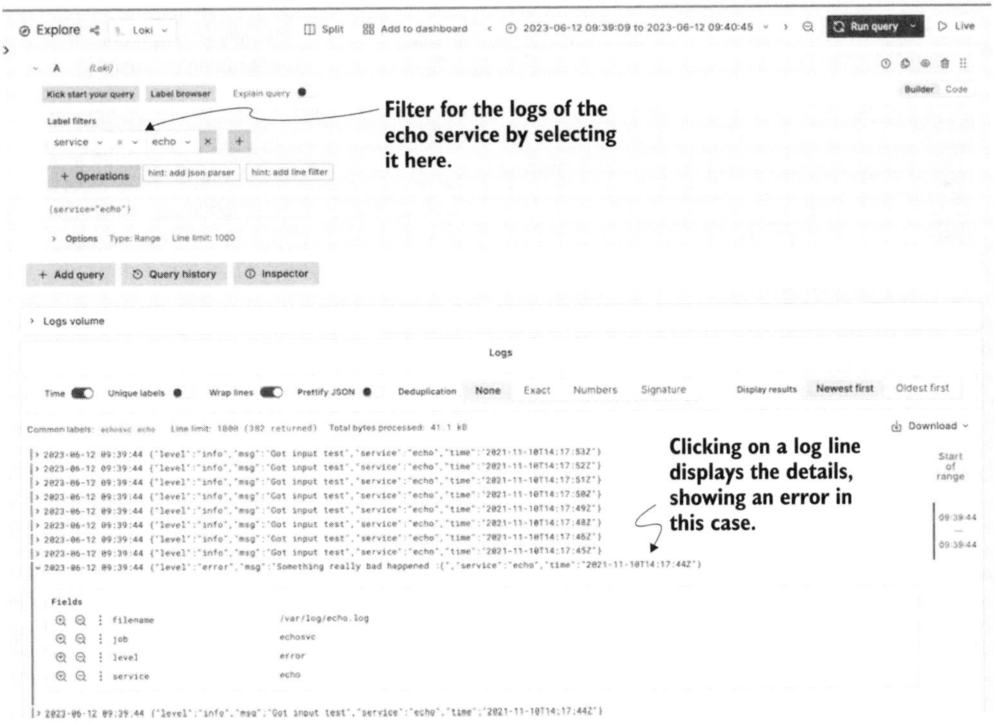

Figure 2.2   Exploring logs in Loki

The Loki data source explore view is quick and simple to filter for certain log levels. For example, you could add another label filter, such as `level="error"`, to only show error log lines.

> **TIP**   To see what is running, use `docker-compose top` (in the directory that contains the docker-compose.yaml file) or `docker ps` (anywhere). Additionally, to tear down everything, removing all containers again, use the `docker-compose -f docker-compose.yaml down` command.

With this, we've completed our practical logs scenario. Now, we can move on to a discussion on the values logs bring to the table and what the costs (in terms of resources and efforts) concerning logs look like.

2.3.3 Costs and benefits

In this subsection, we will take a closer look at the costs and benefits of the logs signal type. Table 2.1 shows an overview of the costs.

Table 2.1 Overview of the costs of logs

	Overhead	Considerations
Instrumentation	Small and simple to add a log line	Widely adopted and supported by programming languages
Agent	Some runtime, lots of options, and few standards for formats (syslog, OTLP)	A runtime footprint, ingestion performance, reliability, and security
Destination	Long-term storage can be expensive.	Data temperature (access recency or frequency) can guide retention

INSTRUMENTATION COSTS OF LOGS

The costs of logs are relatively low for instrumentation, well understood, and widely supported. All programming languages and their libraries allow users to emit logs. Readability, and with it maintainability, has not greatly suffered by adding log lines.

Let's have a concrete look at the instrumentation costs from a developer's point of view. The original code in listing 2.1 has 24 lines of code, and the code instrumented with logs in listing 2.3 has 32 lines of code. Taking the two LOC numbers together, we can calculate the B2I ratio and arrive at a value of 1.33, which is not too bad.

TELEMETRY COSTS OF LOGS

There are some costs associated with collecting and routing logs to a central location, which is typically necessary in a distributed system. Depending on the option you are using here, it may cause ingestion (network traffic) costs.

When selecting a certain agent, ask yourself the following:

- What is the runtime footprint (CPU and memory consumption)?
- What is the ingestion performance? For example, how many log lines per second can the agent handle?
- In terms of reliability, is there a guaranteed delivery of every log line (if this is necessary at all)?
- Is there an appropriate level of security, from encryption on the wire (TLS) to multitenancy support?

TIP If you're unsure about how to measure log agent performance, have a look at chapter 7 of Phil Wilkins' *Logging in Action* (Manning, 2022; https://www.manning.com/books/logging-in-action).

The following are a few examples of log routers:

- The Cloud Native Computing Foundation (CNCF) project's Fluentd (https://github.com/fluent/fluentd) and Fluent Bit (https://github.com/fluent/fluent-bit).
- The CNCF project OpenTelemetry offers an experimental log router called Collector (http://mng.bz/AoJK).
- Cloud provider–specific agents, such as Amazon CloudWatch agents (http://mng.bz/ZqJO), Azure Monitor agents (http://mng.bz/2DNd), or Google Cloud operations suite agents (https://cloud.google.com/monitoring/agent/).
- Proprietary agents, such as Elastic's Logstash (https://github.com/elastic/logstash) and Filebeat (http://mng.bz/1qEV), the Datadog agent (https://docs.datadoghq.com/agent/), or the Splunk Universal Forwarder (https://docs.splunk.com/Documentation/Forwarder).

To avoid exceedingly high costs in this phase, as well as in the destinations, you may wish to prune logs here. Some pruning strategies you might want to consider include

- *Sampling*—That is, dropping a certain percentage of the events, based on a heuristic
- *Filtering based on type*—For example, dropping DEBUG level logs in prod

There are commercial offerings, such as Cribl (https://cribl.com/), that can help define and apply pruning strategies at scale, across providers.

DESTINATION COSTS OF LOGS

Once logs from different microservices arrive at a central location (the destination, such as Splunk, CloudWatch, OpenSearch, or Datadog), the main cost type is storage. At scale, logs can be very expensive, so usually, you don't want to keep everything around forever. It is better to decide the retention period of logs based on the *data temperature*:

- *Hot data*—Your working set—that is, logs you're using in the current time frame to troubleshoot or develop. It has to be readily accessible and fast to query. Usually, that spans from days to weeks.
- *Warm data*—Something you might need but is not necessary immediately accessible or queryable. The retention period here might be months or even years.
- *Cold data*—All the (log) data you don't actively use. You may need to keep these logs lines around for regulatory reasons. It is best to store that kind of log data in cheap, reliable, and durable object storage, such as in Amazon S3 Glacier. It may take minutes or hours to access the data, but given that you seldom, if at all, use it, that's a tradeoff you can live with.

BENEFITS OF LOGS

Now that you have an idea about the costs of logs, let's briefly talk about their benefits. First off, logs are universally adopted and understood. Every developer knows how to emit log lines, and there's fantastic support for logs in every programming language, often in the standard library or in the wider ecosystem (third-party packages, modules, or libraries).

The second main benefit of logs is that, due to their textual nature, a human can usually interpret the meaning; however, there is still a requirement for a developer to be able to write actionable log lines (https://logz.io/blog/logging-best-practices/), such as formatting, context, and so on. Beyond that, all you need is to find a log line, and you can interpret it. There are two approaches to finding relevant log lines:

- Traditionally, every log line (or log item) was *full-text indexed*. Systems like Elasticsearch or OpenSearch as well as many commercial offerings take this approach. This is great, since you can search for everything; however, it comes with scalability and cost challenges.
- Recently, *label-based indexing* has become popular. Rather than indexing the entire text of a log line, you only need to index the labels (or tags) that provide the context (e.g., this is from service `foo`, and it is about and `error` condition). The most popular example of this approach is Grafana Loki (https://grafana.com/oss/loki/), inspired by Prometheus.

With this, we've reached the end of our logs cost and benefit discussion, so let's move on to use cases for logs in the context of observability.

2.3.4 *Observability with logs*

What can we do with logs, and how is what we just saw in the hands-on part related to observability?

As a developer, you can use logs

- For debugging an existing code base (for which you either own the source code or can reverse engineer it).
- To perform testing (e.g., soak tests, performance tests, or chaos engineering) and see where and how your microservices break apart.

Further, in a DevOps or SRE role, logs

- Help identify the service and code responsible for a bug or outage with the goals to (a) stop the bleeding (restart or take it offline) and (b) fix the issue in the code identified.
- Provide context (e.g., identify who made which change when) as well as address regulatory or security-related concerns. The Log4j vulnerability CVE-2021-44228 (https://nvd.nist.gov/vuln/detail/CVE-2021-44228) and CVE-2021-45046 (https://nvd.nist.gov/vuln/detail/CVE-2021-45046), which we saw at the end of 2021, are good examples of security-motivated use cases.

2.4 *Metrics*

Metrics are numerical signals, typically sampled at regular time intervals. They usually consist of a name, a value, and some metadata. The name identifies the metric (e.g., temperature), the value is the observation we're interested in (say, `2.5`), and the metadata provides context (e.g., `room_42` for location-related context). The unit of the observation can be encoded in the name or provided as metadata. Last but not least, the metric is timestamped, either explicitly by the producer of the metric or at ingest (server side).

Traditionally, semantics would often be encoded in a hierarchical manner, but with the advent of Kubernetes and Prometheus, the label-based, flat organization scheme became more mainstream. This label-based scheme is more flexible and extensible. The following example demonstrates the difference:

```
room_42.sensor_window.temperature 2.5
```
A metric using a hierarchical scheme

```
temperature[location="room_42", sensor="window"] 2.5
```
The same metric, using a label-based scheme. If one wanted to add another aspect, such as the position, with the label-based scheme, it would be as easy as adding a new label (e.g., position="top"), whereas with an hierarchical scheme, one would need to reconsider the entire name.

We usually differentiate between low-level or systems metrics and application-level or business metrics. The former are resource usage metrics, like CPU utilization or allocated main memory, and the latter include things like requests handled per second or revenue generated per user. In general, low-level metrics can often be automatically gleaned, whereas application-level metrics require a human to assist in definition and exposure.

Another aspect of metrics, again popularized by Prometheus, is the pull-versus-push approach for metrics. The gist is that, in a cloud-native setup where one deals with containers or functions that are short lived, the discovery is better centralized and the central entity collects the metrics (or scrapes, as Prometheus folks would say—technically, it means calling an HTTP API endpoint to retrieve metrics) rather than having the applications push the metrics to a central place.

When determining which metrics are important to consider, the community came up with several approaches and recommendations. The following are most notable:

- *The utilization, saturation, errors (USE) method*—Created by Brendan Gregg (see https://www.brendangregg.com/usemethod.html), this method is great for low-level metrics and often used in the context of performance engineering and root cause analysis.
- *The rate, errors, duration (RED) method*—Created by Tom Wilkie (see http://mng.bz/PzJ9), this method focuses on the number of requests served, the number of failed requests, and how long requests take. This is useful for application-level cases.
- *The four golden signals of monitoring*—Established by Google engineers (see http://mng.bz/JgJ0), the four signals are latency, traffic, errors, and saturation, which is like RED and USE combined.

From a consumption point of view, we can say that metrics often are graphed (in dashboards) or are used as triggers for alerts in the context of monitoring and analytics. But metrics are also useful and, indeed, used as an input for programs. For example, a horizontal pod autoscaler (HPA) in Kubernetes may scale the number of replicas up or down, based on some custom metric, such as the number of requests handled by a service.

2.4.1 *Instrumentation*

Let's see how we can extend our echo service to emit metrics. Listing 2.7 shows the echo service instrumented with metrics. To be precise, we're using the Prometheus Go library for the instrumentation. Note that listing 2.7 only shows the relevant fragments, not the complete Go code, which is available via the code repo in code/ch02/metrics/main.go (http://mng.bz/wvWq).

Listing 2.7   Example Go program, instrumented to emit Prometheus metrics

```go
func handleEcho(w http.ResponseWriter, r *http.Request) {
    message := r.URL.Query().Get("message")
    log.WithFields(log.Fields{
        "service": "echo",
    }).Info("Got input ", message)
    if rand.Intn(100) > 90 {
        log.WithFields(log.Fields{
            "service": "echo",
        }).Error("Something really bad happened :(")
        invokes.WithLabelValues(strconv.Itoa(http.StatusInternalServerError)).Inc()    ◁
        w.WriteHeader(500)
        return
    }
    invokes.WithLabelValues(strconv.Itoa(http.StatusOK)).Inc()    ◁
    fmt.Fprintf(w, message)
}
var (
    registry = prometheus.NewRegistry()    ◁
    invokes  = promauto.NewCounterVec(    ◁
        prometheus.CounterOpts{
            Name: "echo_total",
            Help: "Total invocations of the echo service endpoint.",
        },
        []string{"http_status_code"},
    )
)
func main() {
    rand.Seed(time.Now().UnixNano())
    registry.MustRegister(invokes)    ◁
    log.SetFormatter(&log.JSONFormatter{})
    http.HandleFunc("/echo", handleEcho)
    http.Handle("/metrics", promhttp.HandlerFor(    ◁
        registry,
        promhttp.HandlerOpts{
            EnableOpenMetrics: true,
```

Increments our metric with the context-specific label carrying the HTTP status code

Sets up the Prometheus registry

Defines our metric

Registers our metric

Defines the /metrics endpoint handler

```
        },
    ))
    log.Fatal(http.ListenAndServe(":4242", nil))
}
```

At this point, you know how to instrument the echo service to emit metrics, but how do these metrics arrive at a destination where you can consume them? Let's take a look in the next section.

2.4.2 *Telemetry*

We are now in the position to execute the echo service locally and expose the Prometheus metrics:

```
$ ./echosvc
```

We can scrape the metrics of our echo service using Prometheus (http://prometheus .io/), which, in turn, can act as a data source in Grafana as the destination. To set up the destination, use the Docker Compose manifest file shown in the next listing (which references listing 2.9) to set up Prometheus and Grafana.

Listing 2.8 Using docker-compose.yaml to stand up Prometheus and Grafana

```
version: "3.5"
networks:
  prom:
services:
  prometheus:
    image: prom/prometheus:latest
    ports:
      - "9090:9090"
    volumes:
      - ./prom-config.yaml:/etc/prometheus/prometheus.yml
    networks:
      - prom
  grafana:
    image: grafana/grafana:latest
    ports:
      - "3000:3000"
    networks:
      - prom
```

Like we've seen for logs, we also need to configure the telemetry agent for metrics. In this case, we this do by defining the Prometheus scrape config, as shown in the prom-config.yaml file in the following listing.

Listing 2.9 Prometheus configuration file prom-config.yaml

```
global:
  scrape_interval: 5s
  evaluation_interval: 5s
```

```
    external_labels:
        monitor: 'lab'
scrape_configs:
  - job_name: 'prometheus'
    static_configs:
    - targets: ['localhost:9090']
  - job_name: 'lab'
    static_configs:
    - targets: ['host.docker.internal:4242']
```

Next, add Prometheus as a data source in Grafana, as shown in figure 2.3, using http://prometheus:9090/ as the URL.

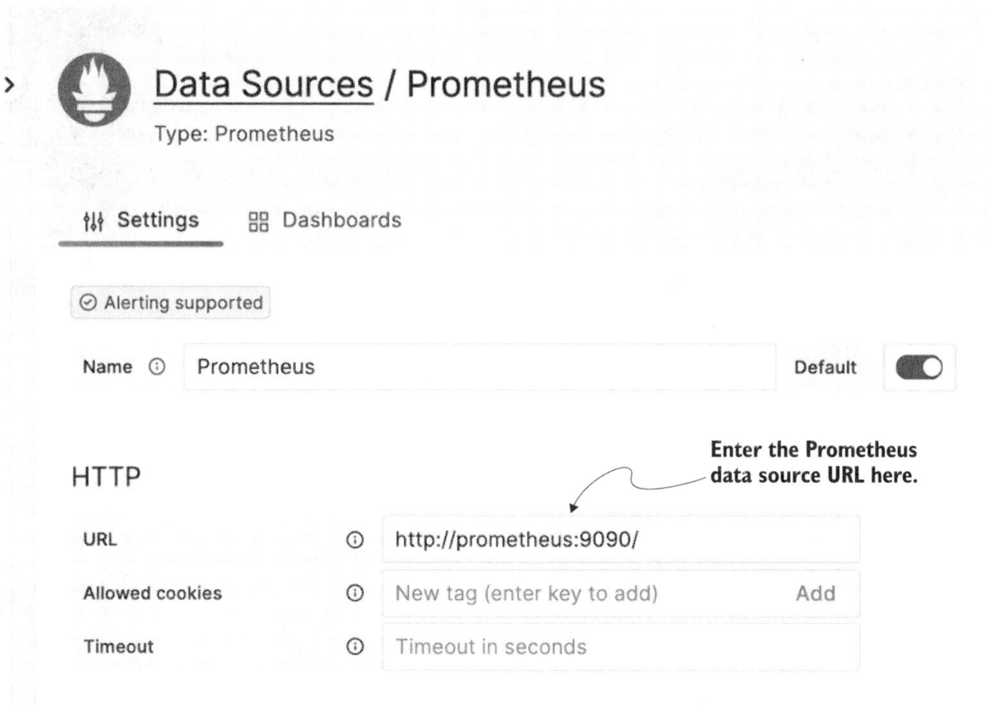

Figure 2.3   Adding and configuring the Prometheus data source in Grafana

Now, you can again use the Explore tab to consume the metrics the echo service exposes. Select Prometheus as the data source, and you should see something similar to what is shown in figure 2.4 if you enter the following PromQL (http://mng.bz/ qrGw) query, which represents the error rate of our service:

```
sum (rate(echo_total{http_status_code="500"}[5m]))
/
sum (rate(echo_total[5m])) * 100
```

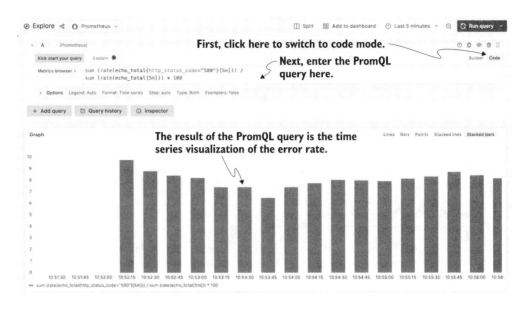

Figure 2.4   Exploring metrics with Prometheus

The preceding PromQL query is the canonical way to capture the error rate. By dividing the errors (HTTP status code 500) by all of the data points, you have a flexible yet complete way to capture errors. In this case, the error rate is a low single-digit rate and should, on average, be 10%, since that's what we have the service configured with in listing 2.7. Next, let's discuss the pros and cons of metrics.

2.4.3   Costs and benefits

We now have a closer look at the costs and benefits of the metrics signal type. Table 2.2 shows an overview of costs associated with metrics.

Table 2.2   Overview of the costs of metrics

	Overhead	**Considerations**
Instrumentation	Auto-instrumentation, if possible	Increasingly supported in programming languages
Agent	Prometheus, OpenTelemetry collector, and OpenMetrics as emerging standard	What to collect and autopruning
Destination	Cardinality, long-term storage, and federation	What to ingest and data temperature for retention

INSTRUMENTATION COSTS OF METRICS

Concerning the costs of instrumenting code with metrics, we can distinguish two cases:

- Using auto-instrumentation usually requires little effort, such as including a library or configuring it (e.g., with Prometheus [http://mng.bz/7Dr9]; Open-Telemetry [https://opentelemetry.io/docs/instrumentation/]; and, increasingly, eBPF based).
- Manual instrumentation requires more effort than auto-instrumentation but also offers more control over which metrics you want to expose in which manner. Typically, these instrumentations should be one-offs, and for a class of metrics (business-level metrics), this kind of instrumentation is the only viable one.

The readability, and with it the maintainability, of the code can suffer with manual instrumentation.

Let's now have a concrete look at the instrumentation costs from a developer's point of view: the original code in listing 2.1 has 24 lines of code, and the code instrumented with metrics in listing 2.3 has 56 lines of code overall. To isolate the metrics-caused instrumentation costs from the total (logs + metrics) instrumentation cost, we need to subtract the 8 lines of code from the logs-caused instrumentation. We then arrive at a value of 48 lines of code.

Taking these two LOC numbers together, we can calculate the B2I ratio and arrive, for the metrics, at a value of 2. This B2I value is slightly higher than what we had with logs (1.33), but it is still not worrisome.

If you want to learn more about good practices concerning metrics instrumentation, I recommend you peruse the following resources:

- CNCF SIG Instrumentation guidance on instrumenting Kubernetes (http://mng.bz/mVer).
- CNCF TAG observability whitepaper input with guidelines for developers on how to implement new metrics (https://github.com/cncf/tag-observability/issues/18).

TELEMETRY COSTS OF METRICS

Agents for metrics have considerations similar to those that we discussed for logs. There is, in addition, the challenge around the cardinality—that is, the number of different values possible in the dimensions of a metric that can contribute to a (dramatic) increase of the costs.

Examples of metrics agents include the following:

- CNCF Prometheus, especially in agent mode (https://prometheus.io/blog/2021/11/16/agent/)
- The CNCF OpenTelemetry collector (https://opentelemetry.io/docs/collector/) and, more specifically, collectors from OpenTelemetry distributions, such as the AWS Distro for OpenTelemetry Collector (http://mng.bz/5wBB)

DESTINATION COSTS OF METRICS

One of the most challenging aspects of metrics is what we call *cardinality explosion*, which we will discuss in detail in chapter 5. What does this mean on a high level? Well, in many cases, the dimension of a metric only has a small set of possible values. For example, the number of HTTP status codes (https://httpstatuses.com/) may be limited to a couple dozen:

```
myapp_http_requests_total{code="200", handler="/helloworld"} --> 42
myapp_http_requests_total{code="404", handler="/cryptomining"} --> 5
...
```

This doesn't cause any issues, as the time series databases are well able to handle it, from a storage and query perspective. But what if you decide to encode the user ID into a label as follows?

```
myapp_http_requests_total{code="200", handler="/ex1", uid="9876" } --> 567
```

Congratulations! You have just introduced the potential for cardinality explosion. Why? Well, imaging your service becomes popular and you end up having to deal with tens or hundreds of thousands—or maybe even millions— of users.

There can be as many values for the `uid` label as you have users, which is very expensive for the time series database to deal with, both in terms of storage and query performance, if possible at all (usually, you will see your queries getting slower in such a case). There's really only one solution: keep your dimensions in control.

Another source of costs in the destination comes when there are many sources. Say you have a fleet of Kubernetes clusters and want to centrally query the metrics. You would need to consider how you go about long-term storage and federation (http://mng.bz/6Ddo) of your metrics, something we will get back to in more detail in chapter 5.

BENEFITS OF METRICS

By the very nature of metrics, their numeric values enable all sorts of automation. For example, you don't have to manually track a metric by looking at a dashboard, but you define a condition (e.g., "goes above this value for at least 3 minutes") and get a notification if and when this is the case. That kind of automation is usually called *alerting*.

Then, there's the wide area of establishing a baseline. (How does the metric "normally" look—what range, max, and min does it have?) One can employ fancy methods here as well, and there's a whole area, called *anomaly detection*, dedicated to the topic of why something looks abnormal. Again, we return to this topic in greater detail later in the book.

Popular destinations for consuming metrics include the following:

- Frontends, such as low-level/debug offerings, including the Prometheus UI or PromLens (https://github.com/promlabs/promlens-public)
- Universal data sources frontends, such as Grafana (https://github.com/grafana/grafana)
- Commercial or integrated offerings, including CloudWatch, New Relic, Datadog, and so on
- Object storage, such as an S3 bucket, for later analysis

With this, we've reached the end of our metrics cost and benefit discussion, so let's move on to metrics use cases for observability.

2.4.4 Observability with metrics

What can we do with metrics, and how is what we just saw related to observability? In a DevOps or SRE role, we can do the following:

- *Establish baselines for signals, based on metrics*—Further, you can define anomalies and expectations via alerts and get notifications if certain values are exceeded (this is more of a traditional monitoring use case for metrics, since the questions are already known up front).
- *Track metrics over time and study histograms*—This can help for capacity planning or scalability conversations.
- *Define operational and tactical goals*—Usually, this is called *service level objective* (SLO) (e.g., "serve less than 12% errors, over a period of a week"). To assess whether the goal has been met, one uses a measurement—usually called a *service level indicator* (SLI)—such as the error rate (ratio of errors to overall requests). Chapter 10 is dedicated to SLOs, so feel free to skip ahead now if you want to learn more.

Now, let's take a look at how to deal with traces.

2.5 Traces

When you hear the term *traces*, it can mean that you have to disambiguate things first—that is, be sure to ask what someone really means when referring to traces. In general, we can differentiate between two cases—local or distributed:

- In the case of local "traces," the more widely used and established term is *profiles*. We use *tracing* and *sampling* (regarding a profile) interchangeably. This is related to capturing certain characteristics of the execution of a process in the context of a single machine, such as kernel-level events or user space function calls along with execution time and resource usage, including CPU and memory, such as in the case of using `strace` to see syscalls. If you go a step further and do this sampling over a period of time, you will end up with what is called *continuous profiling* (CP; e.g., what the eBPF-based Parca (https://www.parca .dev/) project offers. We will discuss the concept of CP, its use cases, and its tooling in detail in chapter 9.

- Distributed traces are used to propagate a context across a number of microservices along a request path in the context of a distributed system, such as a containerized microservice. After the request is completed, you can stitch together the separate service executions, often visualized in a waterfall view or a graph view showing the service invocations, often called *service map.*

NOTE The term *waterfall visualization* is neither new nor unique to distributed tracing. If you look at the in-browser developer tooling available nowadays, you will find that it uses a similar representation to show how long the browser spends handling events (http://mng.bz/o1Od), such as DOM elements handling, or networking-related actions, such as downloading style files or images.

Now, let's take a high-level look at distributed traces, but if you're interested in the details, you can skip ahead to chapter 8, where we will dive deep into the topic. In a nutshell, distributed tracing is all about capturing and visualizing how a request moves through your microservices, potentially across different machines and involving different protocols such as HTTP or gRPC. Two terms you will often come across in this context are

- *Trace*—Represents the end-to-end processing of the request as it moves through the participating microservices. A trace can have multiple spans.
- *Span*—Represents the execution in one particular service along the request path, with the root span as the first span in a trace and child spans as the subsequent (nested) ones.

But how does this work? When a request enters the system, a unique identifier (the trace ID) is generated. Then, depending on the protocol the services used to communicate, such as HTTP or gRPC, this trace ID along with some payload is sent on to the children. This is what we call *context propagation* across processes in a networked setup.

The distributed tracing solution abstracts away the technical details of how the propagation is implemented as well as takes care of stitching all the spans together and delivers them to a central place where you then can view, query, and analyze the traces.

Combining distributed traces with what logs offer yields some interesting insights:

- You can look up the active trace context, pinpointing interesting sources quickly.
- If you attach a log event to the span, you can directly jump from the waterfall/timing visualization to the relevant log message of a component. This

means you don't have to search for log messages and can get away with less indexing overhead.

Now, let's see how we can put that knowledge into practice, starting with emitting spans in our example app.

2.5.1 *Instrumentation*

Listing 2.10 shows the relevant lines of our echo service in the context of instrumentation with traces. Note that we are using OpenTelemetry here to emit the spans, which we will discuss in greater detail in chapter 4.

Listing 2.10 Example Go program, instrumented to emit traces

```go
func handleEcho(w http.ResponseWriter, r *http.Request) {
    message := r.URL.Query().Get("message")
    log.WithFields(log.Fields{
        "service": "echo",
    }).Info("Got input ", message)
    ctx, cancel := context.WithCancel(context.Background())
    defer cancel()
    tr := otel.Tracer("http-api")
    _, span := tr.Start(ctx, "echo")           ⵦ⎯ Starts a new span
    defer span.End()                                  when invoked
    if rand.Intn(100) > 90 {
        log.WithFields(log.Fields{
            "service": "echo",
        }).Error("Something really bad happened :(")
        invokes.WithLabelValues(
            strconv.Itoa(http.StatusInternalServerError)).Inc()
        span.SetAttributes(
            attribute.Key("http-status-code").String(
                strconv.Itoa(http.StatusInternalServerError)))   ⵦ⎯
        w.WriteHeader(500)                          Sets the error code
        return                                      as an attribute (signal
    }                                               metadata) of the span
    invokes.WithLabelValues(
        strconv.Itoa(http.StatusOK)).Inc()
    span.SetAttributes(
        attribute.Key("http-status-code").String(
            strconv.Itoa(http.StatusOK)))   ⵦ⎯ Sets success as
    fmt.Fprintf(w, message)                      an attribute
}                                                (signal metadata)
                                                 of the span
func main() {
    rand.Seed(time.Now().UnixNano())
    registry.MustRegister(invokes)
    log.SetFormatter(&log.JSONFormatter{})
    http.HandleFunc("/echo", handleEcho)
```

```
    http.Handle("/metrics", promhttp.HandlerFor(
        registry,
        promhttp.HandlerOpts{
            EnableOpenMetrics: true,
        },
    ))
    tp, err := tracerProvider("http://localhost:14268/api/traces")     ◁──┐
    if err != nil {
        log.Fatal(err)                                    Sets up the OpenTelemetry
    }                                                       config for Jaeger as the
    otel.SetTracerProvider(tp)                                  trace provider
    log.Fatal(http.ListenAndServe(":4242", nil))
}
```

Now, let's start the service and generate some spans.

2.5.2   Telemetry

We can now execute the echo service locally and ingest traces like so:

```
$ ./echosvc
```

We can ingest the traces of our echo service using Jaeger (https://www.jaegertracing
.io/), which we then use as the data source for Grafana.

   To set up the destination, use the Docker Compose manifest file shown in the following listing to set up Jaeger and Grafana.

Listing 2.11   Using docker-compose.yaml to stand up Jaeger and Grafana

```yaml
version: "3.5"
networks:
  jaeger:
services:
  jaeger:
    image: jaegertracing/all-in-one:latest
    ports:
    - "6831:6831/udp"
    - "16686:16686"
    - "14268:14268"
    networks:
    - jaeger
  grafana:
    image: grafana/grafana:latest
    ports:
    - "3000:3000"
    networks:
    - jaeger
```

Next, add Jaeger as a data source in Grafana, as shown in figure 2.5, using http://jaeger:16686 as the URL.

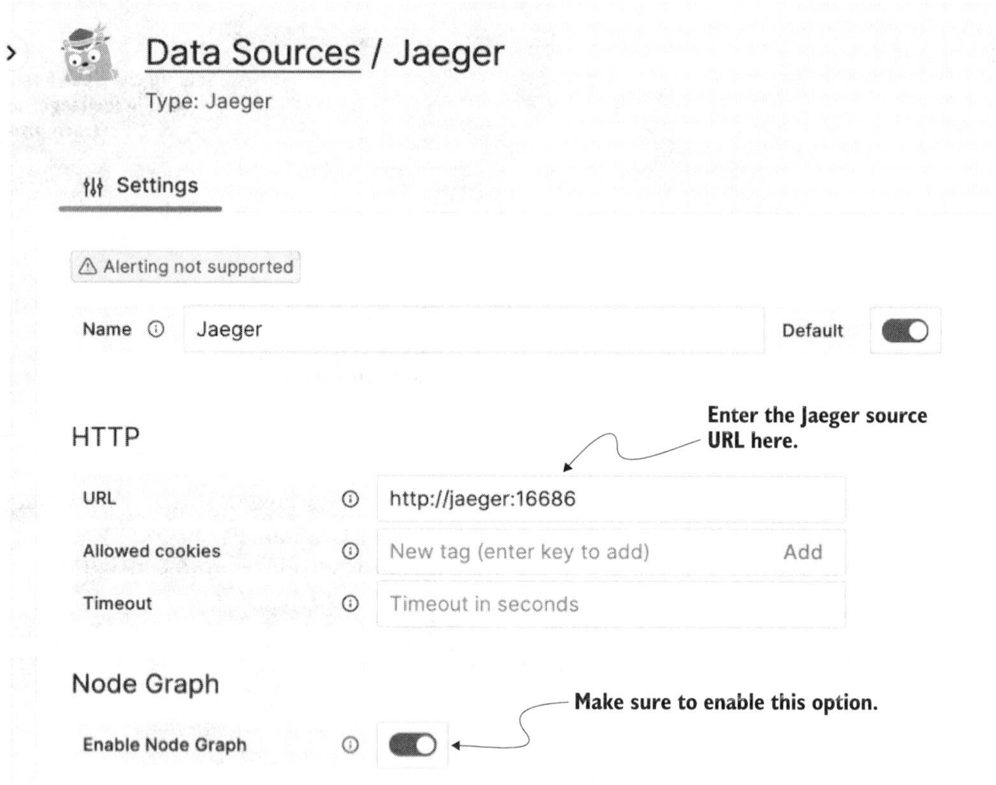

Figure 2.5   Adding and configuring the Jaeger data source in Grafana

Now, you can again use the Explore tab. Select Jaeger as the data source; switch to the Search tab (in the Query type field); select `echosvc`; and if you now select one of the traces by clicking on a Trace ID, you should see something similar to what is shown in figure 2.6 (in the Trace View, right-hand side). In the next subsection, we'll have a look at the costs and benefits of traces.

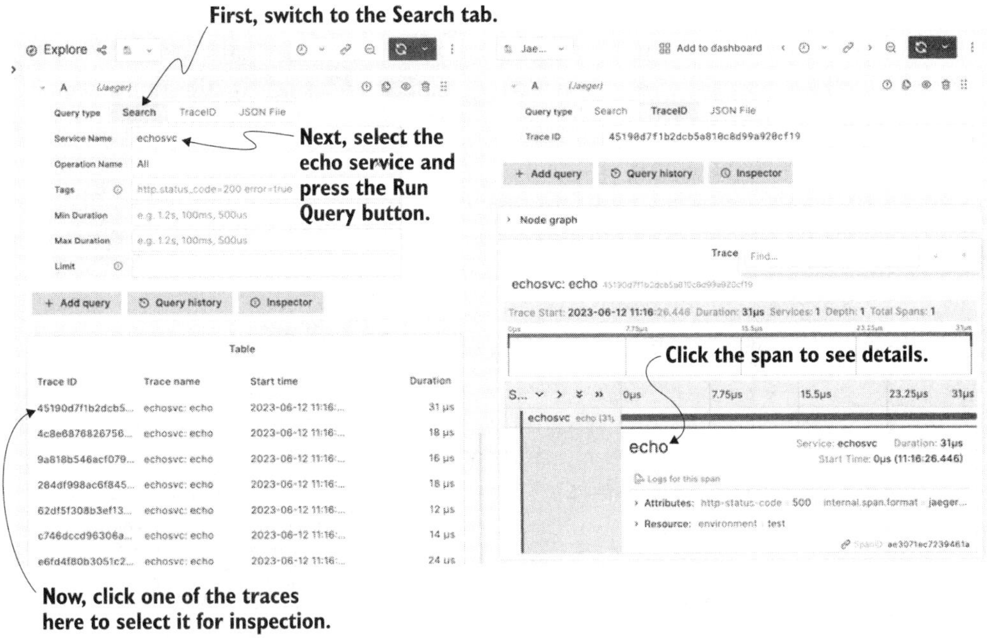

Figure 2.6   Exploring traces with Jaeger: detailed trace view

2.5.3   Costs and benefits

Let's take a closer look at the costs and benefits of the traces signal type. Table 2.3 provides a cost overview of traces.

Table 2.3   Overview of the costs of traces

	Overhead	Considerations
Instrumentation	Some effort and auto-instrumentation	OpenTelemetry uptake and legacy
Agent	Sampling strategy and latency overhead	Use OpenTelemetry collector
Destination	Dedicated storage layer and query and analytics	Lots of commercial offerings and some OSS (e.g., Tempo and Jaeger)

INSTRUMENTATION COSTS OF TRACES

The instrumentation costs of traces, from a developer's point of view, look as follows: the original code in listing 2.1 has 24 lines of code, and the code instrumented with traces in listing 2.10 has 99 lines of code overall.

Now, to isolate the traces-caused instrumentation costs from the total (logs + metrics + traces) instrumentation cost, we need to subtract the 8 LOC from the logs-caused instrumentation as well as the 24 LOC that the metrics instrumentation contributed.

We arrive at a value of 67 LOC for the traces instrumentation alone. Taking the two LOC numbers together, we can calculate the B2I ratio and arrive at a value of 2.79, which is almost double of logs alone (1.33) and slightly higher than metrics instrumentation alone (2).

TELEMETRY COSTS OF TRACES

One major consideration (and this topic could also fit in the instrumentation section previous, but I chose to talk about it here) is sampling of traces. We will discuss this topic in greater detail in chapter 8.

Sampling, in the context of distributed tracing, means to either capture or discard a certain trace a source emits. We usually differentiate between

- *Head-based (sometimes called up-front) sampling*—The agent discards a fixed number of traces. It's deterministic and helps when you're focusing on network costs; however, you may miss interesting traces (anomalies, errors, etc.).
- *Tail-based sampling*—The idea is to defer the sampling decision to when the trace is complete. But how do you know when the trace is done (stragglers)? It usually requires the agent to keep more state around and can lead to a more complex setup as well as higher resource usage (network + storage costs) compared to the simpler up-front sampling decision.

In addition to the runtime overhead (resource consumption) we have seen with logs and metrics already, there's also a tiny latency overhead in the communication path in the case of traces. This is due to the fact that context propagation costs time and bandwidth in the sources as well as on the wire.

DESTINATION COSTS OF TRACES

The distributed tracing solutions in general use data stores that allow you to deal with sparse, timestamped data. In general, traces need to be indexed so that you can search or filter for a particular service or can order by duration. This typically means the storage (backend) needs to be able to index certain span characteristics, such as service name, tags, and other metadata (e.g., the HTTP method).

There are different approaches used in the wild to realize trace storage and retrieval, which can be grouped as follows:

- Dedicated data stores, such as ClickHouse (https://clickhouse.com/)
- General-purpose NoSQL data stores, such as Cassandra, HBase, or Elasticsearch/OpenSearch, that are used with domain-specific schemas and logic to accommodate needs
- Object storage–based backends (e.g., using S3 buckets) that come with querier/ingester logic, such as with Grafana Tempo

The costs of the backends in tracing, like metrics, usually fall into one or more of three buckets: ingestion (how many traces with what payload are inserted), processing (sometimes called *scanning* or *traces retrieved*), and long-term storage costs (retention policies). We will discuss backends in detail in chapter 5.

The actual, overall costs depend on the use case and your policies, so it's not possible to come up with meaningful guidance that is generally applicable. Take, for example, a case where you equip all your developers with access to the distributed tracing solution versus the case where only operations or on-calls get to benefit from it.

BENEFITS OF TRACES

In a microservices setup, you shouldn't view distributed tracing as optional. You get the dynamic high-level call graph/service map of how your services actually communicate, and you can drill into the request paths, without having to manually (time-stamp-based) correlate service calls via log events.

Popular distributed tracing frontends include the following:

- The Zipkin (https://zipkin.io/) built-in UI
- The Jaeger (https://www.jaegertracing.io/) built-in UI
- Using Grafana with various data source plugins (e.g., Jaeger, Tempo, and X-Ray)
- Various plug-ins for Kibana or OpenSearch dashboards

There's a range of commercial (some SaaS and some OSS) offerings that combine back-end/storage and frontend, covering traces among other signal types. We will dive deep into this topic in chapter 6. With this, we've completed the traces cost and benefits discussion. Let's now look at use cases for traces in the context of observability.

2.5.4 *Observability with traces*

What can we do with traces, and how is what we just saw related to observability? In a developer or QA/test role,

- Developers can use spans to identify slow services and optimize request latencies based on this information.
- QA employees can use traces to troubleshoot a dev/test or preproduction environment to catch performance regressions.
- Developers and testers benefit from distributed traces in debug situations—for example, when a customer reports an issue and live (production) workloads need to be investigated.

In a DevOps or SRE role,

- Based on an alert or a customer reporting an issue, on-calls often find themselves in a first-responder role. They need to be able to search for and identify services or components that could be the cause of the problem.
- For SREs, to assess the overall or component health, trace aggregates (e.g., p90 or p95 values) serve as indicators or input data for recommendations for developers.

With this, we've completed our survey of signal types and use cases. Next, let's move on to some good practices that generally apply.

2.6   *Selecting signals*

When collecting signals, be sure to consider the following things:

- Why should I capture this signal? From an ROI perspective, does the signal yield an actionable insight, or does it contribute to the noise (and, even worse, potentially cause network and storage-related costs, without offering any benefit)?

- How long should I store the signal (retention period)? This depends chiefly on the task at hand (e.g., troubleshooting, on-call, or optimization), but there may also be external factors that influence the decision on how long to retain a signal. For example, in the financial industry, you may be required to keep transaction logs for a certain period of time, in order to be, say, Payment Card Industry Data Security Standard (PCI DSS) compliant.

- For numerical signals, such as metrics, what is the "normal" value (or value range)? This is usually used as a baseline. You may consider automating the process of establishing the baseline, potentially using machine learning techniques. In this context, if a signal is not in its normal range, anomaly detection (https://github.com/AICoE/prometheus-anomaly-detector) is your friend.

- Beware of signal hoarding; keeping around all metrics or logs, just because you may need them one day (without a strategy), can be expensive and negatively influence the ROI.

- Label consistently across signal types (e.g., Loki, Prometheus, and Parca).

With this general collection of good practices and considerations regarding selecting signals, we have reached the end of the chapter.

Summary

- To generate actionable insights, for observability, we rely on different telemetry signals, most importantly logs, metrics, and traces.

- You need to decide what signals to collect, store, and use, based on their utility and costs.

- Logs are signals with a textual payload that capture an event, usually consumed by humans.

- Ideally, logs should be structured (e.g., expressed in JSON) and come with a schema, but in reality, the situation can be messy, due to the many formats and protocols in use.

- Metrics are numerical signals, useful for automation (e.g., for dashboarding and alerting).

- The Prometheus format has established itself as a standard in cloud-native systems.

- Distributed traces are signals that capture and visualize how a request moves through your microservices, showing service duration and success state.

- All signals come with costs and benefits, ranging from the instrumentation effort to the telemetry agent to the destinations. This is something you need to consider on a case-by-case (workload) basis in the context of ROI.
- You have seen the signal types in action, end to end, from the instrumentation in the context of a sample app to routing via an agent to the destinations.
- We reviewed shortcomings and good practices in choosing what signals to expose and in what manner for a given use case or task, such as troubleshooting or optimization.

Sources

This chapter covers

- What we mean by signal sources
- The types of sources that exist and when to select which source
- Gaining actionable insights from selecting the right sources for a task
- How to deal with code you own and how and when to instrument
- Understanding supply chain visibility

From an observability point of view, the system under observation (SUO) is made up of a collection of *sources*. These sources emit telemetry signals, such as logs, metrics, and traces, which we discussed in chapter 2 and which form the basis for actionable insights for humans and machines alike.

In the context of cloud-native systems, things tend to move fast—new open source projects are launched, providers add features to their products, and cloud providers introduce new services. It is for this reason (that is, the iteration speed found in cloud-native systems) that we won't go into great detail about specific offerings, their APIs, or their features. What is important and what I'd like to focus on is to enable you to understand which sources are at your disposal and which ones you may wish to select for a certain task.

In this chapter, we will categorize sources using a simple and widely used trichotomy: compute, storage, and network. On a high level, this looks as follows:

- *Compute*—Runtime environments, such as a virtual machine (VM), including those that are general purpose and language specific, like the Java VM, as well as the compute unit, like a microservice running in a container or a function supported by AWS Lambda
- *Storage*—Relational databases (PostgreSQL, MySQL, etc.), NoSQL data stores (Redis, MongoDB, DynamoDB, etc.), file systems (local and networked, like NFS), as well as object stores (e.g., S3)
- *Network*—Network interfaces; gateways; load balancers; virtual private networks (VPNs); and entire isolated cloud provider networks, such as a virtual private cloud (VPC)

In this chapter, we will cover a wide array of technologies. The goal is not to cover each of the signal types per source in detail but to provide you with an overview and a general idea of what to expect as well as information about where to learn more about each source.

3.1 Selecting sources

Remember that the goal of observability is to gain actionable insights, which starts with knowing what sources and signals to consider. On the upside, each source we select contributes signals we can directly use or correlate with other signals. On the other hand, each source that we take into account requires investments: from the instrument costs to agents required to ingest the signals to storage costs in the destinations.

One important thing to consider in the context of sources is what source is relevant to a task or role at hand. An efficient strategy for selecting signal sources is to work backwards, on a per-task or use-case basis. For example, the task at hand might be on-call for infrastructure operations, and you might primarily care about the overall CPU, RAM, and file system utilization. Another example might be improving the latency of an API request as a developer, where you require visibility into network-related sources.

Not only must you consider which sources you select but also which signals from a source you use and to what extent. Consider, for example, the case of a serverless Kubernetes offering, where the control plane and the data plane are both managed for you. Take etcd, where the Kubernetes control plane keeps its state in this context: given that you don't have access to it, you can't change anything in the setup (e.g., rebalance or scale etcd). Because of this immutability, detailed metrics are not as valuable, whereas an overall health indicator is.

However, there are tradeoffs you need to consider; for example, while you might not control how autoscaling happens, having good visibility into how often or when it happens can aid troubleshooting. At the very least, it should help you to determine if the problem is on the provider side or in your app.

We can differentiate between sources you own—and, hence, you're free to instrument—and sources you don't own. Typically, the sources you don't own—and, hence, aren't free to instrument—make up the majority of the sources. This ranges from the compute runtime to storage and network to libraries and other services you use and depend on in your own code.

OK, that was enough theory. Now, let's get our hands dirty, starting with compute-related sources.

3.2   *Compute-related sources*

This section reviews compute-related sources. We will have a look at different types of compute, their main characteristics from an observability angle, and what signals are relevant for which roles.

3.2.1   *Basics*

In the context of cloud-native environments, we're usually faced with a variety of options when it comes to compute. Ultimately, we care about the features we can deliver to business stakeholders. So in an ideal world, we would be able to focus on the application level, which is core to the business, and outsource as much of the heavy lifting (e.g., security patches and operating system upgrades, which are typically not core to the business) to our service provider of choice.

There are oftentimes, however, good reasons that we want to or must own a larger part of the infrastructure stack than we may desire—from compliance requirements to the need for controlling certain aspects of compute (like GPU- or I/O-related). No matter where exactly the line between the infrastructure and application level is, in your case, a good understanding of the responsibilities (e.g., who owns upgrades or security aspects) is the basis for a successful cloud-native operation.

Depending on your role (operations, developer, architect, release engineer, etc.), you might view compute in different ways. Some common ones include the following:

- The unit of deployment (a VM, container, or function)
- Server-centric versus serverless compute
- Monolithic apps versus service-oriented (microservices)

Figure 3.1 shows the spectrum of compute with some common cloud-native example setups. The unshaded boxes in each setup stand for the respective infrastructure components and the shaded boxes for the application-level components.

> **NOTE**   In reality, in any given production environment, you will come across a combination of compute. This may be due to technical reasons (e.g., a move to the cloud and, with it, a containerization of the service), or it could be due to business reasons, such as an acquisition or merger, where different architectures need to be integrated. No matter the reason, it means you almost

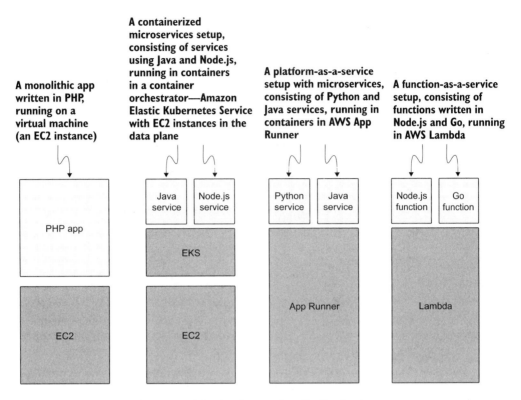

Figure 3.1   A spectrum of compute, infrastructure, and application level

always have to be prepared to deal with a variety of sources and what looks like a good tool or approach for, say, monitoring a monolith is likely not a good fit for a container.

Table 3.1 provides an overview of the coverage of signals across compute-related sources.

Table 3.1   Observability readiness for compute-related sources

Signal	Coverage	Example sources
Logs	All sources	EC2 instance, Docker daemon, and Lambda function
Metrics	Many sources	EC2 instance and Kubernetes metrics pipeline
Traces	Some sources	Node.js function in Lambda

Let's now have a closer look at concrete compute-related sources and their characteristics, in terms of signals. A VM is an established and widely used way to run arbitrary code with certain isolation guarantees with respect to other tenants on the underlying (physical) machine. There are also language-specific VMs, such as the

Java virtual machine (JVM). The JVM represents a rich signal source, exposing logs (https://openjdk.java.net/jeps/158) as well as a number of metrics, from heap memory usage to threads, and you have many tools at your disposal to monitor the JVM performance (https://sematext.com/guides/java-monitoring/).

One thing most Linux systems (bare metal and VMs) have in common these days is that they are using systemd, so let's have a look at certain aspects that are, in general, applicable to systems where users have access to the operating system. Rather than relying on textual logs, systemd comes with its own subsystem, called `journalctl`, which uses a binary format to store logs, with the advantage that the access is faster and the storage is more compact than text. However, this comes with the disadvantage that the traditional text-based tools (e.g., `tail`) don't work anymore.

The `journalctl` tool supports a rich interface, allowing for interactive as well as one-shot-style queries. For example, to show the logs of the systemd unit `example` for the past 12 hours,

```
journalctl --since "12 hours ago" -u example.service
```

A widely adopted concept in logging libraries and frameworks across programming languages is that of *log levels*, representing how severe or granular a certain message is. For example, with `journalctl` you could use `--priority=3` to limit the output to logs with a priority of `Error` (or higher priority).

We will now consider VMs as part of the infrastructure and cover specific characteristics in the context of other compute-related sources, such as Kubernetes. For all cases in which you have access to the VM—that is, besides serverless environments—it is generally true that you can view and query the system logs of the VM. Let's have a look at a concrete example and, with it, a proprietary solution for logs: consider an EC2 instance like the one that follows (note that the output is edited to fit; relevant parts are annotated):

Details about the boot process of the VM, including supported hardware

```
$ aws ec2 get-console-output --instance-id i-0c87223xxxxx --output text
i-0c87223xxxxx    [    0.000000] Linux version 5.8.0-1041-aws
(buildd@lcy01-amd64-017) (gcc (Ubuntu 10.3.0-1ubuntu1~20.10) 10.3.0,
 GNU ld (GNU Binutils for Ubuntu) 2.35.1)
 #43-Ubuntu SMP Wed Jul 14 14:49:43 UTC 2021 (Ubuntu 5.8.0-1041.43-aws 5.8.18)
[    0.000000] Command line: BOOT_IMAGE=/boot/vmlinuz-5.8.0-1041-aws
  root=PARTUUID=fd4c3fdd-01 ro console=tty1 console=ttyS0
  nvme_core.io_timeout=4294967295 panic=-1
[    0.000000] KERNEL supported cpus:
...
Welcome to Ubuntu 20.10!
[    8.645187] systemd[1]: Set hostname to <ubuntu>.
[    8.650813] systemd[1]: Initializing machine ID from KVM UUID.
[    8.655158] systemd[1]: Installed transient /etc/machine-id file.
...
[  OK  ] Finished Execute cloud user/final scripts.
[  OK  ] Reached target Cloud-init target.
```

Here, systemd kicks in and takes over the VM initialization.

In an infrastructure or platform operator role, you will find the VM-level signals useful, be that for troubleshooting or planning. Developers may not always have access to the sources in this space, with JVM a potential exception. With the basics out of the way, let's first turn our attention to containerized environments.

3.2.2 Containers

Containers are convenient abstractions that provide application-level dependency management. That is, containers leverage Linux kernel features, including namespaces for isolation (e.g., processes, network stacks, or file system mount points) and cgroups for resource usage management. Containers wrap up these kernel features in a simple and usable API, allowing you to launch applications with certain isolation guarantees. They are well suited to package all the dependencies your app has (from programming language libraries to operating-system-level resources to environment variables) into a single artifact, called a *container image*, and run it on a host. For the container host, the general observations for VMs or bare-metal instances apply—that is, usually depending on journald for events, with `journalctl` as its primary interface.

Specifically, for the containers, signals can come from the container runtime, such as Docker or containerd itself. On the other hand, signals come from the running containers—that is, application-level signals.

For logs, different container runtimes offer different levels of support:

- The Docker daemon (https://docs.docker.com/config/daemon/#read-the-logs) features a full-blown solution, depending on the host environment, typically making the logs available via `journalctl` or in a certain file system location, such as under `/var/log/`.
- With containerd, the assumption is that the environment in which it is used (e.g., Kubernetes) takes care of the log management. In other words, it doesn't support its own end-to-end solution; however, if you run containerd as a systemd unit, journald will capture the output, providing you with some basic information.
- The Kubernetes-specific container runtime interface (CRI; http://mng.bz/0KAJ) is platform agnostic and does not directly support logging. Instead, the CRI defers the concrete log support to the container runtime you use, such as containerd (see previous).

Concerning container logs from the application level, we have to step back a bit. Twelve-factor apps consider treating logs (https://12factor.net/logs) as event streams, encourage the apps to log to `stdout`, and don't concern themselves with log routing. This "log-to-stdout" stance is what you find nowadays with containers as well; Docker has full support for container logs (http://mng.bz/Ke8X), enabling you to manage log input and output via log drivers, such as journald, syslog, and Fluentd, as well as cloud provider–specific formats. For example, to send logs from a Docker container directly to Amazon CloudWatch, you would configure the log driver like so:

```
docker run --log-driver=awslogs \
          --log-opt awslogs-region=eu-west-1 \
          --log-opt awslogs-group=docker-test \
          --log-opt awslogs-create-group=true \
     ...
```

If you want to learn more about how to use logs with containers, I recommend reading *Logging in Action* by Phil Wilkins (Manning, 2022; https://www.manning.com/books/logging-in-action, which covers this topic in great detail.

For metrics, there are some options available for containers:

- A rather popular and widely used solution to expose metrics is cAdvisor (http://mng.bz/9D4j), which is used together with Prometheus.
- Telegraf (http://mng.bz/WzRg) supports a Docker plug-in (https://github .com/ influxdata/telegraf/tree/master/plugins/inputs/docker) that generates rich metrics, including container stats, memory, CPU usage, and network-related metrics.
- Docker provides a native (https://docs.docker.com/config/daemon/prometheus/) Prometheus integration, which is limited to the runtime (that is, not covering the app, at time of writing).

Specifically, if you are using the Docker daemon (https://docs.docker.com/config/daemon/), you have the option to get (low-level) access to metrics via its socket, as shown in the following code. The output of the `curl` command is edited down to show some example stats; it's in JSON format, so you can query it directly, by using, for example, `jq`:

Launches a long-running container—in this case, the NGINX server. Note the container ID 82cea007263254659534e47cfb13b951f3426f6d91a16246143480f18a217718 here, which we need in the next step to query the metrics.

```
$ sudo docker run -d --rm  nginx
82cea007263254659534e47cfb13b951f3426f6d91a16246143480f18a217718

$ sudo curl --unix-socket /var/run/docker.sock \
    "http://localhost/v1.40/containers/82cea0072632/stats?stream=false"

{
 ... "system_cpu_usage":18084207160000000,"online_cpus":2,
 ... "rss":1892352,"rss_huge":0,"total_active_anon":1892352,
 ... "total_active_file":0,"total_cache":0,"total_dirty":0,
}
```

Use curl to query the UNIX socket /var/run/docker.sock. The Docker daemon facilitates providing services such as starting or stopping containers. We need to provide the container ID we want to have the metrics for, or at least a part that uniquely addresses the container (82cea0072632, in our case).

Table 3.2 shows some example metrics (from cAdvisor) that you can expect to find, typically from containers and their runtimes.

Table 3.2 Examples of container metrics

Category	Example metric in cAdvisor
CPU	`container_cpu_usage_seconds_total` (cumulative CPU time consumed) and `container_cpu_load_average_10s` (container CPU load average over the past 10 seconds)
Memory	`container_memory_max_usage_bytes` (maximum app memory usage) and `machine_memory_bytes` (memory installed on the host)
File system	`container_file_descriptors` (open file descriptors for the container)
Network	`container_network_receive_packets_total` (cumulative count of packets received)

As a developer, you want to have access to the application-level logs, and you will likely find certain metrics useful, be that to optimize your app in terms of resource usage or for troubleshooting. For operators, having a flexible way to configure log routing is important (requirements of where to send certain types of logs and/or retention may change) as well as being able to use the metrics the runtime exposes to ensure a reliable and efficient usage of the host. Now that we have an idea about the container runtime and application basic signal sources, let's move on to how containers are usually used at scale: a container orchestrator, with Kubernetes being the most popular and widely used example.

3.2.3 *Kubernetes*

From an observability standpoint, Kubernetes is both advanced and limited. To understand this statement, let's step back a bit: on the one hand, Kubernetes defines several APIs and exposes a range of signals; on the other hand, it assumes that you take care of the telemetry and processing parts. That is, without a comprehensive strategy on how to collect, route, store, and query the signals Kubernetes offers, there is little that is available out of the box for you to consume signals.

Figure 3.2 provides a high-level overview of the signal sources available in Kubernetes (https://kubernetes.io/docs/concepts/architecture/), both in the control plane as well as the data plane.

The Kubernetes control plane manages the state of all resources in the cluster, such as workloads, namespaces, nodes, and so on, and allows you to query and change the state of the resources under management. In the data plane, several of omponents work together to launch, health check, report, and terminate the workloads (containers running in pods). Note that while Kubernetes itself comes with the promise of portable workloads, the low-level bits (from load balancers to networked storage) can and do differ across cloud providers, including APIs and formats.

The logs and metrics signal types are already well supported in Kubernetes, with logs (http://mng.bz/8rvK) being more distributed over various places and the community

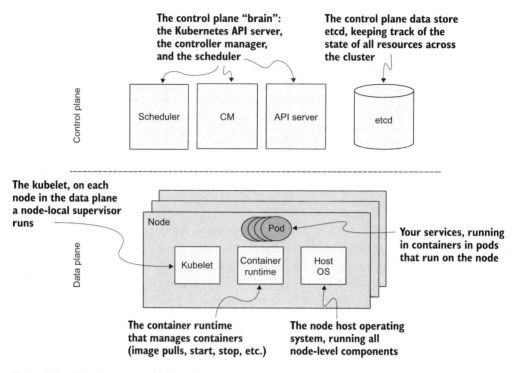

Figure 3.2   Signal sources in Kubernetes

adding support for traces. Let's have a closer look at the different signal types and sources in the Kubernetes context.

Concerning logs in Kubernetes, we can, on a high level, differentiate between the following:

- The system logs (http://mng.bz/EQzq) from the control plane, including the API server, kubelet, and container runtimes.
- The application logs, based on a logging strategy (http://mng.bz/N2DE) you pick (node local or routing based into a central search service, such as OpenSearch).

Depending on the container runtime used, different log management capabilities are available, and as a fallback, you can depend on https://github.com/kubernetes/klog (a Kubernetes-specific Go logging library) being available throughout. Kubernetes doesn't come with a built-in solution for log rotation, either, so this is another decision point, especially concerning portability.

For application logs, Kubernetes supports a simple yet effective way to capture logs that we already know from the section on containers: stdout and stderr. The transient logs are available via the kubectl logs command; however, those are typically not viable for production use, due to their limitations, such as their retention period.

In the context of development or testing, these transient logs Kubernetes offers are rather useful, as you can tell from the following example (note that the output has been edited):

With kubectl logs deployment, we ask for the collective logs from all pods under the control of the deployment. In our example, the deployment is called frontend, and we specifically are interested in the logs of the container ho11y. Finally, we limit the output (displayed log lines) with head.

```
$ kubectl logs deployment/frontend ho11y -f | head -4
{"level":"info","msg":"Using http://d...0","time":"2022-03-25T11:35:51Z"}
{"level":"info","msg":"Using http://d...1","time":"2022-03-25T11:35:51Z"}
{"level":"info","msg":"Using adot:4317","time":"2022-03-25T11:35:51Z"}
{"level":"info","msg":"Init instr... done","time":"2022-03-25T11:35:51Z"}
```

The workload or application-level logs from the ho11y container

To be able to look up logs of your workloads, you need to have a strategy or solution in place that is able to collect logs from the various pods and store and them in a central place. Let's have a look at a concrete setup, assuming you're using Amazon EKS with AWS Fargate in the data plane. In this case, the logging (http://mng.bz/D4Gy) setup is reduced to using a Kubernetes ConfigMap resource as an in interface to configure Fluent Bit as a log router that ships logs, for example, to CloudWatch. This would look as follows (output shortened):

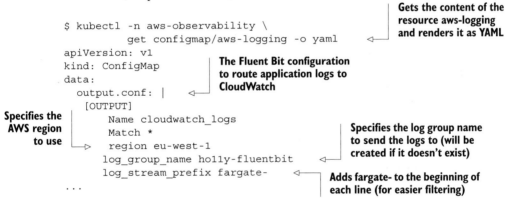

```
$ kubectl -n aws-observability \
        get configmap/aws-logging -o yaml
apiVersion: v1
kind: ConfigMap
data:
  output.conf: |
    [OUTPUT]
        Name cloudwatch_logs
        Match *
        region eu-west-1
      log_group_name ho11y-fluentbit
      log_stream_prefix fargate-
...
```

Gets the content of the resource aws-logging and renders it as YAML

The Fluent Bit configuration to route application logs to CloudWatch

Specifies the AWS region to use

Specifies the log group name to send the logs to (will be created if it doesn't exist)

Adds fargate- to the beginning of each line (for easier filtering)

To consume the logs from the command line, you could, for example, use the `aws logs get-log-events --log-group-name ho11y-fluentbit` … command or the AWS console, as depicted in figure 3.3.

There are many options available to route and consume Kubernetes logs, such as the popular end-to-end setup using Elasticsearch and Kibana (http://mng.bz/lWKj) or the OpenSearch-based variant, as well as newcomers like Grafana Loki, which we will cover in detail in chapter 5.

In the Kubernetes control plane, as shown in figure 3.2, there are several components, such as the API server or etcd, that produce logs. Another source of logs in the Kubernetes control plane is the node-level supervisor (kubelet), usually available via

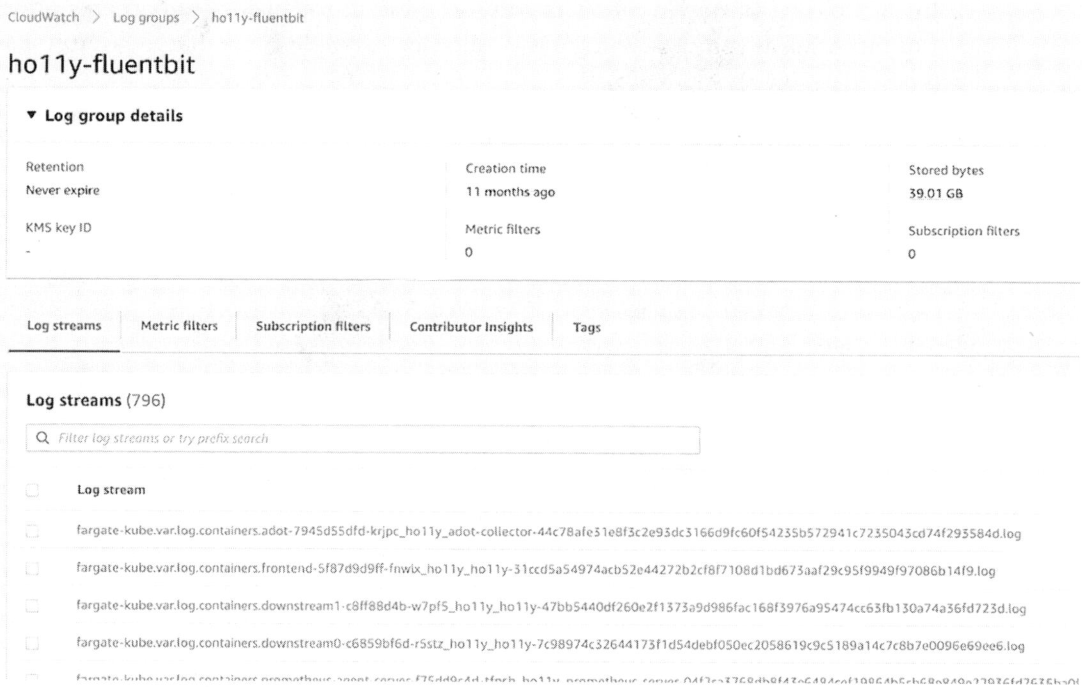

Figure 3.3 Consuming Kubernetes application-level logs in the CloudWatch console

journald. Here, it's most important to consider whether to use a managed service or run Kubernetes yourself.

For managed services, the control plane logs are of a more informational nature, since you typically don't have access to the control components (potentially useful when interacting with the cloud provider support team):

- In Amazon EKS, control plane logs (http://mng.bz/BmOv) are configurable and land in CloudWatch by default.
- In Azure AKS, several resource logs (http://mng.bz/d1gD) for control plane components are available.
- In Google GKE, you can manage both system and app logs (http://mng.bz/rWNg), with the former including control plane components.

Audit logs (http://mng.bz/V1ZX) are another source of logs in Kubernetes, capturing user-generated activities as well as control plane–related ones. These audit logs provide a detailed record of who issued each change as well as in-cluster authentication events and are often relevant, or even required, for regulated workloads and environments.

For metrics, Kubernetes uses the Prometheus exposition format (http://mng.bz/x4V8) to emit metrics, defined in the metrics pipeline (http://mng.bz/Aopp), which is part of the control plane. In contrast to logs, the definition and management of metrics is centralized. You can directly query those raw metrics in the Prometheus exposition format using the `kubectl get --raw` command, for debugging purposes. The following code provides an example (edited to fit):

Access the /metrics endpoint to get raw metrics, filter with grep for metrics that have apiserver in it, and limit with head to five lines.

```
$ kubectl get --raw /metrics | grep --color=auto apiserver | head -5
# HELP apiserver_admission_controller_admission_duration_seconds [ALPHA]
  Admission controller latency histogram in seconds, identified by name
  and broken out for each operation and API resource and type (validate
  or admit).
# TYPE apiserver_admission_controller_admission_duration_seconds histogram
apiserver_admission_controller_admission_duration_seconds_bucket{
name="CertificateApproval",operation="UPDATE",rejected="false",
type="validate",le="0.005"} 9.729562e+06
apiserver_admission_controller_admission_duration_seconds_bucket{
name="CertificateApproval",operation="UPDATE",rejected="false",
type="validate",le="0.025"} 9.729568e+06
apiserver_admission_controller_admission_duration_seconds_bucket{
name="CertificateApproval",operation="UPDATE",rejected="false",
type="validate",le="0.1"} 9.729568e+06
```

The metric shown here, apiserver_admission_controller_admission_duration_seconds, is a histogram type for a control plane component (the admission controller).

Traces are the most recently added signal type in Kubernetes. It uses OpenTelemetry (http://mng.bz/Zq6m) to capture and expose traces (at time of writing) of the API server.

3.2.4   *Serverless compute*

In this section, we take a look at signal sources in the context of serverless compute offerings. These serverless compute environments are usually preferable from an operational perspective compared to managing servers yourself; however, there are cases where you can't use them. Some of these situations include use cases with requirements to control certain low-level settings, such as Linux kernel modules or hardware configurations, for performance reasons. Another class of use cases comes from regulatory requirements, if certain certifications required for financial industry or health care industry workloads are not available.

If you can, however, make use of serverless compute for your workload, you should strongly consider it. Let's begin by discussing the general characteristics of serverless compute and implications of the environments on the observability aspects.

No (ACCESS TO) SERVERS

By definition, *serverless* means you don't deal with servers—that is, you do not provision or maintain servers. Naturally, these servers still exist in the accounts of your provider, but now, it's their responsibility to maintain them. One implication is that you typically don't have `ssh` access to a server, and hence, many of the statements related to `journalctl` in the previous section do not apply. What you, in contrast, are dealing with are APIs that allow you to consume logs or metrics and provider console dashboards that allow viewing the same in a browser.

NO PATCHING

From an operational point of view, an important part of the maintenance you are outsourcing to your serverless compute provider is security patches, usually on the operating system and (language) runtime level. This means, while you still want to track vulnerabilities (especially on the application level), there is less work required on your end, besides testing.

AUTOSCALING

One prominent expectation in serverless compute is autoscaling. This means either vertical (using VMs with more or less CPU/RAM) or horizontal (adding or removing identical machines), changing the compute capacity in order to accommodate changing load. Serverless compute lets you handle autoscaling without having to worry about the details of the scaling models, which in turn reduces the number of metrics you need to ingest.

PAY AS YOU GO

Typically, being serverless comes with a pay-as-you-go model. In other words, if you do not use the capacity, you should, theoretically, not need to pay for it. There are exceptions to this (e.g., fixed fees for an orchestrator such as Kubernetes), and the billing granularity may be a factor as well. The implication here is that you need to make sure to track costs in an automated manner (including alerts), especially if you take the autoscaling into account.

From an observability point of view, serverless environments, in general, mean less effort is required, since a large part of the operational work is outsourced to the provider. A potential downside is the lack of visibility—if an OS or VM signal is not explicitly exposed, there is no way for you to access it.

CONTAINERS VS. FUNCTIONS

Serverless compute offerings come, roughly speaking, in two flavors: container centric and function as a service (FaaS). Let's take a quick look at what the major cloud providers offer in this space.

The container-centric serverless offering in Amazon Web Services (AWS) is AWS Fargate, which you can use as the data plane in the context of two container orchestrators, either in Amazon ECS on AWS Fargate (http://mng.bz/Rxrj) or Amazon EKS on AWS Fargate (http://mng.bz/2DR8). Depending on the orchestrator you're using, different signals are available. For example, EKS on Fargate offers a Fluent Bit–based log routing solution (http://mng.bz/D4Gy) as well as metrics (http://mng.bz/1qZ1) via CloudWatch, and ECS on Fargate offers monitoring (http://mng.bz/PzBY) via CloudWatch as well as metrics in Prometheus format.

AWS Lambda (http://mng.bz/JgWK) is the FaaS serverless compute offering. As depicted in figure 3.4, it provides a unified and comprehensive observability (http://mng.bz/j129) approach that includes AWS X-Ray (http://mng.bz/wv12). In this context, you should consider how you can save on Amazon CloudWatch Logs costs (http://mng.bz/qrVJ) as well.

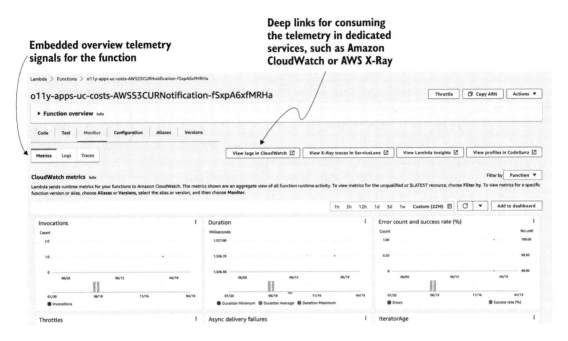

Figure 3.4 AWS Lambda monitoring in the console

There are a number of serverless compute offerings available in Microsoft's cloud, most prominently Azure Container Instances (http://mng.bz/7Dge), which has Azure Monitor (http://mng.bz/mVl4) support, covering CPU, memory, and network usage as well as comprehensive log management. Further, there is the Azure Container Apps (http://mng.bz/5wMa) serverless offering with integrated observability (http://mng.bz/6DaA). Azure Functions (http://mng.bz/o1dp) is the FaaS offering. It integrates with Azure Application Insights (http://mng.bz/nWB2) for logs and metrics as well as OpenTelemetry-based tracing support.

Google Cloud Run (https://cloud.google.com/run/) is the container-centric serverless offering of Google's cloud, optimized for stateless services. It comes with Google Cloud's operations suite (https://cloud.google.com/products/operations—formerly Stackdriver) integration, supporting logs, metrics, traces, and profiles. Google Cloud Functions (https://cloud.google.com/functions/) is Google's FaaS offering, again using Google Cloud's operations suite for observability. With this, we conclude the compute-related sources and move on to state in all its forms.

3.3   *Storage-related sources*

Next, we will take a closer look at storage-related sources. These sources range from relational databases to file systems. In general, since few people have to write their own storage systems, in this category, it's mostly about identifying what signals are available, in what form, and for what period of time (retention).

3.3.1   *Relational databases and NoSQL data stores*

Any useful real-world application typically has some state. In the context of cloud-native systems, there are several different relational database management systems (RDBMS), such as PostgreSQL and MySQL, as well as NoSQL datastores (e.g., DynamoDB, Redis, and MongoDB) used in microservices, depending on the requirements, such as strong consistency, scalability, and access patterns.

Regardless of the type of database, from a user point of view, the most important question to answer is how fast a query is processed. There are several techniques databases employ to speed up query processing, from using indexes to caches. In general, you want to treat the database as a black box, unless your role is specifically focused on this part, such as a database admin. To learn a little more about relevant metrics on a high level, check out the article, "Top 6 Database Performance Metrics to Monitor in Enterprise Applications," by Omed Habib (http://mng.bz/vn24).

RELATIONAL DATABASE MANAGEMENT SYSTEMS

The most common signal types found in the context of an RDBMS are logs and metrics, with traces also being increasingly available. Capturing the database query metrics, such as most frequent or slowest query as well as database performance (e.g., caches and sessions), provides the basis for operations.

High Performance MySQL, Fourth Edition, by Silvia Botros and Jeremy Tinley (http://mng.bz/4Dyj) is a great resource to learn about the kinds of signals MYSQL provides. It can also be used as a basis to generalize the relevant signals to other RDBMSs, such as Maria DB (https://mariadb.com/kb/en/server-monitoring-logs/). Let's take a look at a concrete example: in figure 3.5, you can see the Amazon Redshift performance monitoring, using Grafana as a frontend.

You can collect relevant database metrics yourself (e.g., the popular RDBMS PostgreSQL):

- Using Prometheus with the PostgreSQL Server Exporter (http://mng.bz/QP1v)
- Using a dedicated tool, like pgMonitor (https://github.com/CrunchyData/pgmonitor)

Another option to handle RDBMS performance metrics is to outsource this task to a vendor, be that an observability-focused vendor, like Dynatrace (http://mng.bz/XNQa), Datadog (https://www.datadoghq.com/blog/postgresql-monitoring/), or New Relic (http://mng.bz/yQ6d). Alternatively, you can use what your cloud provider of choice offers, with AWS (see figure 3.5), Azure SQL Database (http://mng.bz/MBAB), or Cloud SQL Insights (http://mng.bz/a1Ym).

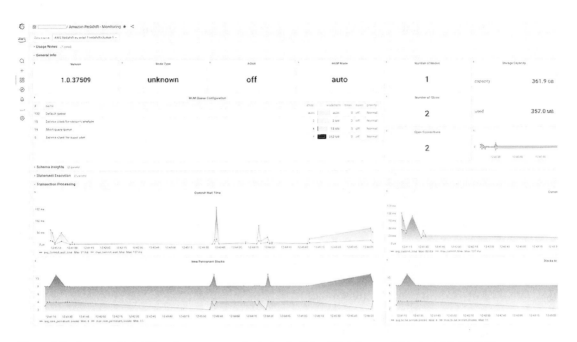

Figure 3.5   Amazon Redshift performance monitoring using CloudWatch as a data source in Grafana

With SQL, a declarative language, you state what the desired operations are, not how to execute them. The RDBMS executing your SQL query has a dedicated component called the *query planner* (https://sqlite.org/queryplanner.html), which takes care of optimizing the SQL query, taking indexes and other factors into account. You can learn about details of the query planning, for example, via the EXPLAIN statement in PostgreSQL (https://explain.depesz.com/s/Q6sQ).

NoSQL
NoSQL data stores have not been around as long as relational databases (less than 20 years compared to 50+ years in the case of RDBMSs). While, for logs, the same considerations apply as for RDBMSs: for performance metrics, we are faced with different characteristics. The emphasis in the context of NoSQL is less on query planning because the lack of relations means query planning matters less. Most important in the NoSQL context are access patterns and what is going on in the storage layer.

Given the breadth of NoSQL datastores (from key–value and document datastores, such as Redis, MongoDB, and DynamoDB, to graph datastores, like Neo4j or Amazon Neptune, to search engines, including Elasticsearch/OpenSearch), we won't go into great detail here, but a few examples may highlight good practices:

- "How to Monitor Redis with Prometheus" by David de Torres Huerta (https://sysdig.com/blog/redis-prometheus/)
- "Monitoring for MongoDB" (http://mng.bz/pPrK)

- "Top DynamoDB Performance Metrics" by Jean-Mathieu Saponaro (https://www.datadoghq.com/blog/top-dynamodb-performance-metrics/)
- "Monitoring Elasticsearch With Sematext" (http://mng.bz/e1KV)

Next up, we'll cover two universal yet simple storage systems: file systems and object stores.

3.3.2　*File systems and object stores*

We will now move on to two storage-related sources that are widely used in cloud-native systems, typically for binary large objects (BLOB), such as images, videos, or documents (PDFs, Word documents, etc.). An important use case for local file systems in cloud-native contexts (e.g., Linux `ext4` or Window NTFS) is that of scratch space or, in other words, for managing temporary files. Networked file systems, such as NFS (https://datatracker.ietf.org/doc/rfc3530/), and object stores are oftentimes used for long-term storage, since they are in contrast to locally attached non-ephemeral storage (i.e., life cycles extend beyond the instance, container, or function existence).

The central place for all sorts of logs, from application logs to system logs, in Linux is the `/var/log` directory, and the dominant tooling for managing local logs is increasingly `journalctl`. I highlight the *local* here, since `journalctl` (by design) does not support shipping logs off a machine, leaving this as an exercise for the operator. We will revisit this issue in chapters 4 and 5, when we talk about log shipping from an agent and back-end destinations perspective.

From an infrastructure operator point of view (e.g., a Kubernetes platform admin), the most important file system signal is the amount of free space left on the root device, and various bad things can happen (https://sre.google/workbook/eliminating-toil/) if you run out of disk space. A simple way to check available disk space on a Linux system is the `df` (https://man7.org/linux/man-pages/man1/df.1.html) command. Take the following example:

Uses the -h option to print sizes in powers of
1024—that is, in a more human-readable format

```
$ df -h
Filesystem      Size  Used Avail Use% Mounted on
/dev/root       7.7G  3.7G  4.1G  47% /
tmpfs           3.8G     0  3.8G   0% /dev/shm
tmpfs           1.5G  904K  1.5G   1% /run
tmpfs           5.0M     0  5.0M   0% /run/lock
tmpfs           4.0M     0  4.0M   0% /sys/fs/cgroup
tmpfs           767M  4.0K  767M   1% /run/user/1000
```

We can see here that a little less than half of the disk space (47%) is used up on this machine.

You can gather further relevant file system metrics with low-level tooling, such as `iostat` and `nfsstat`, or using higher-level tools and agents, like Prometheus (https://prometheus.io/docs/guides/node-exporter/) or, in the case of OpenTelemetry, the Host Metrics receiver (http://mng.bz/OxRw).

For cloud-native applications, object stores are the workhorses, used for virtually anything from small files (JSON) to large BLOBs, such as images. Typically, these object stores offer a simple HTTP API to store and list objects. Different cloud providers offer a range of signals from object stores, usually at least logs and metrics—for example, Amazon S3 (http://mng.bz/Y1Xz), Azure Blob Storage (http://mng.bz/GylD), and Google Cloud Storage (https://cloud.google.com/storage/docs/access-logs).

We've now completed a brief review of storage-related sources, which is mostly relevant for infrastructure operators and is secondary for developers. We now move on to a kind of signal source that you will have to pay attention to, no matter what your role is: networks and their signals.

3.4 Network-related sources

In this section, we will look at all sorts of network-related sources, from low-level interfaces to virtual networks. As with storage, these sources are mostly owned by others (e.g., your cloud provider of choice) and, by their nature, are high-volume sources, meaning you have to deal with a lot of noise.

3.4.1 Network interfaces

Physical network interfaces or virtual interfaces, such as the loopback interface, form the lowest layer of network-related sources. Depending on the environment (think serverless data planes or FaaS), you may or may not have direct access to these interfaces. By *direct access*, I mean being able to use commands such as `ip` (http://mng.bz/zXo1) to query interface and routing information.

To demonstrate the difference between having direct access to the network interface information and when that's not the case, imagine you have an EC2 instance (e.g., as part of a Kubernetes cluster data plane) that you can `ssh` into and then execute (the output is edited to fit):

Using the ip command, list network interfaces, their configuration, and status.

```
$ ip link show
1: lo: <LOOPBACK,UP,LOWER_UP> mtu 65536 qdisc noqueue state UNKNOWN mode
    DEFAULT group default qlen 1000
    link/loopback 00:00:00:00:00:00 brd 00:00:00:00:00:00
2: ens5: <BROADCAST,MULTICAST,UP,LOWER_UP> mtu 9001 qdisc mq state UP mode
    DEFAULT group default qlen 1000
    link/ether 0a:78:c2:54:1f:39 brd ff:ff:ff:ff:ff:ff
    altname enp0s5
3: docker0: <NO-CARRIER,BROADCAST,MULTICAST,UP> mtu 1500 qdisc noqueue state
    DOWN mode DEFAULT group default
    link/ether 02:42:18:7d:57:00 brd ff:ff:ff:ff:ff:ff

$ ip route
default via 172.31.32.1 dev ens5 proto dhcp src 172.31.40.108 metric 100
172.17.0.0/16 dev docker0 proto kernel scope link src 172.17.0.1 linkdown
172.31.32.0/20 dev ens5 proto kernel scope link src 172.31.40.108
172.31.32.1 dev ens5 proto dhcp scope link src 172.31.40.108 metric 100
```

Using the ip command, list routing information, such as the default gateway.

While you do have visibility into network interfaces (both configuration and dynamic information) in the case of a VM or a physical server, in the context of a cloud function or lambda function, you do not.

3.4.2   *Higher-level network sources*

In contrast to network interfaces, higher-level network sources, such as load balancers, are usually directly accessible in terms of having access to the relevant signals, most importantly metrics (health and performance related). Load balancers, both L3/4 and L7 (that is, HTTP level) typically provide a wealth of signals—for example, the Amazon Application Load Balancer (ALB; http://mng.bz/0KvJ) supports logs, metrics, and traces. For a concrete example, see figure 3.6, which is derived from an open source observability demo (https://github.com/observe-k8s/Observe-k8s-demo). The same is the case for the Amazon API Gateway (http://mng.bz/9Dpj) in front of lambda functions. One important aspect in this context is the health of the backends and how to make sure they are up—and, hence, traffic can be routed to them. For example, an `HTTPCode_ELB_504_Count` code from the ALB (http://mng.bz/Wz4g) indicates that backend resources didn't respond in time or, as shown in figure 3.6, various usage-related metrics. Further, you should consider that certain orchestrators, such as Kubernetes, introduce network abstractions (http://mng.bz/8reK)—for example, an Ingress resource—allowing you to manage higher-level network resources in clusters along with signals that may or may not be exposed with the abstractions.

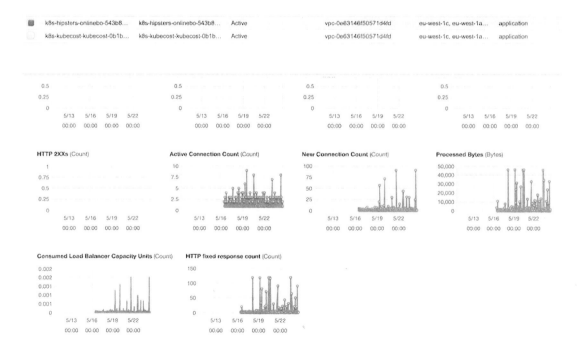

Figure 3.6   Screenshot of the ALB-monitoring console, showing usage metrics

Another high-level source in the network space is the virtual private network (VPN) or, when directly provided by a cloud provider, virtual private cloud (VPC). For an example source, you can use Amazon VPC flow logs (http://mng.bz/EQNq), which provide details about IP traffic going into and coming from network interfaces in a VPC, for a range of security-related use cases. In figure 3.7, you see an example depiction of VPC flow logs exported to an S3 bucket and using Athena for querying (http://mng.bz/6n9D).

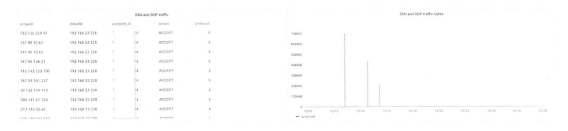

Figure 3.7   Screenshot of VPC flow logs rendered in Grafana, showing SSH and RDP traffic

With this, we've completed the infrastructure-related sources. Now, we can move on to a source type that you typically have a lot more control over: your code.

3.5   *Your code*

We now switch gears and focus on code you own and can instrument. There are two aspects to this:

- *The (business) code you write yourself*—This refers to developing new features from scratch or fixing bugs in your own code.
- *The code you depend on in your code*—This includes programming language standard libraries or third-party libraries. These libraries typically abstract low-level operations or common functionality, including storage and network access.

For the second case, your dependencies, you may, in certain cases (e.g., regulatory requirements and business reasons), decide to own it end to end. For example, you may decide to maintain a private fork of an open source project, so you can iterate faster or issue quick fixes.

In addition, supply chain aspects are important to consider—which (third-party) dependencies you should take into account, from what sources they come, and so on. For visibility into where dependencies come from, you can use tools like Backstage (https://github.com/backstage/backstage) and OpenLineage (https://openlineage.io/).

In this context, we often talk about developer or development observability (e.g., practices to consider and use CI/CD pipelines as signal sources [http://mng.bz/D4Ey]) as well as emerging dedicated tooling in this space, such as what Digma (https://github.com/digma-ai/digma) and Sprkl (https://sprkl.dev/) envision. The general direction is to make developers more productive by providing insights into code changes and their impacts on the application, using a variety of signals.

3.5.1 *Instrumentation*

We already covered the costs and benefits of instrumenting your code in detail in chapter 2 for logs, metrics, and traces. Depending on the programming languages you use (i.e., interpreted versus compiled), you're faced with different efforts to emit multiple signals. When possible, you should use auto-instrumentation, and it's usually a good idea to standardize on OpenTelemetry, to avoid reinstrumentation work when switching signal destinations. We will cover this in greater detail in chapter 4.

3.5.2 *Proxy sources*

In cases when you don't own the code but still want to get some signals out, you can use proxy sources. For example, consider the following cases in the context of scraping metrics with Prometheus:

- You want to add metrics from a message queue, like Kafka or an IoT device, to the mix, so you would run one of the many exporters (http://mng.bz/lWDj) that Prometheus can scrape.
- An alternative situation may arise where you do own the code (e.g., in the context of a batch job or Lambda function), which is a short-running process. Prometheus, on the other hand, assumes a long-running process it can scrape at any time; in this case, you'd use the Pushgateway (https://github.com/prometheus/pushgateway) to compensate for the impedance mismatch. You can learn more about this via the KubeCon EU 2022 talk "Fleeting Metrics: Monitoring Short-lived or Serverless Jobs" by Bartek Płotka and Saswata Mukherjee, available via YouTube (https://www.youtube.com/watch?v=rt4JiK995s8).

A proxy could also be an adapter (e.g., from a log file to `stdout`) to make certain signal types, like logs, compatible and usable in a cloud-native setup.

With this, we have completed the discussion of sources in our cloud-native setup, from compute to storage to network to your own code, and now we move on to the question of how the signals arrive at various destinations for consumption. In short, we move on to agents.

Summary

- Sources are anything in the system under observation that emits telemetry signals, such as logs, metrics, traces, and profiles.
- If you own a source (e.g., the application code you write, running in a container), then you can instrument it; otherwise, you need to work around it, dealing with what the owner of the source emits.
- We can differentiate between sources types: compute, storage, and network.

- Containers and functions can be challenging source types, due to their short-lived nature.
- Serverless environments mean there is less effort but also less control, from an observability standpoint.
- Storage-related sources come with broad logs; metrics support; and, to a lesser extent, traces, but profiling is available.
- For RDBMSs, query planning (analysis) is crucial. For NoSQL data stores, access patterns and storage layout are the most important areas to pay attention to.
- For file systems, it is most important to pay attention to the available disk space (for operators).
- Network-related sources can be noisy, due the high volume of events. Filtering by source, destination, or application can be challenging.
- Higher-level network sources, such as load balancers, are usually more valuable and accessible than lower-level sources, such as NICs.
- When instrumenting your code, be aware of supply chain issues (dependencies).
- For traces and metrics, always use auto-instrumentation as a baseline, and then decide based on ROI where and what to manually instrument.

Agents and instrumentation 4

This chapter covers

- What we mean by agents and instrumentation
- What types of agents exist, for what signal types
- What OpenTelemetry is and how you can benefit from it
- Criteria for selecting an agent

In this chapter, we will focus on how to get the signals from the sources we discussed in chapter 3 to the destinations, which we will be focusing on in chapters 5 and 6. Since observability is all about getting actionable insights from the signals the systems under observation expose, without the agents and instrumentation, there would be little to observe.

In a nutshell, in this chapter, we will learn how to instrument code (and automate that task) as well as select and deploy agents that collect, aggregate, filter, downsample, redact, and route logs, metrics, and traces.

The telemetry industry is, at the time of writing, in the midst of a tectonic shift. This transformation from vendor-specific or signal-specific instrumentation and agents to an industry standard called OpenTelemetry started in 2019. In the context of this book, we consider vendor-specific as well as signal-specific agents as traditional agents, in contrast to OpenTelemetry.

Cloud providers, from AWS to Azure to Google Cloud, as well as observability vendors, from Datadog to Splunk to New Relic to Lightstep to Dynatrace to Honeycomb to Grafana Labs, have decided to assemble behind OpenTelemetry. This effectively means the telemetry industry has decided to make telemetry table stakes, to commoditize it, and, instead, compete on the destinations (storage and query as well as frontends).

OpenTelemetry covers, in order of maturity and at the time of writing, traces, metrics, and logs. Going forward, the community has decided to also cover profiles (resource usage and timing within a process) in OpenTelemetry. See also our discussion in chapter 2.

Since logs are still a work in progress in 2022, I will use vendor-specific or signal-specific setups to demonstrate logs in this chapter. For metrics and traces, on the other hand, I will show you how to benefit from the open and vendor-agnostic standard that OpenTelemetry and its agent, the collector, is.

4.1 Log routers

First, we will have a look at log routers. These agents allow you to collect logs from various sources, be that on a system level or your applications, and send them to a central place for lookup. In this context, you often hear also about log forwarding, log collection, and log aggregation. However, to keep things simple, we will gloss over the details and lump all these together as *log routers*.

At time of writing (2023), vendor-specific agents, such as Splunk's Universal Forwarder or the Datadog agent, as well as signal-specific agents, including Fluentd/Fluent Bit or the widely used Logstash. Expect that to change and move to OpenTelemetry, going forward.

We will differentiate between system logs and application logs. System logs come from, but are not limited to, the following sources (refer to our discussions in chapter 2 for details):

- The operating system (e.g., in Linux, from `/var/log` and `journalctl`)
- The Kubernetes control plane (http://mng.bz/BmWv) logs (including from the API server, etcd, and controller manager) and the worker node logs (http://mng.bz/d10D), such as from the kubelet or the container runtime
- User activity and API usage logs, like the ones provided by AWS CloudTrail (https://aws.amazon.com/cloudtrail/)
- Infrastructure automation logs (e.g., from HashiCorp Terraform or AWS CloudFormation)

Application logs, on the other hand, are what you emit in your code. You may end up using different agents for system logs and application logs; however, if possible, you should try to standardize by choosing one, for example, from the ones discussed in the following sections. This is mostly for operational reasons, as it means there will be less to patch (think of the Log4j challenges, for example) and upgrade.

NOTE   In case you're not familiar with the Log4j challenges I mention here (or maybe you've forgotten about them), CVE-2021-44228 (https://nvd.nist .gov/vuln/detail/CVE-2021-44228), informally known as Log4Shell, was a zero-day vulnerability in Log4j, discovered in November 2021. It caused a lot of work (to apply the security patches) in a lot of places, from internal IT to cloud providers, and serves as an example of how much operational impact such a thing can have.

While logs are stable from an API and model perspective, in OpenTelemetry it may still take until mid-2024 until they are supported throughout in the SDKs and distributions. This means you will need a temporary strategy until you can, eventually, migrate to OpenTelemetry.

OK, that's enough theory. Let's see log routing in action. First up is a popular choice in the context of containers: Fluentd and Fluent Bit.

4.1.1   *Fluentd and Fluent Bit*

The CNCF projects Fluentd (https://www.fluentd.org/) and Fluent Bit (https:// fluentbit.io/) are popular cloud-native agents that started out in the logging domain. Initially, there was only Fluentd (written in Ruby and C), offering a rich ecosystem (with over 1,000 plug-ins) but coming with a relatively big memory footprint (dozens of MB) for the agent.

In 2014, the folks behind Fluentd, Treasure Data, acknowledged the need for a lightweight log router specifically for constraint environments (containers, IoT). This insight led to the development of Fluent Bit (written in C) with a memory footprint of a couple of hundreds of KB and many fewer plug-ins than Fluentd (less than 100).

At time of writing, Fluent Bit is expanding its scope from logs-only to other signal types, such as metrics and traces. For details, have a look at the GitHub issue "Fluent Bit v2.0 Is Coming" (https://github.com/fluent/fluent-bit/discussions/5993). We will focus on the logging aspects, in this section, however, since there are still many WIP items in flight. Let's have a look at a basic usage example in a containerized setup and discuss some properties along the way.

To demonstrate log routing, we're using an OpenSearch with Docker Compose (https://opensearch.org/docs/latest/opensearch/install/docker/) setup. Don't worry about OpenSearch for now; we will cover it in detail in chapter 5. Just think of it as the place logs can be sent to and which you can use to look up, search for, and query log lines. For example, you may be interested in all ERROR-level logs lines from a specific microservice, within a certain time range (say, the last 24 hours).

In figure 4.1, you can see our example logging pipeline—we're using `holly` (http://mng.bz/rWxg) as the log signal source running in a Docker container. The container is exposing port 8765 for its HTTP API and uses the Fluentd logging driver to send log lines to Fluent Bit (the main log router), ingesting log lines into OpenSearch as the log backend destination, which you then can query and visualize in OpenSearch Dashboards.

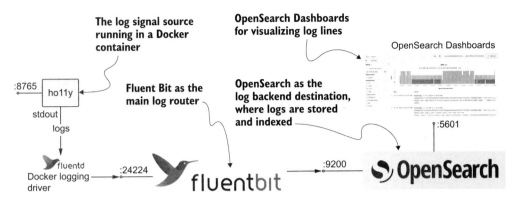

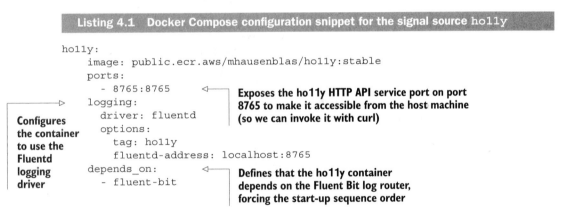

Figure 4.1 Example logging pipeline using Fluentd and Fluent Bit

Moving on to the implementation, we're once again using Docker Compose to stand up the pipeline, which is defined in the ch04/fluent-bit/docker-compose.yaml file. Let us review the pipeline step by step. I've configured the ho11y container in the Docker Compose file in a way that it is using the `fluentd` logging driver (since using Fluent Bit as the driver is not directly support there, yet).

Listing 4.1 Docker Compose configuration snippet for the signal source ho11y

```
ho11y:
    image: public.ecr.aws/mhausenblas/ho11y:stable
    ports:
      - 8765:8765          ◁——   Exposes the ho11y HTTP API service port on port
    logging:                     8765 to make it accessible from the host machine
      driver: fluentd            (so we can invoke it with curl)
      options:
        tag: ho11y
        fluentd-address: localhost:8765
    depends_on:            ◁——
      - fluent-bit                Defines that the ho11y container
                                  depends on the Fluent Bit log router,
                                  forcing the start-up sequence order
```

Configures the container to use the Fluentd logging driver

Next up is the Fluent Bit configuration, as seen in the following listing. As you can see, this takes, as one parameter, a file called fluent-bit.conf, which we will discuss later in this chapter.

Listing 4.2 Docker Compose configuration snippet for Fluent Bit

```
fluent-bit:                              Defines where the Fluent Bit
    image: fluent/fluent-bit:1.9.8       configuration (routing info)
    volumes:                                    can be found
      - ./fluent-bit.conf:/fluent-bit/etc/fluent-bit.conf   ◁——
    ports:
      - "24224:24224"       ◁——   Makes sure we open port 24224 so that we can listen on
      - "24224:24224/udp"          incoming log lines from the Fluentd logging driver in Docker
```

Last but not least, let's see how the logs' backend OpenSearch is configured (in the Docker Compose file in the following listing) in a single-node setup along with the frontend/UI, OpenSearch Dashboards.

Listing 4.3 Docker Compose configuration snippet for OpenSearch (and Dashboards)

```
opensearch-node1:
    image: opensearchproject/opensearch:2.1.0
    container_name: opensearch-node1
    environment:
      - cluster.name=opensearch-cluster
      - node.name=opensearch-node1
      - bootstrap.memory_lock=true
      - "OPENSEARCH_JAVA_OPTS=-Xms512m -Xmx512m"
      - "DISABLE_INSTALL_DEMO_CONFIG=true"
      - "DISABLE_SECURITY_PLUGIN=true"
      - "discovery.type=single-node"
    volumes:
      - opensearch-data1:/usr/share/opensearch/data
    ports:
      - 9200:9200        ◁───  Exposes port 9200 so that we can
                               ingest log lines (from Fluent Bit)
  opensearch-dashboards:
    image: opensearchproject/opensearch-dashboards:2.1.0
    container_name: opensearch-dashboards
    ports:
      - 5601:5601        ◁───  Exposes port 5601 to make OpenSearch Dashboards
    environment:               (frontend/UI) accessible from the host machine
 ┌─▷   - 'OPENSEARCH_HOSTS=["http://opensearch-node1:9200"]'
 │      - "DISABLE_SECURITY_DASHBOARDS_PLUGIN=true"
 │
 Configures OpenSearch Dashboards (frontend)
 to use OpenSearch (backend for logs)
```

At this point, we've effectively implemented the logging pipeline shown in figure 4.1. Now, let's have a closer look at the Fluent Bit configuration itself. As depicted in listing 4.4, I'm using the Forward (https://docs.fluentbit.io/manual/pipeline/inputs/forward) input plug-in in Fluent Bit, taking in the log stream from Fluentd (from the Docker runtime) and, via the OpenSearch output section, configuring Fluent Bit to route the log lines to OpenSearch.

Listing 4.4 Fluent Bit configuration

Here, we're configuring the
Forward plug-in capable of
receiving log items from Fluentd
(from the Docker log driver).

The Forward plug-in will listen
on all network interfaces (that
is, 0.0.0.0).

```
[INPUT]
    Name forward        ◁──
    Listen 0.0.0.0      ◁──
    Port 24224          ◁──
```

The default port for the
Forward plug-in (that
Fluentd connects to)

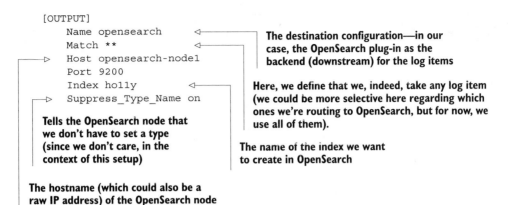

```
[OUTPUT]
     Name opensearch                    ◁
     Match **                           ◁
  ▷  Host opensearch-node1
     Port 9200
     Index holly                        ◁
  ▷  Suppress_Type_Name on
```

The destination configuration—in our case, the OpenSearch plug-in as the backend (downstream) for the log items

Here, we define that we, indeed, take any log item (we could be more selective here regarding which ones we're routing to OpenSearch, but for now, we use all of them).

Tells the OpenSearch node that we don't have to set a type (since we don't care, in the context of this setup)

The name of the index we want to create in OpenSearch

The hostname (which could also be a raw IP address) of the OpenSearch node

Phew, that was a lot of configuration! Now, it's time to launch the pipeline and generate some log lines. First off, we need to launch the Fluent Bit–OpenSearch combo:

```
docker-compose -f docker-compose.yaml up
```

In a different terminal session, launch a simple load generator (in Bash shells) like so:

```
while true ; do \
  curl -s -o /dev/null -w "%{http_code}"
➡  localhost:8765 ; \                    ◁
  sleep 1 ; \                            ◁
done
```

Uses curl to invoke holly and generate log lines, discarding the output and only showing the HTTP status code returned

Pauses for 1 second and then repeats from the top

Now, you can navigate to http://localhost:5601/. You should see the Welcome page of OpenSearch Dashboards (in the ELK stack—Elasticsearch, Logstash, and Kibana—the equivalent component would be Kibana). Click on the burger icon in the upper-left corner (the three lines), and select Stack Management followed by Index Patterns; you should see something like what is shown in figure 4.2.

Next, click on Create Index Pattern, and in the input box that's labeled Index Pattern Name, enter holly and then click Next Step. Then, in the Time Field dropdown list, select @timestamp followed by clicking the Create Index Pattern button. The result you should see is something like what is depicted in figure 4.3.

Now, head back to the OpenSearch Dashboards home page, click on the burger icon in the upper-left corner (the three lines) and then click Discover. You should then see something akin to what is shown in figure 4.4.

You now have a functioning logging pipeline based on Fluent Bit as a log router at your disposal. From this point on, feel free to drill into log lines or use the Dashboards Query Language (DQL; https://opensearch.org/docs/latest/dashboards/dql), a domain-specific query language, to find data in OpenSearch indexes, to query for specific terms in the holly logs.

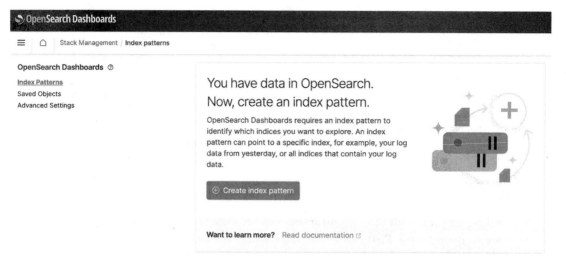

Figure 4.2   Creating an index pattern in OpenSearch Dashboards

Index patterns / ho11y

ho11y

Time field: '@timestamp'

This page lists every field in the **ho11y** index and the field's associated core type as recorded by OpenSearch. To change a field type, use the OpenSearch Mapping API

Fields (14)	Scripted fields (0)	Source filters (0)

Name	Type	Format	Searchable	Aggregatable	Excluded	
@timestamp	date		●	●		
_id	string		●	●		
_index	string		●	●		
_score	number					
_source	_source					
_type	string					
container_id	string		●			

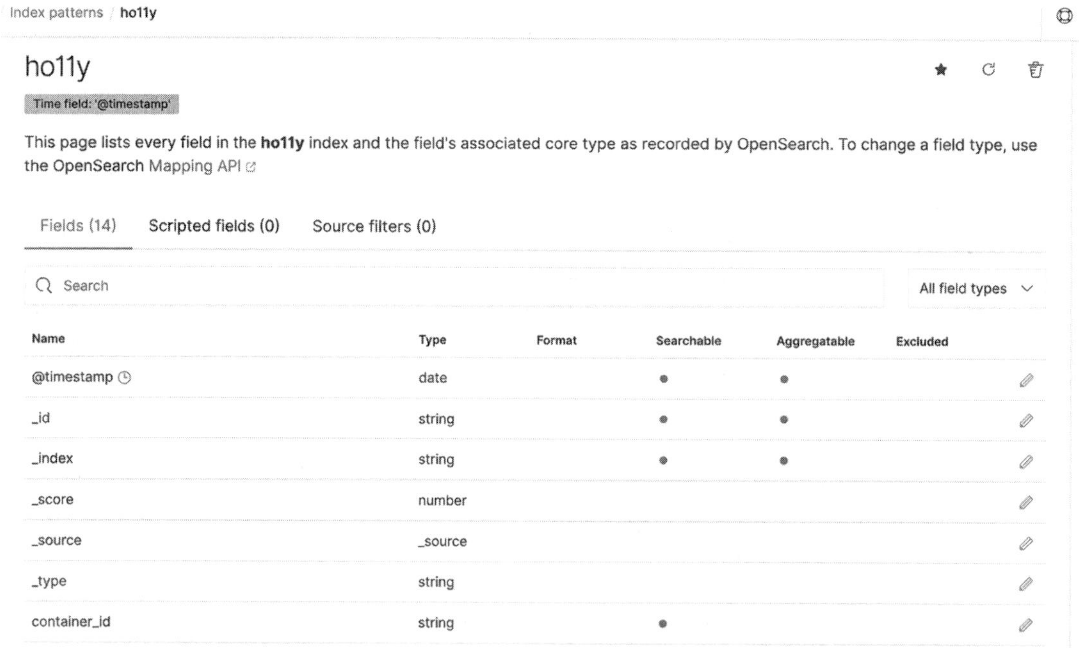

Figure 4.3   The resulting index pattern in OpenSearch Dashboards

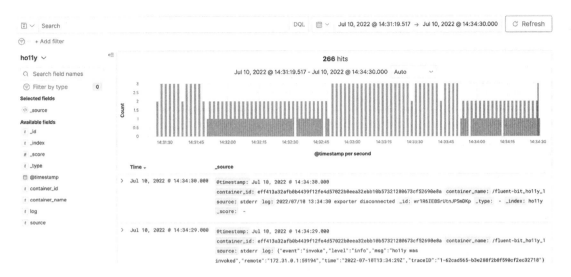

Figure 4.4   OpenSearch Dashboard's Discover view, with our `holly` index selected

If you're interested in understanding how exactly Fluentd and Fluent Bit work in greater detail and best practices for building log routing pipelines in the context of containers (especially Kubernetes), I highly recommend studying the wonderful Manning book *Logging in Action* by Phil Wilkins (2022; https://www.manning.com/books/logging-in-action).

4.1.2   *Other log routers*

We have seen Fluent Bit in action, but this is not our only option. There are, indeed, a number of both commercial and open source log routers available, such as these:

- The Beats (https://github.com/elastic/beats/tree/master) family as well as Logstash (https://github.com/elastic/logstash), part of the Elastic Stack.
- Data Prepper (https://github.com/opensearch-project/data-prepper), an AWS open source project that allows for stateful processing.
- syslog-ng (https://www.syslog-ng.com/products/open-source-log-management/) is a syslog implementation that ingests messages from systemd journal by default, applies filters, and sends them to files.
- rsyslog (https://www.rsyslog.com/) is an open source tool for routing and filtering log messages over an TCP/IP network, introduced as a replacement for syslogd.
- Graylog (https://www.graylog.org/) is a log management software company that provides logging solutions, with a focus on security use cases.
- Cribl (https://cribl.io/) is a cloud offering with powerful ingest and process capabilities.

Remember, as OpenTelemetry matures and logs continue stabilizing, make sure you have a migration strategy in place to move off of whatever log routing agent you are currently using with the OpenTelemetry collector. Let's now move on to metrics.

4.2 *Metrics collection*

In contrast to logs, the landscape is less fragmented concerning metrics. Over the past years (effectively, with the rise of Kubernetes, since 2016), the dominant player is the Prometheus project, which put forward both the way metrics are collected as well as the way metrics are represented on the wire—the *exposition format*. Let's first have a look at Prometheus and then take a quick peek at other established agents in the metrics space.

> **NOTE** While Prometheus established pull-based collection—that is, the agent queries the metrics source via an HTTP endpoint defaulting to `/metrics`— the situation is more nuanced in the context of OpenTelemetry. There, the ingress part is still pull based; however, the egress part (toward the backend destination), is typically push based. We will get into the details in the next section on OpenTelemetry.

4.2.1 *Prometheus*

Prometheus (https://prometheus.io/) is a graduated CNCF project that grew up in tandem with Kubernetes, where it also is predominantly used. It covers the ingestion, storing, and query and federation interfaces for metrics, including a simple UI. Further, part of the Prometheus project is alerting capabilities (a separate binary but tightly integrated).

In chapter 2, we had a general discussion about metrics. Now, let's have a closer look at how Prometheus does things, in greater detail.

A time series in Prometheus is uniquely identified by its metric name and a number of (optional) key–value pairs referred to as *labels*. A metric name captures the general feature you want to measure. For example, `api_requests_total` could be used for the total number of API invocations. Labels, on the other hand, represent Prometheus's dimensional data model. Let's say you want to capture two dimensions with the API invocation metric: the HTTP method used and what the URL path was. You could use the two labels `method` and `path` for this, resulting in the following, for example:

```
api_requests_total{method="GET", path="/some/interesting/thing"}
```

There are different types of metrics Prometheus supports, including counters, gauges, and histograms, and while Prometheus has naming conventions for metrics and labels (https://prometheus.io/docs/practices/naming/), it doesn't define or enforce semantics for them. The lack of defined semantics in Prometheus is, in practice, not a huge problem, since Prometheus offers a feature called *relabeling* (https://prometheus .io/docs/prometheus/latest/configuration/configuration/#relabel_config), which allows you to standardize on naming.

With relabeling, you can add, remove, or modify labels on a per-target basis. A concrete example would be to rename a label to standardize on a label name. Let's assume our source would expose the URL path under the label `handler`, but we want to use `path` in our setup. In this case, we want to do the following relabeling:

```
api_requests_total{method="GET", handler="/some/interesting/thing"}

=>

api_requests_total{method="GET", path="/some/interesting/thing"}
```

You can do this with a relabeling rule that you would define in your Prometheus scrape config (https://prometheus.io/blog/2015/06/01/advanced-service-discovery/ #scrape-configurations-and-relabeling), like the following:

```
- source_labels: [handler]         ⟵    Matches the handler label name and adds
  action: replace                        the path label with the same label value
  target_label: path
- regex: "handler"                 ⟵    Once done, it drops the handler label name, leaving
  action: labeldrop                      path as the one label capturing the URL path.
```

> **Tip**
> If you want to try out relabeling interactively, you can visit https://relabeler.promlabs .com/ and use the relabel rule (in the left-hand Relabeling Rules input box) and the following as an input for the right-hand side (Object Labels):
>
> ```
> method: "GET"
> handler: "/some/interesting/thing"
> ```
>
> When you now click the Analyze Rules button, you should see the rule engine in action, yielding the expected result.

Further, to improve query performance, you can define recording rules (http:// mng.bz/V1vX) in your Prometheus scrape config. This feature allows us to precompute frequently used or expensive expressions, effectively trading space for time, saving the result as a new time series. Let's assume we want to use a recording rule for capturing the server-side error rate of our API invocation example (with `api_ requests_total` being a counter metrics type):

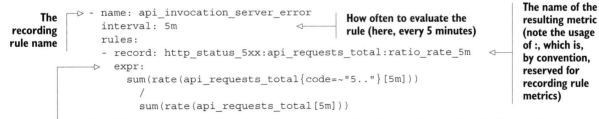

The recording rule name
```
- name: api_invocation_server_error
  interval: 5m                          How often to evaluate the
  rules:                                rule (here, every 5 minutes)
  - record: http_status_5xx:api_requests_total:ratio_rate_5m
    expr:
      sum(rate(api_requests_total{code=~"5.."}[5m]))
      /
      sum(rate(api_requests_total[5m]))
```

The name of the resulting metric (note the usage of :, which is, by convention, reserved for recording rule metrics)

The PromQL expression to evaluate at the current time, resulting in a new time series with the metric name defined by the preceding record value—http_status_5xx:api_requests_total:ratio_rate_5m, in our case

You can use Prometheus in two ways (that is, you're using the same binary, with different configurations):

- Prometheus server (default mode)
- Prometheus agent mode (https://prometheus.io/blog/2021/11/16/agent/), optimized for scraping and remote read–write for federation

We saw Prometheus in action already in chapter 2, but as a reminder, the core of Prometheus is its scrape config. This is where you define what Prometheus should scrape (its targets) and how it is supposed to find the targets (service discovery) as well as, optionally, recording and alerting rules. For example, to scrape the metrics that Prometheus itself exposes (i.e., self-scraping), you could use something like the following in your scrape config:

```
global:
  scrape_interval: 30s    ◁──┐

scrape_configs:
  - job_name: "prom"    ◁──
    static_configs:
      - targets: ["localhost:9090"]
```

By default, Prometheus scrapes (calls) targets every 15 seconds, but here, we relax it to 30.

Prometheus adds the job name as a label (here, job=prom) to any metrics time series scraped. This is a provenance good practice and can aid correlation.

We're using a static service discovery method (providing the URL to scrape or call). In this case, since Prometheus exposes the metrics under $host:9090/metrics, we use this as a value for the targets key.

Note that scrape configs continue to be important, going forward, since OpenTelemetry aims to be compatible with Prometheus and allows you to reuse your scrape configs (with minor adaptations). You will see all of this in action in the end-to-end example in this chapter.

If you want to learn more about how to use Prometheus as well as how it works internally, I strongly recommend the ultimate reference: *Prometheus: Up & Running*, by Julien Pivotto and Brian Brazil, *Second Edition* (O'Reilly; http://mng.bz/x458).

4.2.2   *Other metrics agents*

While Prometheus is the established metrics platform in the cloud-native ecosystem, especially in the Kubernetes context, there are other agents you may come across, for various reasons, including legacy usage or because your organization decided to go all in with a certain vendor or project. This includes, but is not limited to, the following agents (in alphabetical order):

- *Collectd (https://collectd.org/)*—Written in C, with this agent, you can collect (operating) system and application performance metrics efficiently. Several cloud providers and ISVs provide integrations with collectd, such as Amazon CloudWatch, Splunk, and Sumo Logic.
- *Grafana Agent (https://grafana.com/docs/agent/latest/)*—Created by Grafana Labs, this agent is optimized for Prometheus metrics. The code for this agent was donated to the Prometheus project and forms the basis of the agent mode in

Prometheus, there. In agent mode, Prometheus deactivates several functions, including the UI, alerting, and local storage.

- *Graphite (https://grafana.com/oss/graphite/)*—Now also under the Grafana Labs umbrella, this agent represents an example of the telemetry of the previous generation of machine-centric monitoring.
- *Nagios (https://www.nagios.org/)*—This is a venerable open source system (including agent) for monitoring machines and networks.
- *StatsD (https://github.com/statsd/statsd)*—Developed by Etsy, this agent is a Node.js tool that has a client–server model, allowing you to collect and aggregate application metrics and send the metrics to backends, such as Graphite.
- *Telegraf (https://github.com/influxdata/telegraf)*—From InfluxData, this is a rich and powerful agent with many plug-ins, originally written for use with their InfluxDB time series open source datastore and now also supporting OpenTelemetry.

This section is intentionally brief, since I think it's important to be aware of other agents in this space; however, in practice, you can expect that in the majority of cases, you will be dealing with Prometheus, in one form or another. If you come across a legacy environment where one of the preceding agents is used, you want to make sure that there is a clear path to migrate to Prometheus or OpenTelemetry in its place.

4.3   *OpenTelemetry*

OpenTelemetry is an incubating cloud-native computing foundation project that started out as a merger of two projects, OpenCensus and OpenTracing, that were focused on distributed traces. OpenTelemetry expanded its scope, starting in 2019, to metrics and logs. The project is the second-largest CNCF project after Kubernetes, and in its core, it is a collection of APIs, SDKs, and tools you can use to instrument, collect, process, and ingest telemetry signals.

It provides a vendor-agnostic model for emitting traces, metrics, logs (and, going forward, also profiles [https://github.com/open-telemetry/oteps/issues/139]) with both backward compatibility (via receivers and exporters) and native functions via a dedicated protocol. OpenTelemetry includes auto-instrumentation support for some popular program languages and runtimes, such as Java/JVM, .NET, JavaScript/Node.js, and Python. If you're interested in the current status of the many components OpenTelemetry has, you can

- Check out the high-level project status (https://opentelemetry.io/status/) page.
- View fine-grained information, since the project keeps track of the detailed compliance of the implementations with the specification (http://mng.bz/Aojp) as well.

Note that in addition to the specifications (APIs and data model), OpenTelemetry comes with a set of semantics, such as the standard names for system/runtime metric instruments (http://mng.bz/Zqmm).

In figure 4.5, you can see the OpenTelemetry concept of signal collection, with a strong focus on correlation. Starting from the bottom and moving to the top, the figure shows the flow of the signals from applications and infrastructure, through the OpenTelemetry collector, eventually ingested into backend destinations.

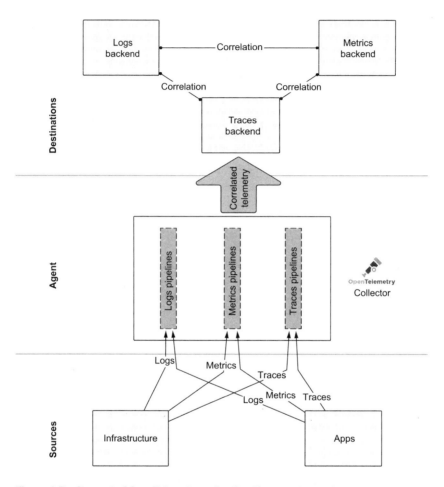

Figure 4.5   Concept of OpenTelemetry collection (from upstream docs; https://opentelemetry.io/docs/reference/specification/logs/overview/)

In the collector, the various signal types (logs, metrics, and traces, currently) are processed in so-called pipelines, dedicated to a signal type. We will discuss this agent's inner workings in greater detail a little later this chapter, but let's first dive into the application code side of the OpenTelemetry house: the instrumentation.

4.3.1 *Instrumentation*

In the context of the code you own, the first thing you want to tackle is emitting signals, using OpenTelemetry. OpenTelemetry provides instrumentation support for 11 programming languages at the time of writing. More specifically, OpenTelemetry supports C++, .NET, Erlang/Elixir, Go, Java, JavaScript, PHP, Python, Ruby, Rust, and Swift.

In OpenTelemetry, instrumentation is organized such that users get a library software development kit for each programming language and, potentially, support for automatic instrumentation. Some languages offer this via separate repos (e.g., Java), while others, like Ruby, maintain a single repo that supports both manual and auto-instrumentation. Remember that instrumentation doesn't come for free. Even in the best case of auto-instrumentation, where you don't have to change your code, there will be a small impact on your app's performance (http://mng.bz/Rx5j).

Let's have a closer look at the different instrumentation methods in OpenTelemetry. We will start with automatic instrumentation, since it's a great starting point and requires less effort.

AUTOMATIC INSTRUMENTATION

With automatic instrumentation, or simply auto-instrumentation, in OpenTelemetry, the steps required are as follows:

1. First, enable auto-instrumentation. You typically need to add one or more dependencies. At a minimum, these dependencies will add OpenTelemetry API and SDK capabilities.
2. Then, configure the auto-instrumentation, either via environment variables (and/or language-specific mechanisms, such as system properties in Java). You must, at the very least, provide a service name to identify the service you're instrumenting and, optionally, other configuration options, including things such as source configuration, exporter configuration, and resource configuration.

OpenTelemetry (at the time of writing) provides auto-instrumentation for generating traces for certain programming languages, including

- Java auto-instrumentation (https://github.com/open-telemetry/opentelemetry-java-instrumentation), which is part of OpenTelemetry, in the form of a JAR file you include (using `-javaagent`). You can configure this agent in a fine-grained manner (http://mng.bz/2DQ8), from sanitizing database queries to capturing predefined HTTP headers, which will dynamically inject JVM bytecode to capture signals from popular Java frameworks.
- JavaScript (https://github.com/open-telemetry/opentelemetry-js), also officially supported via the OpenTelemetry core, also allows yout to use all of your JavaScript apps. Note there are additional, framework-specific SDKs, such as the OpenTelemetry Node SDK (http://mng.bz/1q41), that enable auto-instrumentation.

- Python (http://mng.bz/Pz2Y) is also in the officially supported languages for auto-instrumentation.
- .NET (https://opentelemetry.io/docs/instrumentation/net/automatic/) supports auto-instrumentation as a .NET profiler to inject additional instrumentations at runtime, using monkey patching.
- Go (https://github.com/keyval-dev/opentelemetry-go-instrumentation) is a user contribution, based on eBPF. Strictly speaking, eBPF is a Linux syscall and Virtual Machine (VM), with certain requirements regarding the kernel version and symbol support, allowing you to push down user space functionality into the Linux kernel, triggering it based on events. In this context, it means to automatically capture telemetry signals for you.

Going forward, you can expect auto-instrumentation support for more programming languages as well as supporting metrics. Auto-instrumentation is a good baseline to always consider, since you get some insights essentially for free. However, it has its limitations: auto-instrumentation treats the service as a black box, meaning you won't get business-logic-related signals out of it. For this, you'd need to use manual instrumentation, so let's have look at it.

MANUAL INSTRUMENTATION

Manual instrumentation means that you modify your own code to manually emit signals. The steps required to do so, language agnostically, are

1 Import OpenTelemetry in your code—that is, take on a dependency on the language-specific API and the SDK.
2 For traces and metrics, first, create a provider (usually, there are defaults implemented), which, in turn, allows you to create an instance (along with a name and version).
3 For services (in contrast to a library you may instrument), in addition, configure the SDK, with appropriate options for exporting your signals.
4 After all the setup is complete, focus on the main job: create events (both traces and metric).

NOTE Logs (http://mng.bz/JgrK) don't follow the previously shown pattern. Instead, they leverage existing setups; in other words, while OpenTelemetry takes a clean-slate approach for metrics and traces (via specifying new APIs and providing full implementations of said APIs across the programming languages), the approach with logs is different, in that the focus is on supporting existing logs and logging libraries.

There are many possible use cases and combinations of manual and auto-instrumentation, and if you're, indeed, looking for hands-on guidance on how to use this in the context of your setup, you will find a wide array of excellent articles and tutorials on the web. For example, "OpenTelemetry and Python: A Complete Instrumentation Guide" (http://mng.bz/wvK2), "Auto-Instrumenting Node.js Apps With OpenTelemetry" (http://mng.bz/qrpJ), "Trace Context Propagation With OpenTelemetry" (http://mng .bz/7DAe), and "OpenTelemetry in Java: Tutorial & Agent Example" (https://www .containiq.com/post/opentelemetry-in-java) are all excellent resources. Next up, we have a look at the OpenTelemetry collector—the "universal signal type" agent or "universal telemetry" agent.

4.3.2   *Collector*

OpenTelemetry's agent is called the *collector*. It comprises pipelines that assemble collector components, such as receivers, processors, and exporters, as depicted in figure 4.6. Think of a pipeline as a combination of components that define how and where you get the signals from (receivers), process them at the edge (transform, batch, etc., via processors and connectors), and into which backend to ingest the signals (exporters).

You can define one or more pipelines in a collector. Each pipeline is dedicated to a signal type (e.g., metrics). You can also have multiple pipelines for the same signal type, such as different environments or to enforce different policies. Each of the pipelines acts independently, collecting signals from the sources and ingesting them into backends.

The native way to talk to the collector is via the OpenTelemetry Protocol (OTLP; https://tinyurl.com/mngbz), a general-purpose telemetry data-delivery protocol. The OTLP specification describes the encoding, transport, and delivery mechanisms of signals between the downstream sources, intermediate nodes (like collectors), and backend destinations.

OTLP itself was designed by the OpenTelemetry project and is an incremental improvement over the OpenCensus protocol, focusing on high reliability of delivery and clear visibility when the data cannot be delivered. In addition, OTLP is L7-load-balancer friendly, supporting the correct mapping of imbalanced incoming traffic to balanced outgoing traffic. Further, OTLP allows backpressure signaling from the destinations all the way back to sources, enabling you to build out reliable multihop delivery via intermediate nodes (e.g., OpenTelemetry collectors), each with potentially different processing capacities.

From a protocol perspective, OTLP uses a request–response style: the downstream clients send requests, and the upstream server replies with corresponding responses. OTLP is rather flexible—you can run it over gRPC, HTTP, and (going forward) WebSockets.

While in the future, we may live in a world where everyone and everything natively supports OpenTelemetry—that is, speaks OTLP—this is not yet the case at the time of writing, in 2023. The OpenTelemetry community found a clever way to help jumpstart things: by introducing a vast array of ingress and egress components (receivers and exporters) that can read existing formats and protocols from sources as well as write existing formats and protocols to the destinations.

How does this work, in detail? Let's have a closer look at figure 4.6 now to see how you'd use the OpenTelemetry collector to define signal-type-specific pipelines to collect signals from downstream and ingest them upstream.

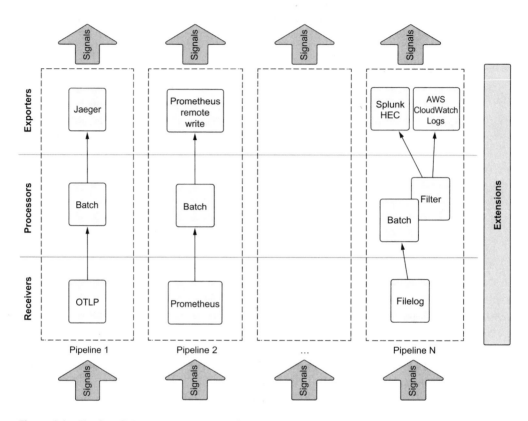

Figure 4.6   The OpenTelemetry collector and its components

Now, we will focus on the pipelines in the collector. Each pipeline uses one or more components:

- In the ingress path, collecting signals from the downstream sources, one or more receivers that can come from two places.
  - For the native OTLP, from the opentelemetry-collector (http://mng.bz/mVM4) repo
  - For all other receivers (Prometheus, Jaeger, Kafka, etc.), from the opentelemetry-collector-contrib (http://mng.bz/5wVa) repo
- The core manipulation component—one or more processors that can come from two places.
  - For a small number of generic processors, such as Batch, from the opentelemetry-collector (http://mng.bz/6DxA) repo

- For all other processors (Filter, Transform, Tail Sampling, etc.), from the opentelemetry-collector-contrib (http://mng.bz/o1gp) repo
- In the egress path, ingesting signals to the upstream destinations, one or more exporters that can come from two places.
  - For the native OTLP (and the logging exporter), from the opentelemetry-collector (http://mng.bz/nWa2) repo
  - For all other exporters (Prometheus Remote Write, Elasticsearch, AWS X-Ray, etc.), from the opentelemetry-collector-contrib (http://mng.bz/vn04) repo

Let's have a high-level look at some example pipelines from figure 4.6:

- The `pipeline 1` is a traces pipeline that can collect traces via OTLP inbound, batch them up, and ingest them into a Jaeger instance.
- The `pipeline 2` is a metrics pipeline that scrapes metrics via the Prometheus receiver inbound, batches them up again, and uses the Prometheus remote write API to ingest them into, say, Thanos or Cortex.
- The `pipeline N` is a logs pipeline that collects log lines via the Filelog (http://mng.bz/rjJE) receiver inbound, then batches them again and filters them, and can then ingest the log lines into two different backend destinations, Splunk and CloudWatch, via the respective exporters.

In addition, the collector also offers several extensions (https://opentelemetry.io/docs/collector/configuration/#extensions) to operate the agent, including health checks, service discovery, and rich telemetry (e.g., logs, metrics in Prometheus format, traces in OTLP, and profiles in `pprof` format).

> **TIP**   There are different ways to deploy (https://opentelemetry.io/docs/collector/deployment/) the collector, usually differentiated between close to the workload (agent mode) and in a central place (gateway mode). Running the collector in gateway mode (effectively, a number of collectors behind a load balancer) can help to enforce policies centrally and support separation of concerns around access control and authentication, including API keys and IAM roles.

Let's have a look at a concrete example that shows the OpenTelemetry collector in action, taking care of both metrics and traces collection and routing; our example setup looks like what is depicted in figure 4.7. We're again using `holly` as the signal generator, exposing metrics in Prometheus exposition format and emitting traces in OTLP format, with the OpenTelemetry collector configured to scrape the metrics and collect the traces and ingest them to respective backend destinations—Prometheus for metrics and Jaeger for traces.

We will now build the overall setup shown in figure 4.7, again using Docker Compose, so let's have a closer look at each of the components in turn. Listing 4.5 shows the sample app `holly`, generating both metrics and traces. Pay special attention to the

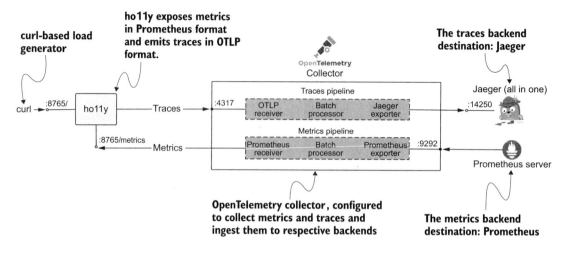

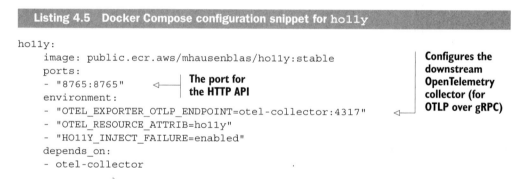

Figure 4.7   Example OpenTelemetry pipeline for traces and metrics

configuration for connecting to the OpenTelemetry collector via the OTEL_EXPORTER_
OTLP_ENDPOINT environment variable.

Listing 4.5   Docker Compose configuration snippet for `ho11y`

```
ho11y:
    image: public.ecr.aws/mhausenblas/ho11y:stable
    ports:
    - "8765:8765"          ⊲── The port for
    environment:                the HTTP API
    - "OTEL_EXPORTER_OTLP_ENDPOINT=otel-collector:4317"   ⊲── 
    - "OTEL_RESOURCE_ATTRIB=ho11y"
    - "HO11Y_INJECT_FAILURE=enabled"
    depends_on:
    - otel-collector
```

Configures the
downstream
OpenTelemetry
collector (for
OTLP over gRPC)

Listing 4.6 shows the OpenTelemetry collector using a custom configuration (otel-
collector-config.yaml) we discuss a little later. We expose all these ports there to
make them accessible from outside of Docker— that is, you can troubleshoot from the
host machine more easily with this setup.

Listing 4.6   Docker Compose configuration snippet for the OpenTelemetry collector

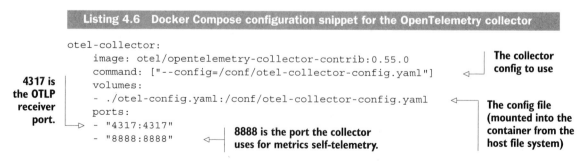

```
otel-collector:
    image: otel/opentelemetry-collector-contrib:0.55.0
    command: ["--config=/conf/otel-collector-config.yaml"]   ⊲── The collector
    volumes:                                                       config to use
    - ./otel-config.yaml:/conf/otel-collector-config.yaml    ⊲── 
    ports:
    - "4317:4317"
    - "8888:8888"   ⊲── 
```

**4317 is
the OTLP
receiver
port.**

**8888 is the port the collector
uses for metrics self-telemetry.**

The config file
(mounted into the
container from the
host file system)

```
-  "9292:9292"
-  "13133"
depends_on:
-  prometheus
-  jaeger
```

9292 is where we expose the Prometheus exporter.

13133 is the port used for collector health checks.

Listing 4.7 shows Prometheus configured as a metrics backend destination to land metrics that we then can query via CLI or using the built-in UI. Note that the Prometheus scrape configuration (prom-config.yaml) referenced here is something we will be discussing a bit later in the chapter (see listing 4.12).

Listing 4.7   Docker Compose configuration snippet for backend Prometheus

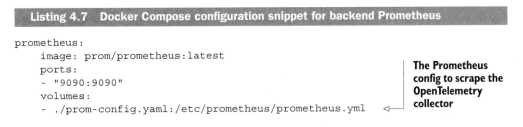

```
prometheus:
    image: prom/prometheus:latest
    ports:
    - "9090:9090"
    volumes:
    - ./prom-config.yaml:/etc/prometheus/prometheus.yml
```

The Prometheus config to scrape the OpenTelemetry collector

Last but not least, listing 4.8 shows how we configure Jaeger, the trace's backend destination. Here the two things to note are port 14250, which we will use in the OpenTelemetry collector as the target to send traces to, as well as the environment variable COLLECTOR_OTLP_ENABLED, which we (at the time of writing, for the version of Jaeger we're using here) still need to set so that the OTLP over gRPC connection between the collector and Jaeger works.

Listing 4.8   Docker Compose configuration snippet for backend Jaeger

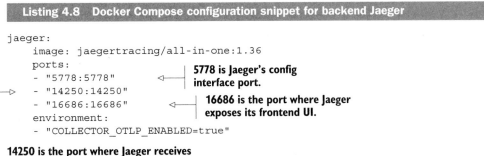

```
jaeger:
    image: jaegertracing/all-in-one:1.36
    ports:
    - "5778:5778"
    - "14250:14250"
    - "16686:16686"
    environment:
    - "COLLECTOR_OTLP_ENABLED=true"
```

5778 is Jaeger's config interface port.

16686 is the port where Jaeger exposes its frontend UI.

14250 is the port where Jaeger receives model.proto, which is OTLP over gRPC.

Now that we know all the components of our setup, let's move on to the configuration of the OpenTelemetry collector and Prometheus. To collect metrics and traces from the sample app, we will configure the OpenTelemetry collector with two pipelines, one for metrics and one for traces, as show in listings 4.9 through 4.11 (splitting the config into receivers, exporters, and the actual services configuration), which you can find in the ch04/otel/otel-config.yaml file.

Let's begin with the ingress path, the receivers.

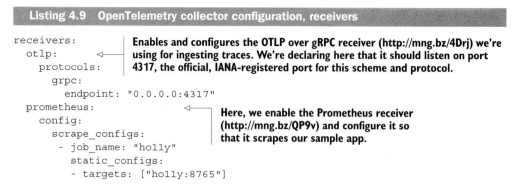

Listing 4.9   OpenTelemetry collector configuration, receivers

```
receivers:
  otlp:              ◁——  Enables and configures the OTLP over gRPC receiver (http://mng.bz/4Drj) we're
    protocols:             using for ingesting traces. We're declaring here that it should listen on port
      grpc:                4317, the official, IANA-registered port for this scheme and protocol.
        endpoint: "0.0.0.0:4317"
  prometheus:        ◁——  Here, we enable the Prometheus receiver
    config:                (http://mng.bz/QP9v) and configure it so
      scrape_configs:      that it scrapes our sample app.
      - job_name: "holly"
        static_configs:
        - targets: ["holly:8765"]
```

Note that Docker Compose makes it so that the `holly` app will be reachable under said name. Let's move on to the egress path, the exporters.

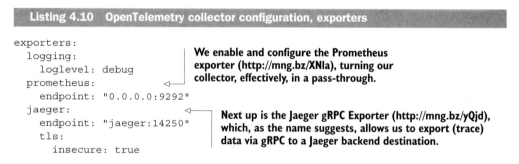

Listing 4.10   OpenTelemetry collector configuration, exporters

```
exporters:
  logging:                        We enable and configure the Prometheus
    loglevel: debug               exporter (http://mng.bz/XNla), turning our
  prometheus:        ◁——          collector, effectively, in a pass-through.
    endpoint: "0.0.0.0:9292"
  jaeger:            ◁——  Next up is the Jaeger gRPC Exporter (http://mng.bz/yQjd),
    endpoint: "jaeger:14250"      which, as the name suggests, allows us to export (trace)
    tls:                          data via gRPC to a Jaeger backend destination.
      insecure: true
```

One thing before we move on: remember that listing 4.8, which showed the Jaeger configuration in Docker Compose, pointed out port 14250? That's exactly what we plug in here, in listing 4.10, so that the OpenTelemetry collector knows where to send the traces.

For the sake of keeping things simple in this example, we're using the Prometheus exporter to allow scraping by a Prometheus server. In a production setup, where federation and long-term storage are relevant, you likely will want to instead use the Prometheus Remote Write Exporter (http://mng.bz/MBGB) here. This enables you to ingest metrics into backends, such as Cortex, Thanos, or managed-OSS services, like Amazon Managed Service for Prometheus (https://aws.amazon.com/prometheus/).

> **TIP**   In the collector config, components (receivers, processors, exporters, connectors, and pipelines) are defined by a component identifier in the `type[/name]` format. You can define components of a given type more than once as long as the identifiers are unique. For example, you could have two metrics pipelines, one called `metrics/dev` and one `metrics/prod`, with different backends.

Finally, we get to use all these receivers and exporters to define our pipelines, as shown in the following listing.

Listing 4.11 OpenTelemetry collector configuration, services (pipeline definitions)

```
service:
  telemetry:        ◁──┐   A good practice in dev/test is to configure the collector
    logs:               │   telemetry to emit fine-grained agent logs and metrics
      level: debug       │   (available via port 8888 on the collector).
    metrics:                    This is where the pipeline definitions
      level: detailed    │      starts; you can have as many as you like.
  pipelines:        ◁──┘
    metrics:        ◁──────────        Here, we define the metrics pipeline using the
      receivers: [prometheus]          Prometheus receiver in the ingress path and
      processors: [batch]              the Prometheus exporter for egress.
      exporters: [logging, prometheus]
    traces:              ◁──────        We configure the traces pipeline that uses OTLP
      receivers: [otlp]                 to ingest traces from ho11y and routes them to
      processors: [batch]               our downstream configured Jaeger instance.
      exporters: [logging, jaeger]
```

WARNING   If you only enable and configure a component such as a receiver or exporter, like we did in the previous steps, but don't use them in a pipeline definition, then it is like the component doesn't exist. The collector simply ignores it, and nothing works as you would expect. This is a very common pitfall I've seen in the wild and, admittedly, run into myself a couple of times.

Also, you might have noticed that in the `exporters` part, there are two entries. The reason is simple: by including the `logging` exporter, you get to see what's going on (e.g., metrics scraped) directly on the screen, since said exporter sends signals to `stdout`.

To wrap up the configuration, let's have a quick look at how downstream Prometheus (our metrics backend destination) is configured (listing 4.8): it scrapes itself, which is a good practice, and most importantly, for our overall setup to work, it scrapes the OpenTelemetry collector via `otel-collector:9292` (this is where we told the Prometheus exporter to expose its endpoint).

Listing 4.12 Prometheus server config, scraping the OpenTelemetry collector

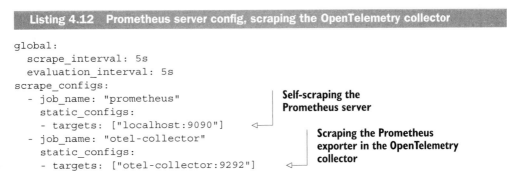

```
global:
  scrape_interval: 5s
  evaluation_interval: 5s
scrape_configs:
  - job_name: "prometheus"              Self-scraping the
    static_configs:                     Prometheus server
    - targets: ["localhost:9090"]   ◁──┘
  - job_name: "otel-collector"              Scraping the Prometheus
    static_configs:                         exporter in the OpenTelemetry
    - targets: ["otel-collector:9292"]  ◁──┘ collector
```

Alright, that was a lot of YAML code to look at. Now, let's run things. Fire up one terminal session and `cd` into `ch04/otel/`, and then do

```
docker-compose -f docker-compose.yaml up
```

NOTE   This time, I've included the poor person's load generator, based on `curl`, in the Docker Compose file, so no further steps are required at this point.

Now, it's finally time to reap the fruits of our hard YAML wrangling, so open up your browser of choice and enter the two URLs for Prometheus (localhost:9090) and Jaeger (localhost:), and you should see something happening.

Switch to Prometheus and enter the PromQL query

```
sum by(http_status_code) (holly_total)
```

You should see (on the Graph tab) something like what is depicted in figure 4.8—that is, the sum of the overall sample app invocations (HTTP API calls), grouped by the HTTP status code returned (it's configured in a way to, on average, cause a 10% error rate).

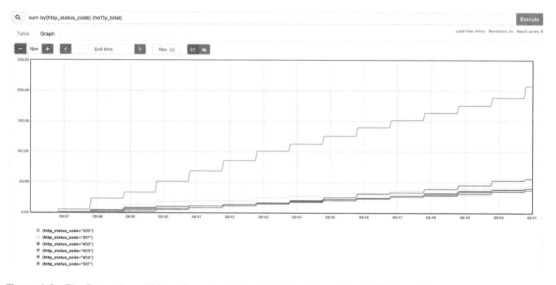

Figure 4.8   The Prometheus UI in action, showing a simple `holly` metric plotted over time

Moving on to traces: in Jaeger, you first have to select the service. You do this by choosing it from the respective dropdown box. Further, in the Tags field, you will enter

```
http.status_code=403
```

This means you're only interested in traces that carry this specific tag—in other words, traces that capture events where an HTTP status code 403 was returned by the `holly` sample app. Now, press the Find Traces button in the left-hand navigation, and the result should be akin to what is depicted in figure 4.9.

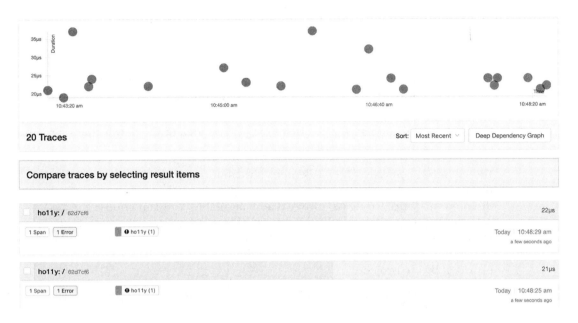

Figure 4.9   The Jaeger UI in action, showing `holly` traces filtered by HTTP 403 status code

Keep in mind that looking at an individual trace in Jaeger is as simple as clicking it in the right-hand list of traces, so go ahead and pick a random one. This should lead you to a view that resembles what figure 4.10 shows.

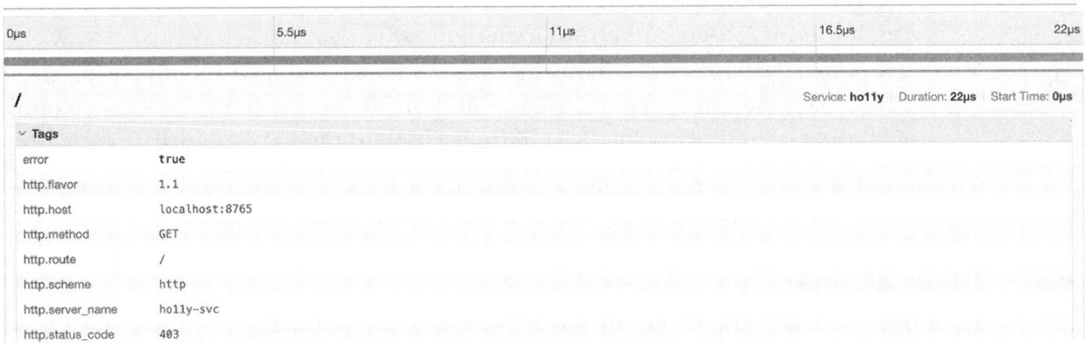

0µs	5.5µs	11µs	16.5µs	22µs

/   Service: **holly** | Duration: **22µs** | Start Time: **0µs**

∨ Tags

error	true
http.flavor	1.1
http.host	localhost:8765
http.method	GET
http.route	/
http.scheme	http
http.server_name	holly-svc
http.status_code	403

Figure 4.10   Drilling into a specific trace in Jaeger, showing all the available details

To sum it all up, in this OpenTelemetry in action walk-through, we have

1   Generated traces and metrics via manual instrumentation.
2   Configured the OpenTelemetry collector to collect these signals and ingest them into two different backend destinations (Jaeger, for traces, and Prometheus, for metrics).

3   Had a look at the signals in the backends. In Prometheus, we plotted the overall invocations by HTTP response code, and in Jaeger, we looked at client-side error spans (containing the 403 HTTP response code).

We will get into the details of working with destinations in later chapters, but here, we focused on the instrumentation and agent aspects in the context of OpenTelemetry.

OK, that was a lot—congratulations on sticking with it! I hope this little Open-Telemetry walk-through gave you a first taste and an idea of the power that's available to you via this universal telemetry agent.

> **TIP**   When it comes to OpenTelemetry distributions (http://mng.bz/a12m), there are several ways you can go about it: you can use the upstream, prebuilt distribution (http://mng.bz/gBnv) readily available, you can choose the distribution of a specific cloud provider or o11y vendor (e.g., the AWS distro [http://mng.bz/5wBB]), or you can decide to roll your own distribution using the OpenTelemetry collector Builder (http://mng.bz/5wVO), a tool provided by the project.

If you want to dive deep into OpenTelemetry, learn where it came from, what the overall vision is, and how to apply it in your setting, I recommend perusing the following books:

- Alex Boten's excellent book, *Cloud Native Observability with OpenTelemetry* (https://www.cloudnativeobservability.com/), providing you more context on Open-Telemetry and many hands-on examples.
- *Practical OpenTelemetry: Adopting Open Observability Standards Across Your Organization* by Daniel Gomez Blanco (Apess, 2023; http://mng.bz/6Dxe), which is an awesome book for learning but also for help introducing OpenTelemetry to an organization (based on his own experiences).
- *Learning OpenTelemetry* by Austin Parker and Ted Young (O'Reilly; http://mng.bz/o1gZ), the most recent book in this space, promises to be a reference book, with the two authors being driving forces behind OpenTelemetry itself.

To round off our agent review, let's have a quick look at established agents that are currently in use and may be replaced by OpenTelemetry in the future.

4.4   *Other agents*

In addition to the Fluent family for logs, Prometheus for metrics, and the Open-Telemetry collector as the universal telemetry agent, there are several established and widely used agents. Most of them have been written by and are distributed by cloud providers, but additionally, some observability vendors have introduced agents, so let's have a quick look at them (the same idea applies: in the fullness of time, all of them likely will be replaced by OpenTelemetry or its collector):

- Amazon CloudWatch Agent (https://github.com/aws/amazon-cloudwatch-agent/) can be used for logs and metrics, supporting AWS's proprietary embedded metric format (EMF; http://mng.bz/nWa5). The CloudWatch agent already supports OpenTelemetry via an embedded collector and has been replatformed on OpenTelemetry (http://mng.bz/G91q). In addition to the CloudWatch agent, AWS already offers an OpenTelemetry-compliant collector via its AWS Distro for OpenTelemetry (https://aws.amazon.com/otel/).

- Azure is in the process of deprecating its Log Analytics agent and Telegraf agents in favor of the new Azure Monitor agent (AMA; http://mng.bz/2DNd). And just like the other cloud providers, Azure is (in the long term) standardizing on OpenTelemetry (http://mng.bz/vn0p).
- Similar to Azure, Google Cloud is moving away from its legacy, collectd-based monitoring agent, in favor of the new Ops Agent (https://cloud.google.com/monitoring/agent/ops-agent), which uses Fluent Bit for log collection and routing, as well as the OpenTelemetry collector, for metrics.
- Vector (https://vector.dev/docs/about/what-is-vector/) by Datadog is an interesting open source project that, to some extent, competes with OpenTelemetry, from the universal signal type support angle; however, it also supports OpenTelemetry. It seems like a good choice of agent if you're all in with Datadog.

Now that we have a good understanding of which agents exist, their coverage, and use cases, let us move on to the topic of how you should go about selecting an agent.

4.5 Selecting an agent

As is often the case, there are several choices available to you. It's important to make sure you pick an agent that is a good fit for your workloads, environment, and organizational capabilities.

It doesn't hurt to consume general material on the topic, such as blog posts and articles—for example, see "Logstash, Fluentd, Fluent Bit, or Vector? How to Choose the Right Open-Source Log Collector" (http://mng.bz/4DrR) or "Who Is the Winner: Comparing Vector, Fluent Bit, Fluentd Performance (https://medium.com/ibm-cloud/log-collectors-performance-benchmarking-8c5218a08fea); however, you should use them as an inspiration or starting point rather than a "buyer's guide." In other words, it is very likely you will have to do your own evaluation, based on your needs and preferences, to properly select an agent. In no particular order, I present you with criteria you can use as, at the very least, a starting point to evaluate agents and pick what's right for you.

4.5.1 Security for and of the agent

Where I work, at AWS, security is the highest priority, so I start with this. It is important to consider both the security *of* the agent and the security *for* the agent, by which I mean the following:

- With security *for* the agent, ask yourself and/or the vendor the following:
  - Who handles CVEs and security patches?
  - Is the agent pen tested and, if so, when (e.g., one-off, regularly, or when major components change)?

– Can you get reproducible builds for artifacts, such as container images of the agent?
– Is the agent's supply chain known and/or documented?

- With security *of* the agent, try to determine the following:
  – Does the agent support TLS/HTTPS and equivalent cryptographically secured traffic?
  – Can you apply policies across a fleet of agents (e.g., credentials, access, and filters)?
  – Are mechanisms in place to deal with sensitive data, such as personally identifiable information (PII), as required by certain legislations, such as in Europe, through the General Data Protection Regulation (GDPR)?

Ideally, you will get this information up front, via a checklist from the open source project, ISV, or cloud provider vending the agent.

4.5.2   *Agent performance and resource usage*

Agent performance—that is, how fast signals can be processed, typically measured via the throughput along with the resources used—is a key evaluation criteria. The following are some examples of such performance-related reports:

- The upstream "OpenTelemetry Collector Performance" docs (http://mng .bz/QP96).
- The AWS Distro for OpenTelemetry Collector (ADOT) collector performance report (http://mng.bz/N2J1).

Zooming in on performance, one important criterion is, in a nutshell, related to the resource footprint of an agent. For example, a criterion might be how much RAM and/or CPU seconds the agent consumes in various phases (e.g., idle, on average, or peak) to collect, mutate, and ingest signals.

Along with this, you want to be able to have breakdowns across signal types in case of a multisignal agent, like the OpenTelemetry collector. Figure 4.11 shows an example screen capture of a Grafana dashboard (https://ref.otel.help/otel-collector-ops/otel-collector-dashboard.json) capturing OpenTelemetry collector resource usage over time.

In the context of resource usage, you want to make sure the resources the agent uses are few compared to your footprint. Don't forget the cumulative effect—that is, while a single agent might only use up a few MB across an entire fleet with several thousands of agents, that might sum up to the high TB range. Most agents nowadays have mechanisms that allow you to control resource usage (e.g., in the case of the OpenTelemetry collector, you can use the memory limiter processor to prevent out-of-memory (OOM) scenarios.

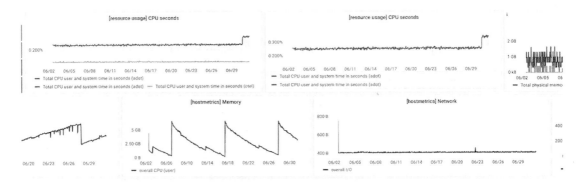

Figure 4.11 Grafana dashboard of OpenTelemetry collector resource usage

4.5.3 Agent nonfunctional requirements

In addition to the functional aspects, it's important to ask yourself the following:

- Is the agent open source, extensible, or backed by a single vendor or community?
- Who watches the watcher, or, put differently, what about the agent telemetry? In 2023 (and beyond), you should expect not only to have access to the agent logs but also get metrics (ideally, in Prometheus format) as well as traces and profiles from your agent.
- Is the agent capable of dealing with one or more signal types? A signal-specific agent means you need multiple agents for 360 coverage.

There is much more to nonfunctional requirements than we've discussed, but again, these questions form the basics, and you may choose to extend them with organizational requirements or preferences when selecting an agent.

Summary

- There are two types of agents: vendor-specific ones, like the Datadog agent, and signal-specific ones (usually open source), like Fluent Bit for logs.
- In this book, we consider vendor-specific and signal-specific agents as traditional agents, in contrast to the open source, all-encompassing OpenTelemetry collector.
- OpenTelemetry is a set of specifications, SDKs, a protocol (OTLP), and agents.
- OpenTelemetry allows you to collect, process, and ingest logs, metrics, traces, and (in the future) profiles in a vendor-neutral way.
- With OpenTelemetry, you get rich metadata both on where the signals came from (resource attributes) and about the telemetry signals themselves.
- Based on the semantic conventions, OpenTelemetry enables you to implement effective correlation in the backends.

- Auto-instrumentation is an important baseline method to automatically generate telemetry without changing the application code.

- If a vendor or programming language (in OpenTelemetry) supports auto-instrumentation, use it.

- Where auto-instrumentation doesn't deliver what you need (business logic), you need to manually instrument your code with an OpenTelemetry SDK.

- Use the OpenTelemetry collector to collect and route traces and metrics, and eventually logs, from any source to any destination, forming a universal telemetry agent.

- Agents need to be secure, performant, and lean (minimal resource usage).

- Selecting an agent can take time and may require some effort but is worth the investment in the long run.

Backend destinations

This chapter covers

- What we mean by backend destinations and what types of destinations exist
- Backend destination options for handling logs, metrics, and traces
- What time series data stores are and what you can use them for
- Introducing columnar data stores and formats along with their use cases
- Considerations for selecting backend destinations

By now, you should know what major signal types exist (see chapter 2), where they come from (see chapter 3), and what options exist to collect and preprocess said signals (see chapter 4). In this chapter, we will dive deep into backend destinations, the targets or sinks for agents. Backend destinations, or backends for short, are the source of truth for your observability questions. They allow you to store and query signals and make them available to frontend destinations (see chapter 6).

Why do I make the distinction between backend and frontend? Well, there are a few examples that fall exactly in one or the other category. For example, Grafana is a pure frontend destination (sometimes also called the *presentation stage*) that queries backend destinations to visualize or alert on signals. The Cloud Native Computing Foundation (CNCF) project Cortex, on the other hand, is a pure backend destination (besides a rudimentary admin Web UI, you only have the API to ingest and query metrics).

Then, there are offerings from dedicated observability vendors, such as Splunk, Datadog, Dynatrace, Honeycomb, New Relic, Lighstep by ServiceNow, AppDynamics by Cisco, and Sumo Logic, which typically combine frontends and backends, providing an integrated experience. In those cases, you can't use the frontend (UI) separately from the backend. There are also mixed cases in the open source space, like CNCF Jaeger (which sports an ingestion pipeline but requires an additional storage system). We will cover these all-in-ones or unified destinations in chapter 6.

Another special case is cloud-provider-native offerings, especially Amazon Cloud-Watch, Azure Monitor (including Application Insights), and the Google Cloud operations suite, which cover a wide range of features and provide integrations with different backends and frontends.

> **NOTE** Like I pointed out in chapter 1, regarding why I am using the logs, metrics, and traces boundaries to present topics, I am making the frontend–backend distinction mostly on a conceptual level. This should aid in your understanding; however, by now, you know that the reality is much messier and more complicated.

Now, let's get into it. In this chapter we will

- Have a look at some commonalities and general backend terminology
- Review options for and usage of logs backends
- Review options for and usage of metrics backends
- Review options for and usage of traces backends
- Discuss columnar data stores
- Discuss how to go about selecting a backend

Ready? Let's dive in!

5.1 *Backend destination terminology*

Backends are the source of truth for all your observability questions, be that a human asking them (ad hoc, based on a hunch) or a piece of code (think an alert that queries a backend to evaluate if a certain condition is met). Before we get into the different types of backends and their pros and cons, we will first step back a bit and look at their common characteristics along with some basic terminology we need for the rest of the chapter and book.

In general, there are three main parts you want to consider with backends, whether that is concerning performance or costs (see section 5.6 for more):

- *Ingestion*—How the signals arrive at the backend. Various protocols and formats exist, such as OpenTelemetry's OTLP or the Prometheus formats.
- *Storage*—Usually, there's the expectation that the signals ingested are stored for a longer time period (weeks, months, or even years), allowing for historical query and data analytics. But this doesn't always have to be the case, as pure in-memory solutions exist (e.g., CNCF Pixie) and have their uses, such as live cluster debugging, keeping only hours of (volatile) data around.
- *Query*—The more exact and common term we use for *asking a backend a question* is to *query the backend*. What exactly *query* means can differ from backend to backend and can range from a declarative style, such as SQL, to an API call, such as is the case with many tracing backends. You will also often come across domain-specific languages (DSLs), such as PromQL, and you'll see several examples of these DSLs in use throughout this chapter. With this in mind, let's move on to the first, and probably most widely adopted, kind of backend, for all sorts of logs.

5.2 Backend destinations for logs

In this section, we will take a cursory look at backend destinations that you can use to ingest logs and query them. As we discussed in chapter 2, logs are timestamped, typically capturing events; have a (hopefully structured) payload; and are primarily meant for human consumption. The sheer number of different log types and formats makes it sometimes difficult to figure out what the optimal backend is. Usually, it depends heavily on the use case and your preferences, such as open source and open standards first, or you might prefer a managed offering over a DIY approach (or the other way round). Having said that, and of course this also applies to the rest of the backends for metrics and distributed traces, let's see what we have here.

5.2.1 Cloud providers

Every cloud provider has, at the very least, a service in their offerings that allows you to land logs—more specially, that is (focusing on the big three hyperscalers):

- Amazon CloudWatch Logs (http://mng.bz/yQjp) organizes different kinds of logs in log groups that, in turn, comprise one or more log streams (think of a never-ending series of events), which are made up of log events. It uses a proprietary way to ingest the logs and offers the embedded metric format (EMF; http://mng.bz/nWa5), a format that allows you to embed custom metrics alongside logs. In other words, EMF is more event-centric (supporting high cardinality) than a pure log format. You can use CloudWatch Logs Insights, which provides a purpose-built query language to query your logs.

- Azure Monitor Logs (http://mng.bz/MBGQ) allows you to collect, organize, and analyze log and performance data from monitored resources in Azure (from resource groups to the app level). It organizes logs in workspaces, with queries written in Kusto Query Language (KQL), which is somewhat similar to what you find in CloudWatch Logs Insights. It sports an interesting feature called *functions*, enabling you to reuse query logic as well as rich export functionality (rule-based with various destinations, from storage to event hub).

- Google Cloud Logging https://cloud.google.com/logging/) is part of the Google Cloud's operations suite, and it includes storage, query, and log routing. As the top-level unit, Google Cloud Logging uses the log to organize entries. The log comprises log entries (events) that can stem from Google Cloud services or third parties (platform-level) as well as applications. What stands out in this context is how flexible the destinations for log routing are: from JSON files stored in Cloud Storage buckets (think the equivalent of S3 buckets) to Big-Query (a large-scale, ad hoc SQL distributed query engine for data warehousing) to Pub/Sub (Google's event stream) to things that are more comparable with what other clouds provide—that is, log "buckets" that support customizable retention periods.

Let's have a look at a concrete logs example using CloudWatch. Examine the following CloudWatch Logs Insights query (where CloudWatch reports it scanned 3.7 GB of data, covering 3.1 million records):

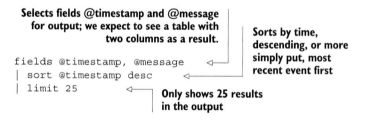

WARNING With the `limit 25` in the preceding CloudWatch Logs Insights query example, we instructed CloudWatch to limit the output displayed to 25, but CloudWatch still needs to scan a large number of logs, depending on the time range selected. The time range, and with it the volume of the data scanned, is something you should always consider. On the one hand, it can take a long time, up to several minutes, for the query to return, which is far from interactive usage; and on the other hand, you're oftentimes charged for the amount of data that has been scanned.

Figure 5.1 shows the result of the preceding CloudWatch Logs Insights query. Typically, cloud providers land all the system-level logs (sometimes called *platform logs*, such as syslog and journald but also cloud-platform/API logs) in their own offerings, which makes it a good default starting point, especially for all nonapplication-level logs. If you're curious how to route your application-level logs to these destinations, refer to chapter 4, where we discussed options and usage for agents. Next up, let's have a look at open source offerings in this space.

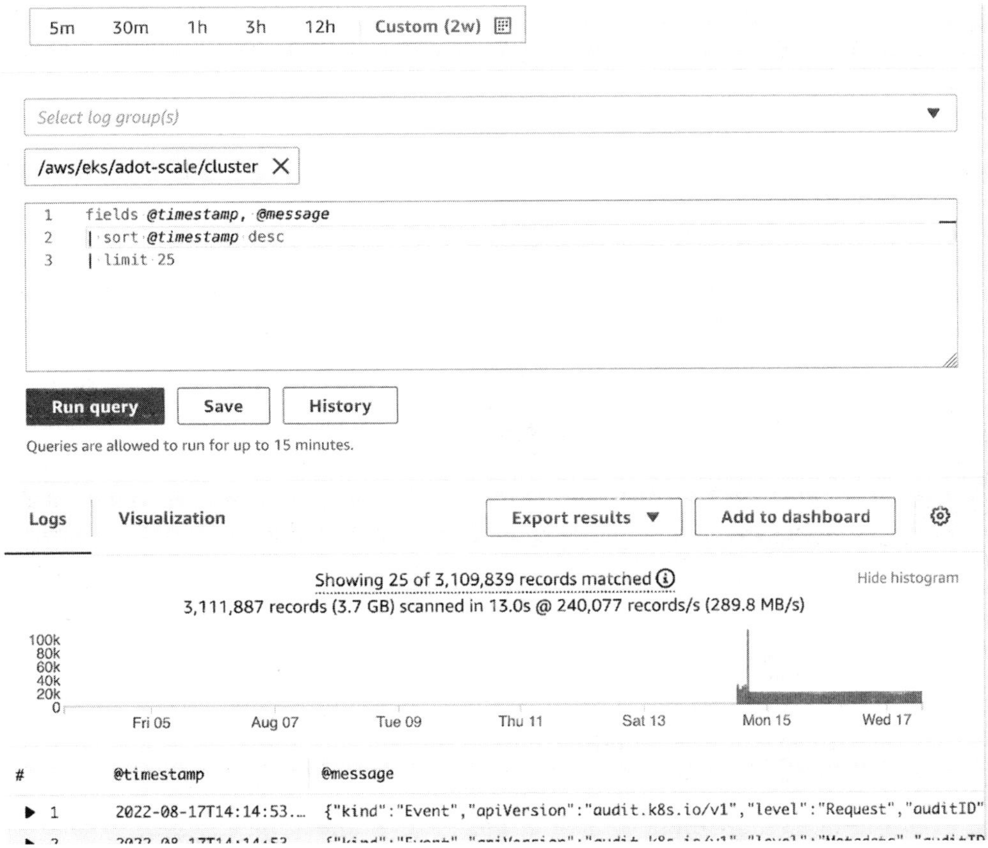

Figure 5.1 CloudWatch Logs Insights query result showing the 25 most recently added log events

5.2.2   Open source log backends

There are not that many widely used, open source–based log backends available (compared to metrics and traces, although as you will see later, log and trace backends share a lot of characteristics, and backends often store them similarly):

- *Elasticsearch and OpenSearch*—I'm lumping Elasticsearch (https://www.eiastic .co/elasticsearch/) and OpenSearch (https://opensearch.org/) together— ES/OS for short, going forward—because it really is a family of two projects and products (managed services) with a common root. They are both extending Apache Lucene (https://lucene.apache.org/), a veteran, comprehensive text search engine written in Java to make it easy to use for signal ingestion and query, even in a distributed setup. OpenSearch started out as a fork of Elasticsearch, sponsored by Amazon, and reached general availability (http://mng .bz/a12j) with its 1.0 version in July 2021. As time goes by, the ES/OS code bases are expected to diverge, but from the get-go, the major difference was the license under which each project was distributed. However, ES and OS have the fact that they are logs-first backends in common (optimized for storage and retrieval of logs). As a reminder, in chapter 4, we used OpenSearch as a destination for the Fluent Bit agent.

I won't cover ES/OS in detail in this book, as there are plenty of resources available on the topic, so if you want to dive deep, I'd recommend reading the excellent second edition of the Manning book *Elasticsearch in Action* by Madhusudhan Konda (2023; https://www.manning.com/books/elasticsearch-in-action-second-edition).

We will get back to the ES/OS topic in the context of traces later in this chapter, since this is a signal type ES/OS have decided to cover nowadays as well (support for metrics is also available; however, it is not as full blown as for the other two types).

- *Grafana Loki (https://grafana.com/oss/loki/)*—This is a horizontally scalable, multitenant log aggregation system, released under the AGPLv3 license, and its design was inspired by Prometheus. It does not index the contents of the logs themselves (as ES/OS do) but rather a set of labels for the ingested log streams. You have seen Loki in action already in chapter 2, and it's certainly something to take a closer look at; currently, few managed offerings based on it exist.
- *ZincObserve (https://github.com/zinclabs/zincobserve)*—This is a search engine you can use for indexing and looking up logs, with a focus on reducing log storage costs.

Now, let's move on to commercial offerings in the space.

5.2.3 *Commercial offerings for log backends*

The commercial offering space for log backends is well set up, and you will find some common features across of all of these, such as paid ingestion, strong multitenancy support, and a wide range of built-in integrations with other signal sources, from apps to cloud provider offerings. The offerings include but are not limited to the following:

- *Splunk (https://www.splunk.com/)*—The established logs incumbent, with a range of enterprise features and strong OpenTelemetry commitment
- *Instana (https://www.instana.com/)*—Acquired by IBM and provides many interesting features and integrations
- *SolarWinds (https://www.solarwinds.com/)*—Acquired formerly independent SaaS offerings Loggly and Papertrail as well as the monitoring offering Pingdom
- *Logz.io (https://logz.io/)*—A start-up with an amazing range of offerings in the cloud-native domain (using OpenSearch and Jaeger)

No matter where you look, logs are always in use, so the question is not *if* but *which* backend you should use. We will get back to the selection criteria later in the chapter, but for now, you can rest assured that you will need a log backend. With this, you have a rough idea what logs backends can do and what options exist so let's move on to metrics.

5.3 Backend destinations for metrics

Time series databases (TSDB) are the bread and butter of storing and querying signals of the metrics type. You can use TSDBs to track a range of different metrics, from low-level systems metrics, such as the memory usage of a container, to application-level metrics, such as the number of invocations of your service.

What is a TSDB, and how does it work? As shown in figure 5.2, the main index is the time. The unit of bookkeeping is the metric that comprises one or more time series. Each time series, in turn, keeps track of a value and, typically, you can have many of these time series active at the same time (in the sense that you can use them

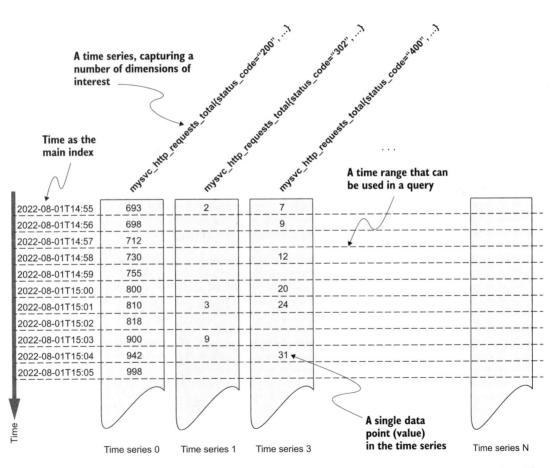

Figure 5.2   Time series database concept, showing N time series of the `mysvc_http_request_total` metric

in a query, with their values readily being available). The typical way to interact with the TSDB is to ask, "In the time frame from x to y, what are the values or value aggregates matching these conditions?"

The main index used in a TSDB is the time, usually divided into equal buckets. To keep things simple, figure 5.2 uses minute intervals, but usually, the intervals can be as small as seconds or milliseconds in granularity.

Each time series has a unique name (e.g., `mysvc_http_request_total{status_code="400"}`), capturing several dimensions of interest. The dimension of interest here is the HTTP status code returned (`status_code`), and many more, like the HTTP URL path, HTTP method, and so on might also be something you want to track. The metric this time series belongs to is of the type `counter`. That means its values increase strictly monotonically, and it captures the overall number of invocations of the `mysvc` service's HTTP API. In this context, the net change between time periods will give you the number of invocations in a period. A single data point, addressed by time and unique time series, represents the value. In our case, as shown in figure 5.2, it means that at time `2022-08-01T15:04`, the TSDB has seen a total of 31 invocations that resulted in a `400` HTTP status code.

Oftentimes, you want to query a time range, rather than a particular instant in time. You can do this by specifying the start (`2022-08-01T14:58`) and end (`2022-08-01T15:01`). You can, for example, ask the TSDB how many invocations of a certain type occurred; in our case, if you're interested in client errors, you'd ask how many `400` HTTP status codes were witnessed in the time frame, and the answer would be 12 (at the end of range, we have 24, and at the start, we had 12).

Cardinality explosion

You might wonder what happens if you start adding dimensions to a metric you want to track, with a metric being the umbrella term for all related time series. In this example, let's say a dimension you're interested in is the user ID.

In contrast to, say, the HTTP status code, which has a small, bounded number of values (a couple of dozens, from 1xx to 5xx), the user ID could have many values. If your app is successful, potentially serving many hundreds of thousands of users, this means the TSDB has to ingest and store hundreds of thousands of time series (for that single metric only, and you may have thousands of metrics you want to track).

This idea of many different values a dimension can take on being multiplied by the number of metrics is what we call *cardinality explosion* and can result in slow query times, since the TSDB needs to inspect each time series in a given time range, for each dimension. That systems property makes TSDBs for certain types of observability use cases not the best fit: at the very least, you should be aware of this and avoid adding dimensions that you know or suspect of "exploding," in terms of their cardinality.

If you would like to dive deeper into the topic of TSDBs and their use cases in general, consider reading the article "What Is Time-Series Data? Definitions & Examples" by Ajay

Kulkarni, Ryan Booz, and Attila Toth (https://www.timescale.com/blog/time-series-data/). Now, let's switch gears and get practical by looking at several open source and commercial offerings you can use as TSDB backends, especially in the context of Prometheus-compatible cases. We covered the Prometheus basics in chapter 4 and will not repeat them here. We will focus on mid- to large-scale production use cases in this chapter—in other words, when a single Prometheus instance typically is not sufficient anymore. Let's again look at the options for cloud providers, open source offerings, and commercial offerings.

> **NOTE** Prometheus is, by design, not horizontally scalable. That is, you can add more RAM and locally attached persistent storage to scale Prometheus vertically to handle more metrics or deal with a longer time period. What you can't expect is that running multiple copies of Prometheus automatically means the telemetry data is managed for you in such a distributed setup.

If you do have use cases such as a fleet of Kubernetes clusters, where you want to land metrics from many machines in a single place (federation), or you want to be able to query long time periods, such as the past three years, and a single Prometheus instance can't handle the task, you are looking for long-term storage (LTS) solutions. The following options can handle these use cases.

5.3.1 Cloud providers

Every cloud provider has, at the very least, a service in their offerings that allows you to ingest metrics as well as some open source or Prometheus-based ones, in addition to their native offerings. The following are some of the most prominent hyperscaler options, offering both platform and application-metrics ingestions:

- *Amazon CloudWatch Metrics (http://mng.bz/gBne)*—Covers metrics from over 100 AWS services (vended metrics) and keeps them around for 15 months, allowing you to query up-to-the-minute data and historical data equally. You can use the property query language as well as SQL (via CloudWatch Metrics Insights) to query metrics as well as alert (called alarms) on certain conditions. It also comes with dashboards that provide insights out of the box.
- *Amazon Managed Service for Prometheus (http://mng.bz/e169)*—A Prometheus-compatible monitoring service that uses CNCF Cortex in its data plane. You can ingest metrics via the Prometheus remote write interface (http://mng.bz/pPe5) and use PromQL to query it.
- *Amazon Timestream (http://mng.bz/Ox0K)*—A serverless time series database service for IoT and operational applications that offers an SQL-based query language and enables you to use it in a more traditional big data use case.
- *Azure Monitor Metrics (http://mng.bz/Y1Bo)*—Allows you to collect, organize, and analyze metrics from monitored resources in Azure. It supports namespaces to logically group time series as well as rich exploration and fine-grained storage and retention options.

- *Google Cloud Monitoring (https://cloud.google.com/monitoring)*—Part of the Google Cloud's operations suite; it enables you to collect metrics, events, and metadata from Google Cloud, AWS, hosted uptime probes, and application instrumentation.
- *Google Cloud Managed Service for Prometheus (http://mng.bz/GyaM)*—Runs Prometheus-based collectors as DaemonSets in Kubernetes and ensures scalability by only scraping targets on colocated nodes and pushing the scraped metrics to the central data store (Monarch). You can use PromQL to query the metrics, for alerts or, for example, as a data source in Grafana.

Figure 5.3 shows an example metrics explorer output—here, the Metrics Explorer being part of the Azure Monitor Metrics service. Next, let's look at open source offerings for metrics LTS and federation.

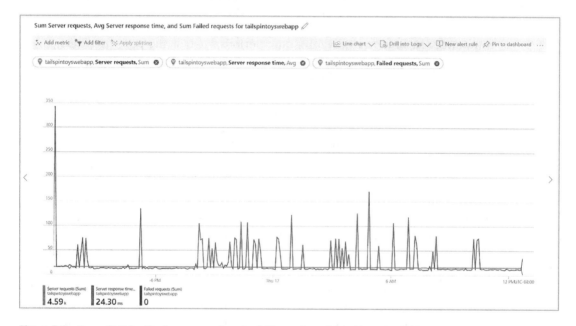

Figure 5.3   Azure Metrics Explorer example output (Azure docs, http://mng.bz/Y1Bo)

5.3.2   *Open source metrics backends*

The metrics backend space is rather crowded, which is good for you, in terms of options available, but it can also be challenging to keep track of developments and make the best decision for workload:

- *CNCF Cortex and Thanos*—Two CNCF projects with different philosophies about how to ingest and query Prometheus timeseries. Cortex (https://cortexmetrics .io/) is used in Amazon Managed Service for Prometheus; and Thanos (https:// thanos.io/), founded by Improbable, is used in a variety of cases by many large companies, from Amadeus to eBay to SoundCloud to Tencent. Cortex has a push approach (using the `remote_write` Prometheus interface) to allow a Prometheus fleet to ingest metrics, whereas Thanos initially had a pull approach (using the `remote_read` API), allowing one to federate metrics from many Prometheus setups (but now, it also supports push).

- *Clymene (https://clymene-project.github.io/)*—A time series data and logs collection platform for distributed systems that allows the storage of signals in different types of databases, such as for logs or metrics. It is a relatively new system, but in its design, it is cloud native.

- *Grafana Mimir (https://grafana.com/oss/mimir/)*—A horizontally scalable, highly available, multitenant, long-term storage option for Prometheus, available under the AGPLv3 license. It started in 2022 as a fork of the CNCF Cortex project, and Grafana Labs has added many improvements, making it part of their SaaS offering as well.

- *Icinga (https://github.com/icinga/icinga2)*—An open source monitoring system that checks the availability of your network resources, notifies users of outages, and generates performance data for reporting. You don't find Icinga widely used in cloud-native setups, but you might still need to be able to interop with it.

- *InfluxDB (https://github.com/influxdata/influxdb)*—A popular open source time series platform spanning a wide range of functionality, including offline process of the data, alerting, and exploration, with good Prometheus compatibility.

- *LinDB (https://github.com/lindb/lindb)*—A scalable, high-performance, and highly available distributed time series database that features its own SQL-like query language, called LinQL.

- *M3DB (https://m3db.io/)*—Originally from Uber, this time series data store is used by Walmart, LinkedIn, and many others. It's capable of handling billions of metrics (see this FOSDEM 2020 talk on its scaling: https://archive.fosdem.org/2020/schedule/event/m3db/) is now also available via Chronosphere as a managed service.

- *Nagios Core (https://github.com/NagiosEnterprises/nagioscore)*—An open source app that enables you to monitors systems, networks, and infrastructure.

- *Netdata* (https://github.com/netdata/netdata)—An open source, high-fidelity infrastructure monitoring and troubleshooting tool (agent and UI).

- *Nightingale (https://github.com/ccfos/nightingale/blob/main/README_en.md)*—A cloud-native monitoring system you can use to wrap and enhance the Prometheus, Alertmanager, and Grafana combo.

- *OpenTSDB (https://github.com/OpenTSDB/opentsdb)*—A distributed, scalable TSDB written on top of HBase. Its heyday was in the mid-2010s, when HBase was widely used.

- *Promscale (https://www.timescale.com/promscale)*—A unified observability backend for Prometheus metrics and OpenTelemetry traces, built on PostgreSQL and a TSDB extension called TimescaleDB (https://www.timescale.com/).

- *QuestDB (https://github.com/bluestreak01/questdb)*—A high-performance, open source SQL database for applications from financial services to observability. It includes endpoints for PostgreSQL wire protocol; high-throughput, schema-agnostic ingestion, using InfluxDB Line Protocol; and a REST API for queries, bulk imports, and exports.
- *Zabbix (https://github.com/zabbix/zabbix)*—An open source distributed monitoring solution. Like others in this list (Nagios, Icinga, and OpenTSDB come to mind), it is not widely used today in cloud-native setups, but you should be aware of it.

Some of the open source projects are packaged and offered as services. Let us move on to this topic now.

5.3.3 Commercial offerings for metrics backends

There are a few offerings dedicated to metrics, including the following:

- *Chronosphere (https://chronosphere.io/)*—Essentially "M3DB as a service." They make good progress in terms of features and OpenTelemetry compatibility.
- *VictoriaMetrics (https://github.com/VictoriaMetrics/VictoriaMetrics)*—A monitoring solution with integrated TSDB that you can use standalone or as a service. While Prometheus compliance (https://github.com/prometheus/compliance) is, at time of writing, a growth area for VictoriaMetrics, the overall offering is cloud native and powerful.

In most, if not all, cases (Kubernetes, ECS), you want and need metrics and, with them, a backend. Choose your backend based on Prometheus compatibility and your specific usage pattern (e.g., ingest, storage, or query distribution).

5.4 Backend destinations for traces

Now, we have a look at various options to ingest and query distributed traces. In this space, you would typically find wide support for OpenTelemetry, although Zipkin support is still needed in some places, such as PHP.

5.4.1 Cloud providers

Just as with logs and metrics, your cloud provider of choice has something to offer if you want to ingest and use tracing:

- *AWS X-Ray (https://aws.amazon.com/xray/)*—Amazon's managed distributed-tracing offering, which allows you to analyze and debug applications. It used to be a standalone service and is now being integrated in CloudWatch. X-Ray has standardized on OpenTelemetry and captures traces from a number of compute and database AWS services as well as apps written in Java, Node.js, and .NET.
- *Distributed tracing in Azure (http://mng.bz/zXWw)*—Part of Application Insights with SDKs for .NET, Java, and Node.js/JavaScript. Application Insights now also supports distributed tracing via OpenTelemetry.

- *Cloud Trace (https://cloud.google.com/trace)*—Google's offering for distributed tracing, which supports Go, Java, Node.js, and Python via OpenTelemetry.

Figure 5.4 provides an example output of Google Cloud Trace, a sophisticated distributed tracing backend. It shows the analytics of traces, specifically the latency distribution. Next, we will cover open source tracing solutions.

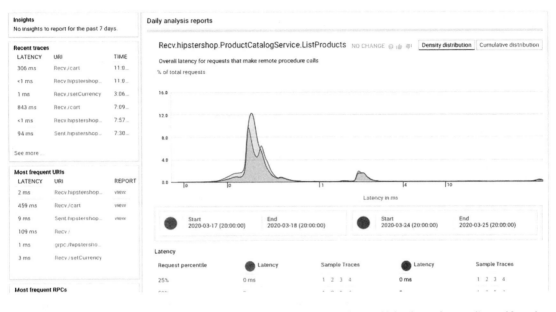

Figure 5.4   Viewing traces in Google Cloud Trace (Google Cloud docs; https://cloud.google.com/trace/docs/trace-overview)

5.4.2   Open source traces backends

Open source tracing solutions do not offer as many options as with metrics backends, but they still offer some choice:

- *CNCF Jaeger and Zipkin*—Both Jaeger (https://github.com/jaegertracing/jaeger) and Zipkin (https://github.com/openzipkin/zipkin) are distributed tracing systems hosted by CNCF. These days, Jaeger seems to be the more actively developed project, but Zipkin is still widely used and supported. I recommend you have a look at the respective communities (Slack and GitHub issues) and make up your own mind. We will cover both in chapter 6.
- *Elasticsearch and OpenSearch*—These options have expanded from logs to support handling traces. Both have excellent frontends (Kibana and Dashboards) that we will, again, cover in chapter 6.
- *Grafana Tempo (https://grafana.com/oss/tempo/)*—A distributed tracing backend available under the AGPLv3 license. It uses object storage (e.g., S3) in the

persistence layer and is integrated with Grafana, Prometheus, and Loki. It supports Jaeger, Zipkin, and OpenTelemetry ingestion.

Now, let's move on to commercial offerings, which are, in contrast to open source offerings, very richly equipped. This starts at correlation features and ranges all the way to sampling and integrations.

5.4.3 *Commercial offerings for trace backends*

Originally called *application performance monitoring* (APM) vendors, nowadays, the tracing aspect (or *observability solution*) is often highlighted. We will cover these offerings in detail in chapter 6.

While distributed tracing hasn't yet reached the same level of adoption as metrics and logs, it's increasingly important for cloud-native setups. Even if you don't have a short-term strategy around it, consider testing it in smaller-scoped projects or products. Now, we'll shift gears to discussing a class of backends that helps address the aforementioned challenge of cardinality explosion: columnar data stores and formats.

5.5   *Columnar data stores*

There are many so-called columnar storage–based engines or simply data stores that you can use as backends for telemetry data. *Columnar* refers to the way the data is laid out in memory or on disk, boosting query performance.

Row-oriented databases, such as MySQL and PostgreSQL, keep all of the data associated with a record in close proximity in memory (or on disk). This means, in general, row-oriented DBs are a good fit for online transaction processing (OLTP) use cases, such as e-commerce, in which you have in-place updates of records. They are optimized for reading and writing rows, which is a great fit when you have many individual transactions with a potential for low data volume, such as is the case when inserting or updating single records in an online web application (e.g., putting a product into a shopping basket, following someone on a social media site, and so on).

Column-oriented or columnar data stores (see Mike Stonebraker et. al., "C-Store: A Column-oriented DBMS." Proceedings of the 31st VLDB Conference, Trondheim, Norway, 2005; see also https://people.brandeis.edu/~nga/papers/VLDB05.pdf) store the data of columns next to each other and are typically a good choice for so-called online analytical processing (OLAP) use cases. These are cases where you have few transactions but are dealing with a high volume of queries. The write path is the ingest of, say, time series data, and the read path is, for example, an ad hoc query over a time range. These columnar data stores are, hence, well suited for historical (time series) data where we want to extract actionable insights, typically in an interactive manner, from large datasets (many billions of rows and, potentially, petabytes of data) or, in other words, observability use cases. Let's have a closer look at this: figure 5.5 shows row-oriented versus column-oriented storage strategies.

Starting with the logical layout, a tabular view on columns (vertical) and rows (horizontal), a particular value has the coordinates c_iR_j (e.g., the value of the third column, second row would be referenced by C2R1). Now, when you are storing the values row-oriented (the left-hand side of figure 5.5), you start in the first row and then move on to the second row, and so on, resulting in a storage layout (on disk or in memory) that stores the first row, the second row, and so on, until the last row. In contrast, when storing the values column-oriented (the right-hand side of figure 5.5), you start in the first column and then move on to the second column, and so on, resulting in a storage layout (on disk or in memory) that stores the first column, the second column, and so on, until the last column.

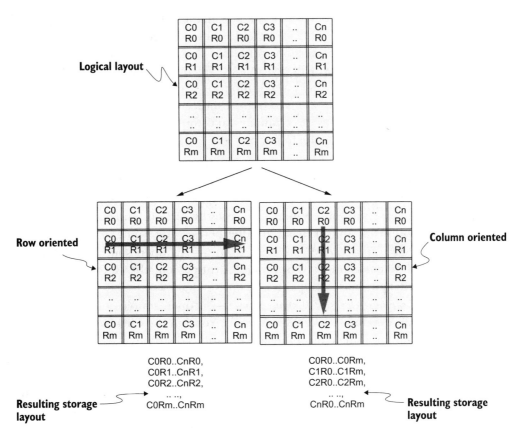

Figure 5.5 **Row-oriented vs. column-oriented storage**

You may be wondering, why bother with column-oriented storage? It turns out, columnar storage has a number of advantages for OLAP use cases, which includes our observability use cases.

In observability use cases, you can have many dimensions of interest, resulting in high cardinality and many columns. For any given query, there may only be a few columns relevant for a query. Columnar data stores allow for faster and fewer scans, since fewer unnecessary values need to be read (that then are immediately discarded, as they don't contribute to an answer).

Further, column-oriented design allows you to apply storage optimization techniques, such as differential storage, like the XOR compression Facebook developed in the context of the Gorilla TSDB (see Tuomas Pelkonen et. al., "Gorilla: A Fast, Scalable, In-Memory Time Series Database." Proceedings of the VLDB Endowment, Vol. 8, No. 12, 2015; see also http://www.vldb.org/pvldb/vol8/p1816-teller.pdf) and run-length encoding (RLE; see D. Abadi, S. Madden, M. Ferreira, "Integrating Compression and Execution in Column-Oriented Database Systems." Proceedings of the 33th International Conference on Management of Data [SIGMOD]; https://doi .org/10.1145/1142473.1142548), yielding a smaller footprint and less resource usage.

In addition to compression, columnar design also enables vectorized execution (multiple data items per CPU cycle) and effective partitioning in the context of a single machine, and sharding a replication for scaling out, allowing you to answer queries over hundreds of millions of rows in subsecond time frames.

Prominent examples of columnar data stores, columnar formats, or services that use this strategy include the following:

- *Apache Cassandra (https://cassandra.apache.org/)*—Written in Java—a C++ variant, ScyllaDB, is also available (https://www.scylladb.com/).

- *Apache Druid (https://druid.apache.org/)*—An open source real-time analytics database with observability use cases by Airbnb, Alibaba, eBay, Lyft, and many more. You can run Druid in Kubernetes (http://mng.bz/0KDp).

- *Apache Pinot (https://pinot.apache.org/)*—An open source real-time distributed OLAP data store used by LinkedIn (http://mng.bz/KeOP), Uber, Slack, Stripe, and many more companies.

- *ClickHouse (https://clickhouse.com/)*—An open source columnar database, originally developed in 2008 by Yandex. You can use ClickHouse for all signal types, both for a single machine and in various distributed settings (sharded and replicated data with Apache Zookeeper as coordinator). When running it on Kubernetes, you should consider using the Altinity Operator for ClickHouse (https://github.com/Altinity/clickhouse-operator). ClickHouse has more-than-decent adoption, including Uber (logs), Cloudflare, and SigNoz, where it is being used as a building block in o11y solutions.

- *FrostDB (https://github.com/polarsignals/frostdb)*—A columnar database allowing for semistructured schemas, using Apache Parquet for storage as well as Apache Arrow for queries, developed as open source by Polar Signals.

- *Snowflake (https://www.snowflake.com/)*—An integrated platform delivered as a service. It features storage, compute, and global services layers that are physically separated but logically integrated.

If you're interested in learning more about the implementation details of some of the aforementioned data stores, I recommend reading the excellent article, "Comparison of the Open Source OLAP Systems for Big Data: ClickHouse, Druid, and Pinot," by Roman Leventov (http://mng.bz/9DRx).

In this context, it's interesting to note that columnar storage is not limited to backends. For example, in OpenTelemetry there is ongoing work to introduce columnar encoding (https://github.com/open-telemetry/oteps/pull/171) in the collector and protocol, to speed up processing and improve performance and scalability.

> **Tip**
>
> The space of columnar data stores and databases, formats, and open source projects has exploded in the past decade. In fact, my first industry job (after some 12 years in research) was in the context of a Hadoop start-up on the now-retired Apache Drill project (which was similar to the open source version of Google's Dremel, which forms the basis of BigQuery).
>
> There are many interesting data stores that you may be interested in, including MonetDB, Hypertable, Apache Kudu, and Greenplum. Covering them in any detail goes beyond the scope of this book. If you want to learn more, I recommend reading Martin Kleppmann's excellent book *Designing Data-Intensive Applications* (O'Reilly, 2017; https://dataintensive.net/) and *Fundamentals of Data Observability* (O'Reilly, 2023; http://mng.bz/jPQz) by the one and only Andy Petrella.

After that much theory, we deserve some action! So let's dive deep into an example with an open source columnar data store that gained a lot of traction in the past few years: ClickHouse.

In this walkthrough, you will (again) use the `holly` generator, configured to send its logs via the Fluentd logs driver to the OpenTelemetry collector with a pipeline using the Fluent Forward receiver (http://mng.bz/WzD4), and the ClickHouse exporter (http://mng.bz/8rZZ) to ingest the logs into ClickHouse, where you then will be able to query the logs using SQL.

Excited? Let's go!

We start off with the Docker Compose configuration shown in the next listing. You know most of the setup already from previous examples, so we will focus on the new parts of this setup.

Listing 5.1   Snippets of the Docker Compose configuration for the ClickHouse setup

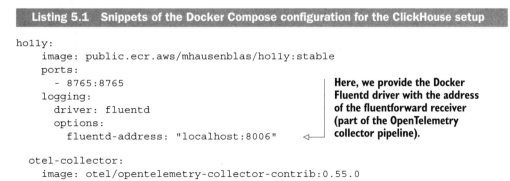

```
holly:
    image: public.ecr.aws/mhausenblas/holly:stable
    ports:
      - 8765:8765
    logging:
      driver: fluentd
      options:
        fluentd-address: "localhost:8006"
```

Here, we provide the Docker Fluentd driver with the address of the fluentforward receiver (part of the OpenTelemetry collector pipeline).

```
otel-collector:
  image: otel/opentelemetry-collector-contrib:0.55.0
```

```
command: ["--config=/conf/otel-collector-config.yaml"]
volumes:
- ./otel-config.yaml:/conf/otel-collector-config.yaml
ports:
- "8006:8006"
```

We need to expose the Fluent Forward receiver port here so that we can receive log lines from Docker.

```
clickhouse-server:
  image: clickhouse/clickhouse-server
  ports:
  - "8123:8123"
  - "9000:9000"
  ulimits:
    nproc: 65535
    nofile:
```

There are several low-level Linux settings, such as the number of processes and files allowed for ClickHouse that we're setting here.

This is where we set up ClickHouse: the port 8123 for the Web UI and port 9000, the default native TCP endpoint for clients (allowing the OpenTelemetry exporter to talk to it).

For more details on the ClickHouse configuration and good practices, see the ClickHouse operations docs (https://clickhouse.com/docs/en/operations/settings), specifically, the excellent article on ClickHouse Networking (http://mng.bz/EQyo). Now, we will move on to the telemetry agent setup. The following listing shows the OpenTelemetry collector configuration I put together for our ClickHouse example.

Listing 5.2   OpenTelemetry collector configuration for the ClickHouse setup

```
receivers:
  fluentforward:
    endpoint: 0.0.0.0:8006
processors:
  batch:
    timeout: 5s
    send_batch_size: 100
exporters:
  logging:
    loglevel: debug
  clickhouse:
    dsn: tcp://clickhouse-server:9000/default
    ttl_days: 3
service:
  telemetry:
    logs:
      level: debug
  pipelines:
    logs:
      receivers: [ fluentforward ]
      processors: [ batch ]
      exporters: [ logging, clickhouse ]
```

We configure the Fluent Forward receiver here to listen on all addresses on port 8006 for TCP connections. If all works, the Docker Fluentd driver will connect here.

Here, we set the batch size to 100 log lines. In practice, this would be much higher, likely in the thousands (depends on how long you want to wait until the logs are accessible in ClickHouse). I chose this low number to speed up things for you to see results.

This is the place where we set up the ClickHouse exporter, configuring it with the address of where the ClickHouse server is running. From the server perspective, our exporter is just another client talking TCP with it. The ttl_days setting limits the time data is kept around (not really important for our demo).

Finally, here, we assemble the pipeline using the components we configured previously.

Phew! That was some YAML wrangling again, so let's get that applied. In a new terminal session, go to ch05/clickhouse/, and then execute (self-contained, no need for
an external load generator) the following:

```
docker-compose -f docker-compose.yaml up
```

Now you can go to http://localhost:8123/play, which is ClickHouse's playground, and
enter the following SQL query (for reference, on my machine, it takes some milliseconds to read around 1,000 rows):

```
SELECT
    Timestamp as ts,                                    We pull out certain columns of interest,
    Body AS payload,                                    especially the associated trace ID.
    JSONExtractString(Body, 'traceID') AS traceID
FROM otel_logs
WHERE
    match(payload, 'invoked') AND                       We do a regex match against the
    ts >= NOW() - INTERVAL 30 SECOND                    body of the log message, requiring
                                                        it to contain the string invoked.

The table the OpenTelemetry                             We limit the output to
ClickHouse exporter set up                              the last 30 seconds.
for us to query.
```

The result of the SQL query execution is what you see in figure 5.6. Note the query
stats in the right area above the output table.

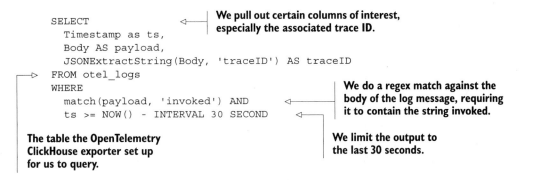

Figure 5.6   The ClickHouse Web UI playground, executing our SQL query, and showing the results

TIP   If you find yourself working more with ClickHouse, then I'd recommend
you check out ClickCat (https://github.com/clickcat-project/ClickCat), a
nice and simple user interface that lets you search, explore, and visualize data
in ClickHouse.

Another (related) category is distributed query engines, which can, among other things, use columnar data formats. These include

- PrestoDB (https://prestodb.io/), open sourced by Facebook (Meta)
- Cloud provider offerings, such as Amazon Redshift (https://aws.amazon.com/redshift/) and Google BigQuery (https://cloud.google.com/bigquery)

In the last part of this chapter, we shift gears and move to a hot topic: out of those many choices, how to best go about selecting one (or more) backends.

5.6   *Selecting backend destinations*

Selecting backends can be tough. To give you a feeling for the sheer number of options, have a look at the CNCF landscape in the Observability and Analysis (https://landscape.cncf.io/card-mode?category=observability-and-analysis) space. It sports many different options, from open source to SaaS.

Now that you have an idea about the spectrum of offerings in the backends domain, let's turn our attention to picking a backend that is a good fit for your needs. Working backward from your workload and your requirements is something I recommend. Also, be aware that it is not uncommon to end up using multiple types of backends in concert. For example, you might use CNCF Cortex for metrics LTS and federation along with OpenSearch for log and trace storage and query. Finally, remember that certain frontends, such as Grafana, as the canonical example, allow you to bring together signals from various backends, effectively building out a single pane of glass for your observability needs. We will discuss this in detail in chapter 6.

We discussed return on investment (ROI) in earlier chapters, and with backends, this is of central importance. Let's dive into the costs aspect first.

5.6.1   *Costs*

In the ROI context, backends require investment, typically in the mid- to long-term range—that is, years. This is due to the fact that data has gravity, meaning wherever the majority of your data resides defines your primary environment (think on-prem versus cloud or between different cloud providers). It costs time and money to transfer data between environments, and you want to avoid unnecessary egress and ingress data transfer costs.

More specifically, the monetary investments for backends can break down into

- *Ingestion costs*—An agent, like the OpenTelemetry collector, ingests (or writes) signals into the backend. For example, for a Prometheus-compatible backend, this may be measured in USD per million samples ingested.
- *Storage costs*—After ingestion, signals need to be stored for long-term retrieval. These costs are usually not the biggest contributor to your bill (most often ingestion or query is).

    Concerning storage, one often useful property is the "retention period." With this, your provider expresses how long your signal will be stored and is available for answering queries. This can be a static or fixed property (e.g., one year) or something that you can configure (potentially, along with downsampling strategies in metrics backends, like CNCF Thanos already offers).

- *Query costs*—Using the signals to answer your o11y questions means you need to be able to look them up, scan them, and query them; these costs can be expressed in samples processed or can be more volume oriented (e.g., GB scanned). Understanding where and how query occurs (besides the maybe obvious ad hoc query you, as a human, perform interactively) is crucial.

  For example, think of the case in which you define an alert or alarm (compare chapter 7), and then a condition is evaluated in regular time periods, causing one or more queries to be executed. Again, at scale, this can sum up, and I have seen surprises (not the good kind) from customers not aware of this.

In addition to these variable costs, there can be flat costs, such as per-seat license costs; however, those are fairly predictable (in contrast to the variable costs, such as ingestions or query) and more commonly found with frontends or all-in-one solutions. One more consideration in the context of the costs of a backend—beyond the actual task at hand, like troubleshooting or performance optimization— is that there may be regulatory requirements to keep certain types of signals (usually logs) around for several years.

> **NOTE** Regulatory requirements around the storage and protection of telemetry signals is especially pertinent in regulated verticals, such as financial industries or health care. You may need to prove this capability in the context of achieving a certification, such as the case of an app that handles credit cards usually requiring Payment Card Industry Data Security Standard (PCI DSS) compliance or privacy requirements in the context of System and Organization Controls (SOC).

Here is one quick word on buy versus build in the context of backends: unless you are an observability vendor (or cloud provider), please consider not building your own backend from scratch. It can take many years to build something reliable and scalable, and if you have N innovation tokens or engineering cycles to spend, they are usually better invested in your core business and what sets you apart from the competition, rather than building the next time series data store.

I do not mean to discourage you from building an internal observability platform based on, for example, integrating various open source backends, with an open source frontend as a single pane of glass. However, you should be aware of the total cost of ownership (TCO), so be prepared to take the costs of your engineering team, support, training, and security patching (to name a few common ones) into account when you make a decision. Let's move on to the topic of open source and open standards next.

5.6.2   Open standards

Building on open standards is a good choice: try to avoid backends that are exclusively accessible via proprietary APIs, or at the very least, have a strategy in mind regarding how you can make these proprietary APIs comply with (industry) standards.

For example, in the context of our observability considerations, support for Open-Telemetry (at least on the road map) is something you want to include in your checklist. Every major cloud provider and ISV already now supports OpenTelemetry—see the respective vendor listing (https://opentelemetry.io/vendors/) on the project home page that details OpenTelemetry support (distributions and OTLP endpoints support).

Not all signal types are equal in this respect:

- Logs tend to have many open standards and formats in use. Standardization is not practical, and hence, standards like OpenTelemetry typically limit themselves to declaring normative mappings from and to established standards, like syslog.
- Metrics are increasingly represented in Prometheus exposition format or its successor, OpenMetrics (which sports exemplars support). Note, however, that there is a lot of old-school stuff, especially from or in non-cloud-native setups, that is still using things like Graphite format, the InfluxDB line protocol, or StatsD.
- Nowadays, it is important to ensure traces are OpenTelemetry compliant.

Next, we will look at a common challenge in the ingestion path.

5.6.3   Back pressure

When looking at ingesting signals at scale, you may come across the challenge of dealing with sources that generate, say, log lines or spans at a high rate. To deal with the back pressure—that is, not overloading the backends—you can use a queue between the source, agent, and backend. This allows you to decouple the producer side (signal source or agent) and consumer side (backend).

For example, you could use Apache Kafka (https://kafka.apache.org/) in the egress path of an OpenTelemetry collector configured with the Kafka Exporter (http://mng.bz/N2zN) component in a pipeline, as we discussed in chapter 4. In this configuration, the collector would serve as a short-term, in-memory queue publishing into a Kafka broker, and the backend could, for example, be an S3 bucket that gets populated on a schedule, via a lambda function. Next, we will cover how to manage too many values.

5.6.4   Cardinality and queries

In this section, we discuss two related problems when selecting a backend: cardinality and queries. We discussed cardinality explosion in the metrics backend section already. What we mean is that a metric's dimension (e.g., session ID or user ID) could potentially take on highly varying values, causing issues when ingesting and storing the metrics (costs) as well as when querying them. In the context of queries, high cardinality might cause slow or hanging queries—that is, a query might time out before returning a result.

The best way to address this problem is to avoid high cardinality when using metrics backends. By avoiding it, I mean carefully controlling which metrics you scrape (or collect) and working backward from what you actually use. For example, your guidance could be that only metrics that are actively used in a dashboard or an alert are "allowed in." You can defer the decision by implementing this logic in the agent—for example, via an OpenTelemetry processor in one of your pipelines.

Alternatively, if you can't or don't want to limit yourself, you can use dedicated data stores that can handle a high volume of metrics, such as ClickHouse or commercial offerings. For example, Honeycomb initially spent a considerable time to build a proprietary data store for high-cardinality signals, from scratch. In their case, it made sense, since that's literally their business model. Again, this is a quick reminder of buy versus build in this context.

In general, query performance (how fast a backend can return results as a reaction to a query) is an important topic; however, details are beyond the scope of this chapter. It does have a time–speed tradeoff in some systems; for example, Prometheus and InfluxDB are fast performers if you're within their cardinality limits and are doing "alerting"- style queries. Distributed systems, on the other hand, tend to be slower in the near term but handle long-range queries (i.e., "tell me how we performed for the last quarter") far better.

If you're interested in setting up your own query performance TSDB benchmark, have a look, for example, at what Aliaksandr Valialkin shared in "High-Cardinality TSDB Benchmarks: VictoriaMetrics vs. TimescaleDB vs. InfluxDB" (http://mng .bz/D4mn).

Concerning the way queries are expressed as well as wire formats, some commonly used query languages, schemas, and formats are as follows (note that I intentionally mix up transport schema and query languages here to keep things simple):

- For the logs signal type:
  - Elastic Common Schema (ECS; http://mng.bz/lWy6) with the query syntax of Elastic-flavored Lucene
  - Grafana Labs' LogQL (https://grafana.com/docs/loki/latest/logql/)
  - CloudWatch Logs Insights query syntax (http://mng.bz/BmJ0)
  - The syslog protocol (https://datatracker.ietf.org/doc/rfc5424/), as per RFC 5424
  - Apache's Common Log Format (https://en.wikipedia.org/wiki/Common_ Log_Format)
  - NGINX access and error log (https://docs.nginx.com/nginx/admin-guide/ monitoring/logging)

- – Graylog Extended Log Format (GELF; https://go2docs.graylog.org/5-0/getting_in_log_data/gelf.html)
  - – The Windows Event Log schema (http://mng.bz/d1AN), as a query format if you're using Windows Event Explorer
  - – Common Event Format (CEF; https://docs.nxlog.co/userguide/integrate/cef-logging.html)
- In the time series databases realm or for the metrics signal type:
  - – PromQL (http://mng.bz/qrGw), the Prometheus query language
  - – The Prometheus exposition formats (http://mng.bz/rW7B) and OpenMetrics (https://openmetrics.io/)
  - – InfluxData's Flux (https://www.influxdata.com/products/flux/), a standalone data scripting and query language
- For the traces signal type, there are no widely established query standards for traces yet, but Grafana Labs is working on this topic. Also, OpenTelemetry OTLP, as the default wire format, is widely adopted in this context.
- For signals of type profiles, `pprof` (https://github.com/google/pprof) is widely used; see also chapter 9, where we will dive deeper into this topic.

Note that for most of the aforementioned signal types (profiles excluded, expected to be available in 2023), the OpenTelemetry OTLP (http://mng.bz/V1KP) is already, or will soon be, the standard way to perform data exchange. In most cases, you want to choose a backend that supports an (open) industry standard, such as OpenTelemetry or OpenMetrics, over proprietary (only) ones, but see also the previous section on open standards, regarding the expected caveats in this context.

With this selection guide, we've reached the end of the chapter on backends. Next, we will discuss frontends (e.g., Grafana) and all-in-one solutions, such as Apache SkyWalking.

Summary

- Backends are the source of truth for your observability questions.
- The backends store signals in a durable and long-term manner, supporting various query languages, typically declarative.
- There are various offerings for logs, metrics, and traces backends. You can choose between what cloud providers offer, open source (and run-yourself) options, and managed offerings from a wide range of providers.
- Some backends (e.g., OpenSearch in the OSS space and most commercial offerings from observability vendors) can handle more than one signal type; however, in practice, one can end up with different backends per signal type.
- Being able to move from one signal type in a backend to another signal type in another—potentially different—backend is crucial to answer arbitrary questions.
- Cardinality explosion is the challenge that a metric dimension can take on many different values (think user ID).

- TSDBs, such as Prometheus, are a great choice for the metrics signal type (numerical aggregates), until you run into cardinality explosion.
- Use columnar data stores and formats for high-cardinality signals and use cases.
- Make sure you have a good idea of what exactly you want to store (e.g., logs versus metrics).
- Due to data gravity, careful selection of your backends is crucial (to avoid large export–import costs when transferring data).
- Be aware of the direct and indirect costs in the ingestion, storage, and query phases when selecting a backend.
- Choose support for open standards concerning query languages and wire formats in backends over proprietary ones to minimize lock-in and maximize interoperability.

Frontend destinations

This chapter covers

- What frontend destinations are and what options exist
- What all-in-one destinations are and available options
- How to go about selecting frontends and all-in-ones

In chapter 5, we had a look at observability backends. Essentially, these are specialized time series databases (TSDBs), general-purpose relational databases with a TSDB extension, or columnar data stores that are able to store logs, metrics, and traces. Once you have ingested the signals in a backend, you can use the backend to answer observability questions, usually referred to as *querying*. This process might be a declarative one, such as is the case with SQL or PromQL, or an imperative one, where you, for instance, tell a traces backend to look up a span by root span ID.

But the storage of signals and being able to query them are only means to an end. Observability is about understanding the system and getting actionable insights from the telemetry signals collected and ingested. So what you really want as a user of an observability solution is to ask ad hoc questions and get (timely) answers.

Ideally, this should happen no matter what the time frame you're asking the question about is or the volume of the telemetry data involved. For example, let's assume you ingest 10 GB of log data and 1 billion traces per day, with a retention period of a year. When you're troubleshooting, you don't want that fact to slow you down (wait for the queries to time out or take minutes to return), as this disrupts your flow, potentially causing you to overlook issues, like finding a bug slower—or not at all.

What is this environment where you ask these (observability) questions? These environments can be frontends and all-in-ones. Frontends are, by design, pure graphical user interfaces (GUIs) that allow you to configure one or more data sources to be used to create dashboards or alerts, such as Grafana. All-in-ones, on the other hand, combine backends and frontends into one indivisible logical unit. In other words, you can't use the GUI of an all-in-one as a standalone but only in combination with the backend(s) the provider designed it for.

So how can you pose different questions, and how are the results presented to you? You've guessed it: it is, indeed, frontend and all-in-one destinations you are using to achieve this. A term that you might come across in the observability community is *a single pane of glass*. In the context of this book, what I mean by this is a single place or application that you can use to consume all your signals, query, and correlate different signal types. Let's get into the deep end with a tour of observability frontends.

> **Tip**
> Reality shows that chasing the single pane of glass as the single most important requirement or priority (which may come from management) is often not the most efficient use of time and money. Can there be a standardization to consume many, if not most, of the signals in a single place? Yes. Will there be exceptions? Also yes. In other words: aim for it by considering one of the solutions presented in this chapter, but allow for flexibility where this is not (easily) possible.
>
> Note that I'm not suggesting that you should give up on the idea of standardizing on one main frontend, such as Grafana (it is very helpful to have all the data in one place, including the support of correlation). However, be prepared that there will always be a case where certain signals or sources are not covered by that frontend, requiring you to use a dedicated tool, in addition.

6.1 Frontends

We will first discuss the two most popular open source frontends: Grafana and Kibana. Next, we will have a look at other open source offerings and commercial offerings used in the observability space.

6.1.1 Grafana

Grafana (https://github.com/grafana/grafana) is nowadays part of Grafana Labs' LGTM stack (https://github.com/grafana)—Loki, Grafana, Tempo, and Mimir—its first and most important asset. Grafana started out as a fork of Kibana (http://mng .bz/x47W), when Grafana Labs' founder Torkel Ödegaard was looking for a UI that focuses on time series data and offers graph-focused dashboards.

Grafana offers several resources, but the three most important are

- *Data sources*—Representing backends you want to use in your dashboards or alerts
- *Dashboards*—A way to organize related visualizations
- *Alerts*—Sending you a notification when a certain thing happens (see chapter 7 for greater detail)

Let us now have a look at Grafana and its top-level resources in action. First, we need to stand up a Grafana instance; we do this with the following Docker Compose file that you launch with the, by now, well-known command `docker-compose -f docker-compose.yaml up` (make sure you first go to `ch06/grafana/`).

Listing 6.1   The Docker Compose configuration for the Grafana instance

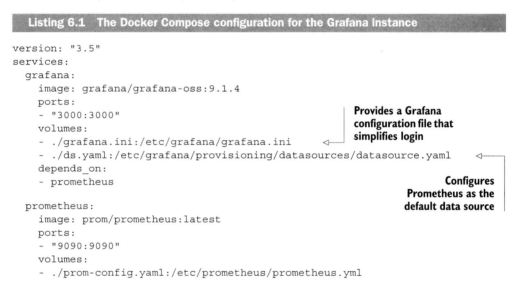

```
version: "3.5"
services:
  grafana:
    image: grafana/grafana-oss:9.1.4
    ports:
    - "3000:3000"
    volumes:
    - ./grafana.ini:/etc/grafana/grafana.ini          ⟵  Provides a Grafana
    - ./ds.yaml:/etc/grafana/provisioning/datasources/datasource.yaml   ⟵   configuration file that
                                                              simplifies login
    depends_on:
    - prometheus
                                                       Configures
  prometheus:                                          Prometheus as the
    image: prom/prometheus:latest                      default data source
    ports:
    - "9090:9090"
    volumes:
    - ./prom-config.yaml:/etc/prometheus/prometheus.yml
```

The grafana.ini file we reference in the Docker Compose file allows us to avoid logging in. Note that at time of writing, Grafana was in version 9; hence, the concepts and screenshots are referencing this version. There were some fundamental changes from Grafana 8 to 9 (unified alerting—that is, alerts being global, rather than on a per-dashboard basis), so keep this in mind when comparing your onscreen output with the screenshots you see here.

Let's begin with Grafana data sources (https://grafana.com/docs/grafana/latest/datasources/, including Amazon CloudWatch, MySQL, Prometheus, and Jaeger, representing backends you can use for visualizations or alerting. If the core data sources are not enough, there are hundreds of plug-ins (https://grafana.com/grafana/plugins/) available, or you can create your own.

Now go to http://localhost:3000/, and then click the gear icon with the Configuration label in the lower part of the left-hand menu. Select the Data Sources menu item. You should see the preconfigured Prometheus data source and, when you click the Add Data Source button, a list of all the available data sources (including potential data source plug-ins you installed).

You can preinstall and preconfigure plug-ins (data sources and visualizations) on Grafana startup. The details are beyond the scope of the book, but as a starting point, here's an example. Let's say you want to preinstall the ClickHouse data source plug-in (assuming you have the `grafana-clickhouse-ds` binary available locally) with Click-House running self-hosted or from one of the SaaS offerings. Using Docker Compose, you'd add the following lines to the docker-compose.yaml YAML manifest in the Grafana section:

```
...
    volumes:
    - ./ds.yaml:/etc/grafana/provisioning/datasources/datasource.yaml
    environment:
      GF_INSTALL_PLUGINS: grafana-clickhouse-ds      ◁─┤ The binary of the plug-in,
                                                         in your local filesystem
```

In addition, you would define the ClickHouse data source in a file called ds.yaml (which is used in the Docker Compose file previous) with the following content:

```
apiVersion: 1
datasources:
  - name: ClickHouse                                 ┌ Defines the type of
    type: grafana-clickhouse-datasource   ◁──────────┘ data source plug-in
    jsonData:                      ◁─────┐ Below, the data source
      defaultDatabase: default           │ plug-in-specific
      port: 9000                         │ configuration
      server: clickhouse
      username:
      tlsSkipVerify: true
      secureJsonData:
        password:
```

If you now do a `docker-compose up`, the ClickHouse data source is automatically added and configured, readily available for you to use in Grafana.

After this short detour on how to provision plug-ins, let's have a look at a concrete data source. After clicking the Add Data Source button (I picked CloudWatch; see figure 6.1, noting that I trimmed out certain lines, so you will see more here), you should see data source–specific configuration options, including authentication, authorization, and various defaults or limits you want to set.

In this view, you can also define whether the data source should be used as the default data source for new dashboards or alerts (the Default toggle is in the upper-right corner), and if you click the Dashboards tab, you will usually (but not always) find predefined dashboards for the data source. You can use those predefined dashboards as is or as a starting point for your own dashboards. Finally, in the bottom row, you will find several buttons, and with the Save & Test button, Grafana performs a simple (data source–dependent) check to see if it can access the data source with the credentials you provided.

NOTE The test that Grafana carries out when you press the Save & Test button is typically very basic. Think of it as a necessary but not sufficient

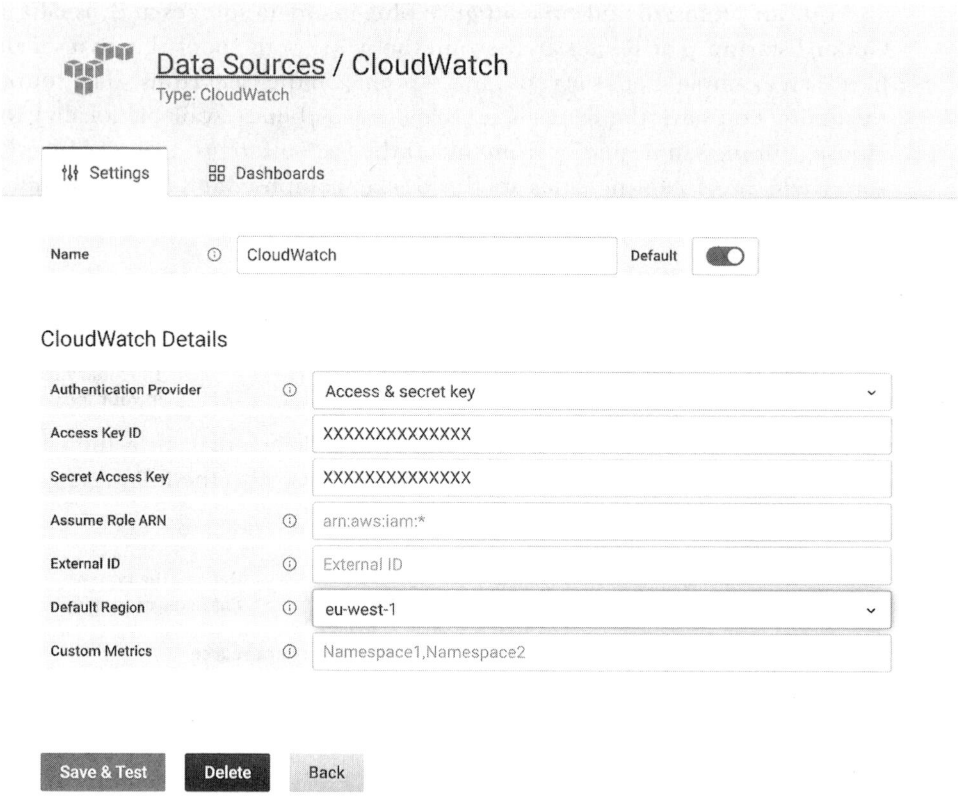

Figure 6.1   An example Grafana data source, showing configuration options

condition: if it passes, you can move on (e.g., using Explore to issue a test query against the data source). If it doesn't pass, you want to check connectivity and whether you have access to the data source, such as by checking IAM roles or API keys.

Grafana dashboards (https://grafana.com/docs/grafana/latest/dashboards/) group panels (https://grafana.com/docs/grafana/latest/panels/), supporting a variety of visualizations (https://grafana.com/docs/grafana/latest/visualizations/), from time series plots to heatmaps to bar charts that are organized into (collapsible) rows. You can make your dashboards much more reusable and flexible by using variables (https://grafana.com/docs/grafana/latest/dashboards/variables/) in a dashboard.

Let's see that in action: first, create a new dashboard (click the menu item that shows four squares with the title Dashboards), and there, click New Dashboard. Now, pick the gear symbol in the upper-right icons row that has the label Dashboard Settings. You should see the dashboard settings now; there (on the left-hand tab selection), click Variables. Here, you can create a new variable by clicking the Add

Variable button. Let's give it the name Test with the type Custom and An Example Dropdown in the label field. This allows us to define a dropdown list of predefined values that our dashboard users can select one or more from. For the values in the Values Separated by Comma option, use `200,301,404`, and the result will be something like you see in figure 6.2.

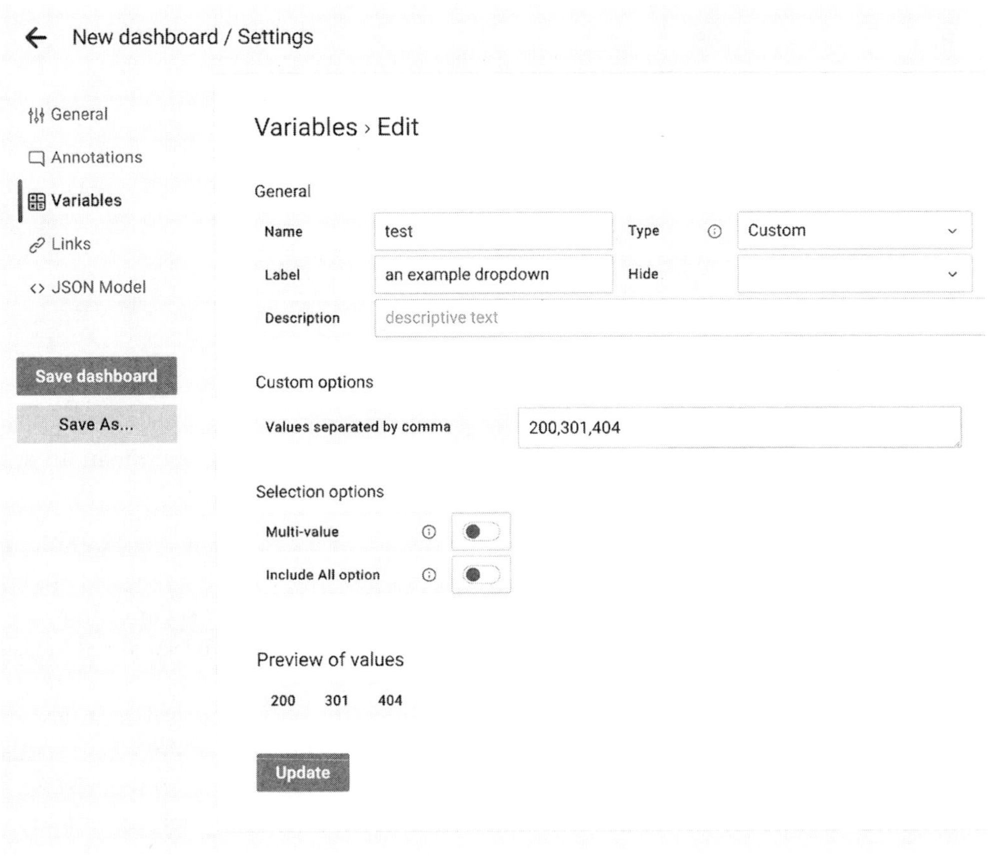

Figure 6.2   Definition of an example Grafana dashboard variable with fixed (predefined) values

When you're done entering, click the Update button. When you now either press the ESC key or click the left arrow in the upper-left corner, you will go back to the dashboard and should see the result of defining the `test` variable, akin to what is shown in figure 6.3.

> **TIP** Through Grafana version 9, consider using the different types of variables (e.g., query, custom, and data source) supported as a way to implement correlation. Starting with Grafana version 10, there is a dedicated correlations

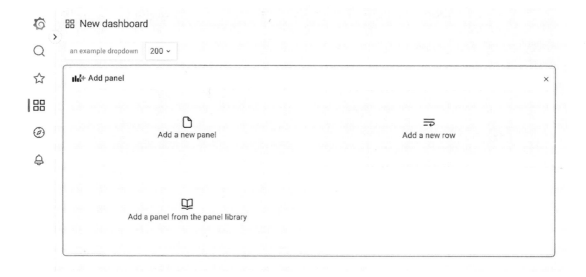

Figure 6.3   Our example dashboard variable `test` rendered in the dashboard

API, including UI support to use variables and transformations in a correlation (http://mng.bz/AoPz).

Now that you have defined the variable `test`, you can use it, for example, in a dashboard query to parameterize it. Let's do exactly that. First, we need a panel that holds the visualization, so create one by clicking the Add a New Panel button. Since we defined Prometheus as the default data source, Grafana picks a suitable visualization (of type time series) for us.

There is also already a placeholder (empty) query there called A. For the following, make sure you're in the Code (and not the default Builder) mode; this is something you can toggle on the upper-right-hand side of the query. Now, enter the following parameterized PromQL query in the Metrics Browser input field:

```
rate(
  prometheus_http_requests_total{code="$test"}[5m]
)
```

This query uses our previously defined Grafana dashboard variable `test` to filter the label values. Put in other words, let the dashboard user select which HTTP status code to query for (with HTTP status code `200` as the default). Figure 6.4 shows the result of the parameterized query in the dashboard editor (press the Apply button in the upper-right-hand corner when you're happy with it and want to try the dashboard).

Figure 6.5 shows the result of the dashboard variable `test` used in our PromQL query, allowing you to select the HTTP status code. If you select a different value, like `301`, it's likely that the panel is empty, which is expected, since no such label values

| Data source | 🔴 Promethe... ⌄ | ⑦ | > | Query optio... | MD = auto = 2768 | Interval = 15s | **Query inspector** |

⌄   A   *(Prometheus)*   ⑦ 📋 ⊙ 🗑 ⠿

Query patterns ⌄   Explain ⬤   **Run queries**   Builder `Beta`   Code

Metrics browser >   `rate(prometheus_http_requests_total{code="$test"}[5m])`

> **Options**   Legend: Auto   Format: Time series   Step: auto   Type: Range   Exemplars: false

Figure 6.4   **The Grafana dashboard variable `test` used in a PromQL query (panel editor)**

exist (unless you've done something in addition to Prometheus or something unexpected happened).

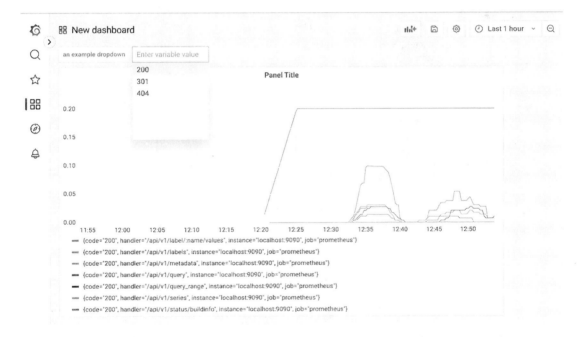

Figure 6.5   **The Grafana dashboard using Prometheus as a data source (with parameterized PromQL query)**

Try playing around with the values for `test` or adding a new variable for the `handler` label. In this context, note that there are sveral variable types beyond the simple example we just used, from data source selection to free text inputs to query variables. The latter allow you to write a query against a specific data source, returning a list of values.

For example, you could write a PromQL query that populates a dropdown list for a new `handler` variable, which you could then use in the extended parameterized PromQL query `prometheus_http_requests_total{code="$test",handler="$handler")`. For another example of a query against a data source to populate the values of a dashboard variable, think of a Kubernetes cluster in which you want to provide your dashboard users with a selection of available namespaces they can choose from, based on a PromQL query.

> **TIP**   As with data sources, you can provision Grafana with dashboards, either directly, as shown previously, or using Terraform (http://mng.bz/Zq8P). There are many great, community-maintained dashboards available via the Grafana dashboard registry (https://grafana.com/grafana/dashboards/) that you can import by reference or via downloading the JSON definitions.

Alerts (https://grafana.com/docs/grafana/latest/alerting/) are the third core Grafana resource. There have been fundamental changes to the topic of unified alerting, introduced in Grafana version 9. We won't discuss alerts in this chapter but, rather, dive deep into the topic in chapter 7.

You don't have to operate Grafana yourself. If you prefer to outsource the heavy lifting of upgrades, security patches, and access controls, there are many choices (at the time of publication):

- Amazon Managed Grafana (https://aws.amazon.com/grafana/) has been around since late 2020 and went into general availability (GA) in September 2021. It comes with support for AWS SSO and SAMLv2, making it easy to give access to the dashboards to any user in your organization.
- Azure Managed Grafana (http://mng.bz/RxYK) has been in GA since August 2022, supporting Grafana version 9 features.
- You can use managed Grafana as part of Grafana Labs' Grafana Cloud (https://grafana.com/products/cloud/) offering, along with a range of other OSS-based tooling, including Grafana Loki for logs and Grafana Tempo for traces.
- Alibaba Cloud offers Managed Service for Grafana (https://www.alibabacloud.com/product/grafana) that provides integration with collaboration tools, including DingTalk and WeCom.

OK, that was a lot of fun. Next up is Kibana (and its OpenSearch variant, Dashboards).

6.1.2   *Kibana and OpenSearch Dashboards*

We discussed Elasticsearch and OpenSearch (ES/OS) as backends in chapter 5. In this context, you have the choice between Kibana (https://www.elastic.co/kibana/), for Elasticsearch and OpenSearch Dashboards (https://opensearch.org/docs/latest/dashboards/index/) for OpenSearch as the respective frontends.

Since OpenSearch Dashboards is a fork of Kibana, there are, as one would expect, many common concepts and features, not considering the difference in licensing. Given the nature and dynamics of the two projects and the managed offerings based on them, I won't cover either Kibana or OpenSearch Dashboards in detail here, but I will point out a number of starting points for you, should you wish to learn more about one of them:

- In chapter 4, we used OpenSearch and OpenSearch Dashboards as backend and frontend destinations for log ingestion and query with the Fluent Bit agent.
- Via the Logz.io blog, there is an excellent Kibana tutorial (https://logz.io/blog/kibana-tutorial/) available, or if you want to invest more time, dive into the Kibana docs (https://www.elastic.co/guide/en/kibana/current/get-started.html), which offer a great onboarding as well.
- For OpenSearch Dashboards, I suggest reviewing the project docs, which offer an OpenSearch Dashboards 101 walkthrough (https://opensearch.org/docs/latest/dashboards/index/), and if you want to learn about OpenSearch Dashboards Notebooks (think Jupyter Notebook; http://mng.bz/2D80), the project blog has you covered.

As a side note, it is interesting to see that Grafana started out as a Kibana fork, radically simplifying the UI with a strong focus on time series data, especially metrics. This caused Grafana to be often used together with Prometheus, which is still the case today. Over the past years, Grafana broadened its scope, now also aiming to cover logs (and traces) visualizations. On the other hand, Kibana and OpenSearch Dashboards were initially focused on logs and are now increasing their support for metrics and traces. Interesting times, indeed!

Just like with Grafana, you can outsource the operations of Kibana and OpenSearch Dashboards to SaaS offerings:

- Elastic offers managed Kibana as part of their observability (https://www.elastic.co/observability/) solution.
- Amazon OpenSearch Service (https://aws.amazon.com/opensearch-service/) offers visualization capabilities powered by OpenSearch Dashboards as well as Kibana (versions 1.5 to 7.10).
- Aiven for OpenSearch (https://aiven.io/opensearch/) supports OpenSearch Dashboards, and you get to choose in which cloud (AWS, Azure, Google, etc.).
- Logz.io has a logs management (https://logz.io/platform/log-management/) offering built on OpenSearch and OpenSearch Dashboards that includes integrations and human-coached AI/ML.

With this, let's have a look at two more open source frontends used in observability setups.

6.1.3   *Other open source frontends*

In addition to Grafana and Kibana/OpenSearch Dashboards, there are two more open source frontends you may want to have a look at when you evaluate options:

- Apache Superset (https://superset.apache.org/), available under the Apache License Version 2.0, positions itself as a data exploration and visualization platform that supports a wide array of databases (http://mng.bz/1qWj), including Amazon Athena, Google BigQuery, ClickHouse, Elasticsearch, MySQL, and TimescaleDB; however, Prometheus support is, at time of writing, not available. It became a top-level Apache Software Foundation (ASF) project in early 2021 and has a number of contributors, including Airbnb (where it started), Dropbox and Lyft.

- Metabase (https://github.com/metabase/metabase) promises to enable "everyone in your company to ask questions and learn from data," which is very suitable for observability use cases. It is released under the AGPL as well as commercial licenses and has a strong SQL focus. You can connect (http://mng.bz/Pzpn) Metabase to a range of databases (including Google BigQuery, PostgreSQL, and Snowflake), and more options are available via partner and community drivers. In addition to the open source DIY model, you can use the commercial managed offering (https://www.metabase.com/pricing/) under the same name, either on-premises or in the cloud. Now, let's move on to the cloud provider and ISV offerings.

6.1.4   *Cloud providers and commercial frontends*

In this space, you will often hear or read the term *business intelligence* (BI)—think observability for business processes. Indeed, many of the offerings in this space stem from there and have been adapted to or are used in the observability context as a specific use case area. Let's have a closer look:

- *Amazon QuickSight (https://aws.amazon.com/quicksight/)*—A cloud BI service by AWS that you can use for dashboarding and reporting. It also supports many popular backends, including Amazon Athena, S3, OpenSearch, and Salesforce.

- *Looker Studio (https://lookerstudio.google.com/overview)*—Google's BI offering as a service, supporting a range of visualizations and connectors to hundreds of backends.

- *Microsoft Power BI (https://powerbi.microsoft.com/en-us/)*—The BI cloud offering of Microsoft that supports data marts and apps with deep integration into the Microsoft office suite. Alternatively, you can use Azure dashboards (https://learn.microsoft.com/en-us/azure/azure-portal/azure-portal-dashboards), which comes with several out-of-the-box integrations with Azure Monitoring.

- *Tableau (https://www.tableau.com/)*—A visual analytics platform you can use in many different setups, from desktop to on-prem to the cloud, supporting a large number of data sources and visualizations.

The commercial offerings mentioned in this section are widely used, mostly by the business side of the house, rather than the engineering team. However, in the context of observability, we do need a comprehensive approach, enabling as many as possible job families to participate and benefit from the system signals.

6.2 *All-in-ones*

Technically speaking, all the cloud provider offerings, including CloudWatch, X-Ray, Azure Monitor, and Google Cloud's operations suite, fall into the all-in-ones category. We covered them in chapter 5, so let's focus here on the other offerings in this space.

There are some open source offerings, with some of them hosted by the Cloud Native Computing Foundation (CNCF) or the Apache Software Foundation (ASF), that offer support for two or more signal types. They come with ingestion and query capabilities, typically allowing different backends to be plugged in or in-memory (nonpersistent) storage.

6.2.1 *CNCF Jaeger*

The CNCF Jaeger (https://github.com/jaegertracing/jaeger) project started out at Uber and was inspired by Google's Dapper project and Zipkin. Nowadays, it is a graduated CNCF project that positions itself as a distributed tracing platform, with built-in support for various backends, including Apache Cassandra; ES/OS; and custom ones, like ClickHouse, via the third-party storage plug-in framework.

Jaeger's overall architecture is a collection of microservices, written in Go, that are working together. The core Jaeger components are

- *Agent (optional)*—A daemon sends traces (over UDP) to the collector, designed to be deployed to all hosts where apps run. The agent is being replaced by OpenTelemetry.
- *Collector*—Receives traces from OpenTelemetry (SDKs or collector) or Jaeger agents and validates, enriches, and stores them in a storage backend.
- *Query service*—Exposes the APIs for retrieving traces from storage and hosts the UI.
- *UI*—The web-based GUI a user interacts with to search for and analyze traces and/or view the system architecture (graph representation of the microservices).
- *Ingester*—A simplified version of the collector that reads traces from Apache Kafka (a popular open source message broker) and writes them to a storage backend.

For experimentations (dev–test use cases), Jaeger also supports pure in-memory storage, readily usable via an the "all-in-one" distribution, combining the core Jaeger components in one package.

Let's see Jaeger in action: we again use a Docker Compose setup and configure Jaeger with ClickHouse as the span storage (listing 6.2). This time we're using a small-scale microservices setup with three `ho11y` instances wired up to simulate a frontend service that calls out to two backend services.

Listing 6.2   The relevant bits of Docker Compose file for Jaeger with ClickHouse setup

```
frontend:
    image: public.ecr.aws/mhausenblas/ho11y:stable          ◁─     The frontend microservice,
    ports:                                                          using ho11y. It's configured to
    - 8765:8765                                                     call the two backends and send
    environment:                                                    traces to the OpenTelemetry
    - "DOWNSTREAM0=http://backend0:8766"                            collector.
    - "DOWNSTREAM1=http://backend1:8767"
    - "OTEL_RESOURCE_ATTRIB=frontend"
    - "OTEL_EXPORTER_OTLP_ENDPOINT=otel-collector:4317"
    - "HO11Y_INJECT_FAILURE=enabled"
                                                  The Jaeger all-in-one distribution
                                                  configured with ClickHouse as the
  jaeger:                                   ◁─    backend, using the gRPC-based
    image: jaegertracing/all-in-one:1.35          plug-in mechanism
    command: [
      "--grpc-storage-plugin.binary=/etc/jaeger-clickhouse",
      "--grpc-storage-plugin.configuration-file=/etc/clickhouse-
    plugin.config"
    ]
    volumes:
    - ./jaeger-clickhouse:/etc/jaeger-clickhouse
    - ./clickhouse-plugin.config:/etc/clickhouse-plugin.config
    ports:
    - "9090:9090"
    - "16686:16686"
    - "14250:14250"
    environment:
    - "SPAN_STORAGE_TYPE=grpc-plugin"            ClickHouse as the backend
                                                 to store traces (and make
  clickhouse:                          ◁───┘     them searchable)
    image: clickhouse/clickhouse-server
    ports:
    - "8123:8123"
    - "9000:9000"
```

We again use the OpenTelemetry collector to collect the traces from our `ho11y`-based microservices setup and ingest them into ClickHouse (via Jaeger). The respective OpenTelemetry collector configuration is shown in the following listing (see also chapter 4).

Listing 6.3   OpenTelemetry collector configuration for Jaeger with ClickHouse

```
receivers:
  otlp:
    protocols:
      grpc:
        endpoint: 0.0.0.0:4317
```

```
exporters:
  jaeger:                          ◁──    The Jaeger exporter configuration
    endpoint: jaeger:14250               (we don't do TLS, so it is
    tls:                                 configured insecure)
      insecure: true
service:
  pipelines:
    traces:                        ◁──    The traces pipeline, using the
      receivers: [ otlp ]                 OTLP receiver and Jaeger exporter
      processors: [ batch ]
      exporters: [ logging, jaeger ]
```

Now, it's time for a `docker-compose up`, and if you now open up http://localhost:16686/ in your browser of choice, you should see something like what is shown in figure 6.6 (in the left-hand side form) if you've first set the Service dropdown to Frontend and entered `http.status_code=404` into the input field labeled Tags.

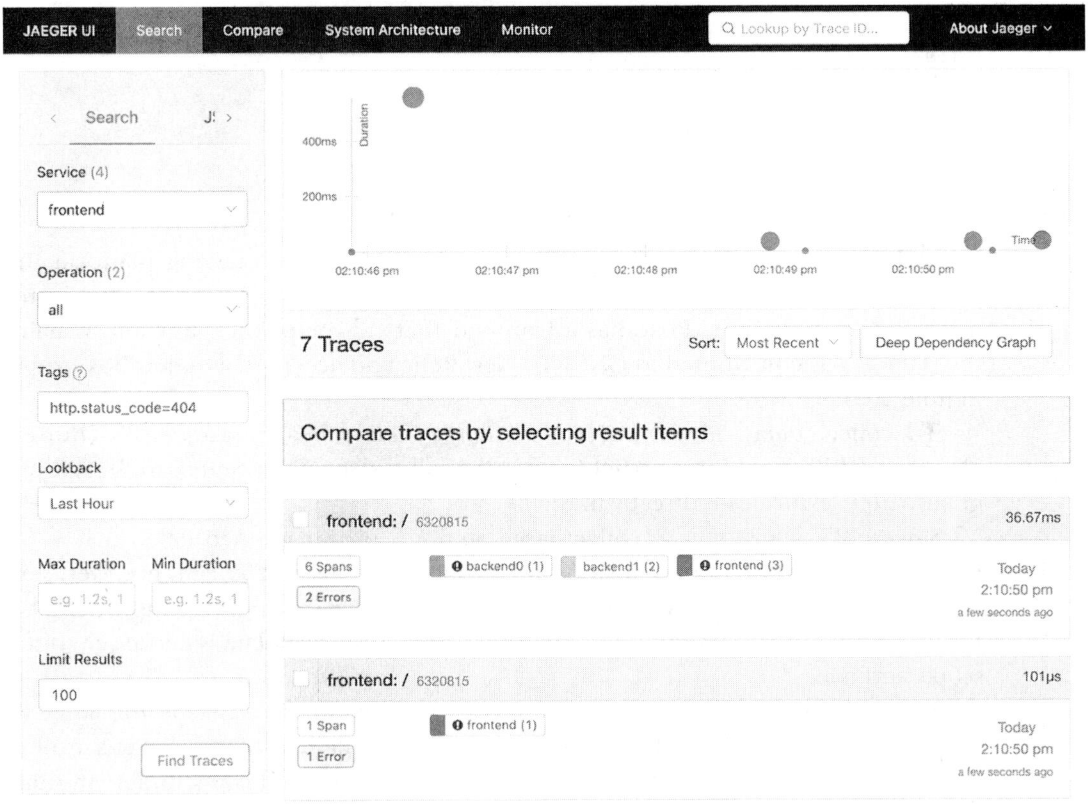

Figure 6.6 Jaeger UI showing all traces for a certain tag (`http.status_code=404`)

Getting an overview of all the traces is useful, but usually, you want to drill down and understand what is going on in the context of a request end to end. To do that, you can click on one of the traces and land in a view shown in figure 6.7. The trace details view gives you the individual spans a trace is composed of in the waterfall model, including duration and high-level metadata, such as type of operation and whether it was successful or not. Let's move on to the another CNCF project in this category.

Figure 6.7   Jaeger UI showing trace details

6.2.2   *CNCF Pixie*

Pixie (https://px.dev/) is a Kubernetes-specific, real-time debugging platform that collects telemetry data, such as metrics, traces, and profiles, without manual instrumentation or redeploys. Pixie has a frontend that can help you query and visualize this data. It was contributed to CNCF by New Relic and accepted as a sandbox project in June 2021.

To collect data without any code changes, Pixie heavily uses eBPF (https://ebpf.io/). eBPF is a Linux kernel feature that allows you to execute sandboxed programs, after verification, directly in the kernel.

Since eBPF allows you to collect large amounts of fine-grained data, such as full request and response bodies, it stores all its data in memory. You can, however, send the telemetry data to any OpenTelemetry-compatible endpoint (http://mng.bz/JgXV) for long-term data retention. In other words, historical data is, by design, out of scope for Pixie.

To query the telemetry data, Pixie uses a rather clever domain-specific language called PxL (https://docs.px.dev/tutorials/pxl-scripts/write-pxl-scripts) that was inspired by Python Pandas. Users can use PxL to query and process Pixie's underlying data however they like. All of Pixie's dashboards are also entirely scriptable, allowing users to build the views and visualizations that work best for them.

Pixie has a lively community with an interesting and promising road map. It sports a number of integrations, from Slack alerts to using it in a Grafana dashboard (via OpenTelemetry export). If you're running a Kubernetes cluster, I recommend taking a closer look at Pixie, as it can be a very useful tool in your tool belt. Now, let's move on to a distributed tracing veteran open source frontend.

6.2.3   *Zipkin*

Zipkin (https://zipkin.io/) is an open source distributed tracing system, written in Java and run by the OpenZipkin volunteer organization. Zipkin has a tracing-focused UI (see figure 6.8) and integrates a range of backends, including ES/OS, Apache Cassandra, and MySQL, with other backends offered as third-party extensions. The Zipkin project was also inspired by Google Dapper and originally created by Twitter, with roots going back to 2015.

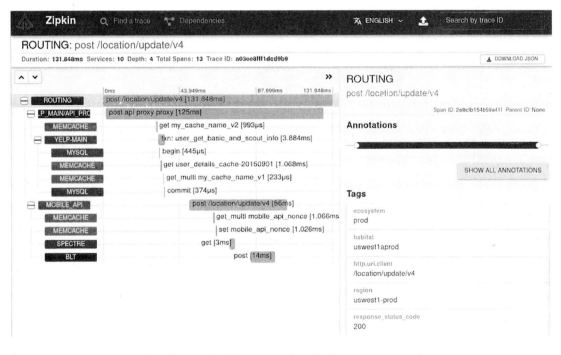

Figure 6.8   A screenshot of Zipkin in action (from the project docs)

I won't go into any detail here concerning Zipkin's architecture, since it is very similar to what we've seen in the context of CNCF Jaeger. If you want to try out Zipkin and see it in action, check out the Zipkin GitHub repo, which has a nice collection of Docker Compose examples (http://mng.bz/wv7P) from using Apache Cassandra as a backend to trace ingestion with Apache Kafka, readily available for you. To view the Docker Compose example, do a `docker-compose up` in the respective directory and then go to http://localhost:9411 and click Run Query to see the results. Next up, we'll cover an exciting Apache Software Foundation (ASF) project.

6.2.4 *Apache SkyWalking*

Apache SkyWalking (https://skywalking.apache.org/) is an ASF open source project that, nowadays, offers support for distributed tracing of distributed systems, like microservices in Kubernetes environments. It started out as a distributed tracing system in China Unicom in 2015 and has been adopted by over 100 companies, including Alibaba, China Merchants Bank, and Huawei. If you want to dive deeper into the topic, check out "Application Performance Monitor and Distributed Tracing with Apache SkyWalking in Datahub" (http://mng.bz/qr7r) by Liangjun Jiang to see it in action. With that, we move on to two all-in-ones that build atop of ClickHouse.

6.2.5 *SigNoz*

SigNoz (https://github.com/SigNoz/signoz) positions itself as an open source alternative to Datadog and New Relic. Currently, it uses ClickHouse as its backend; until mid-2021, it focused on an Apache Kafka and Apache Druid combo (http://mng .bz/7DBv) for storage. See also chapter 5 for more details on these backends. SigNoz is easy to set up and comes with several tutorials, covering topics from consuming Kubernetes infrastructure metrics (http://mng.bz/mV7a) to visualizing JVM metrics from a Spring Boot application.

Let's have a very quick walk-through to see SigNoz in action. All you need for that is to have Docker Compose installed and then execute the following:

```
$ git clone -b main https://github.com/SigNoz/signoz.git && cd signoz/deploy/
$ docker-compose -f docker/clickhouse-setup/docker-compose.yaml up
```

If you now wait a couple of minutes (to give the bundled app some time to generate signals), head over to http://localhost:3301/, and select a trace, you should see something akin to what is shown in figure 6.9 (SigNoz's trace view). Next up is another ClickHouse-based open source all-in-one offering.

6.2.6 *Uptrace*

Uptrace (https://github.com/uptrace/uptrace) is an all-in-one tool that states it support traces, metrics, and logs and uses OpenTelemetry to collect data as well as ClickHouse to persist the telemetry signals with the capability to offload cold data (historical data you don't frequently access) to S3-compatible object storage. For alerting, Uptrace has integrations with several notification channels, including email, Slack, and Telegram.

Uptrace has a positioning and architecture similar to what you've seen with SigNoz, and while at time of writing it seems less mature than SigNoz, there's certainly potential here. I wouldn't be surprised to see even more open source all-in-ones using a similar setup going forward. With this, we conclude the open source offerings and turn our attention to commercial offerings in the space.

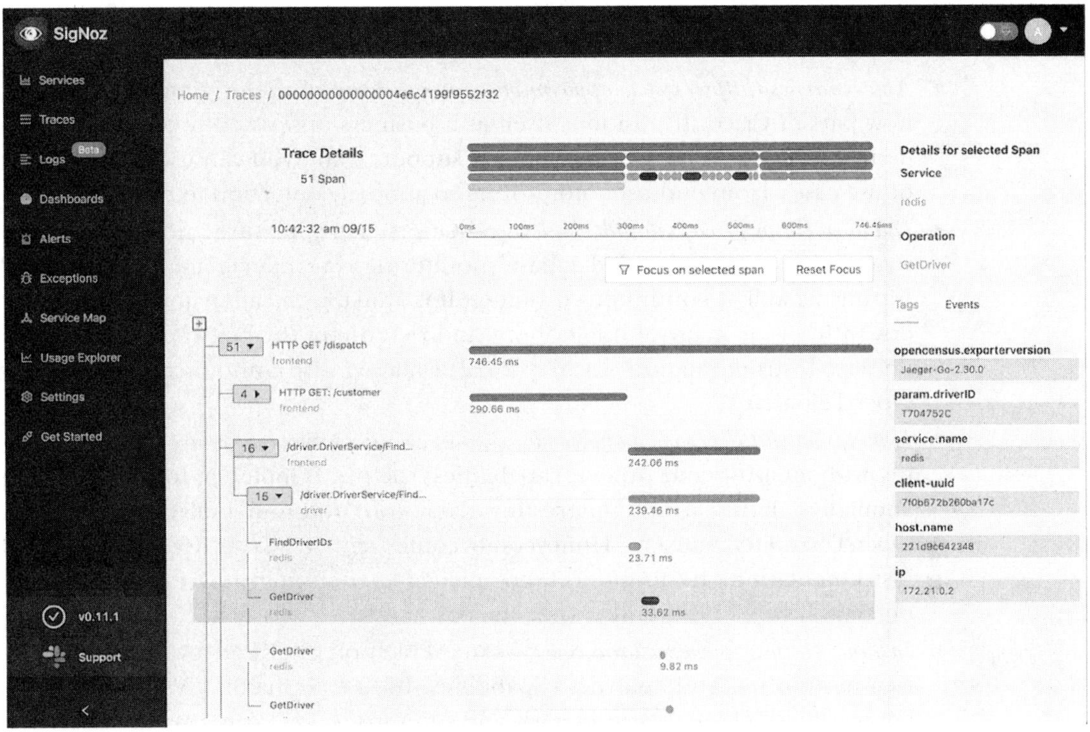

Figure 6.9   A screenshot of SigNoz in action with the traces view active

6.2.7   *Commercial offerings*

Many of the commercial offerings in the all-in-ones category started out years or, in some cases, more than a decade ago. Back then, the label often used for their services was *application performance monitoring* (APM). The term *APM* has been mostly replaced by *observability solution*, since it's more inclusive and, presumably, makes better headlines and advertising search engine optimization (SEO) than APM.

This section is intentionally short, as I don't want to give the impression it's possible to provide a comprehensive review, or even comparison, of all the vendors and their respective offerings. It is, at time of writing, indeed, a busy and crowded space, and we have already witnessed a few consolidations and acquisitions, with more likely to follow in the years to come. What I do want to achieve with the following list is a short summary of the available options, highlighting their strong points and overall positioning. This should enable you to have a few starting points when you make a selection (more on that in the next section). The vendors and offerings of interest in this space include (but are not limited to) the following, in alphabetical order:

- *Aspecto (https://www.aspecto.io/)*—An SaaS offering with a focus on distributed tracing that you can use for root cause analysis by correlating traces, logs, and metrics. The team behind it is active in the OpenTelemetry project, so it's no surprise that Aspecto makes use of it heavily.

- *AppDynamics (https://www.appdynamics.com/)*—One of the original APM players, now part of Cisco. It positions itself as a business observability platform with a dedicated agent (with OpenTelemetry support), and you can use it for a range of use cases, from end user monitoring to anomaly detection to dashboarding.

- *Datadog (https://www.datadoghq.com/)*—Offers many features, including infrastructure, container, and database monitoring; log management; distributed tracing; as well as continuous profiling. It is available via all major cloud providers, with a wide array of integrations and rich out-of-the-box capabilities based on auto-instrumentation. In May 2022, Datadog also announced support for OpenTelemetry.

- *Honeycomb (https://www.honeycomb.io/)*—A cloud-native observability SaaS offering with amazing and unique capabilities, such as BubbleUp, for investigating anomalies. It has a very interesting data store (custom built) and supports OpenTelemetry natively. Honeycomb comes with a strong focus on manual instrumentation. Its founders were pivotal in defining and establishing the observability (o11y) moniker over the past years.

- *Instana (https://www.instana.com/)*—An APM tool, acquired by IBM, that has rich monitoring and analytics capabilities. It, like all major ISVs in this space, bet on OpenTelemetry rather early and supports it now. You can use Instana on AWS, Azure, Google, and IBM Cloud.

- *Lightstep (https://lightstep.com/)*—An SaaS offering that has a unified storage layer (https://lightstep.com/blog/lightstep-metrics-database), allowing it to store different signals; an interesting pricing structure; and lots of activity in OpenTelemetry, upstream. Lightstep was founded by Ben Sigelman (who helped establishing Dapper at Google) and is now part of ServiceNow.

- *Lumigo (https://lumigo.io/)*—A smaller player but a interesting SaaS offering in this space, with competitive pricing. It natively supports OpenTelemetry and has a focus on distributed tracing.

- *New Relic (https://newrelic.com/)*—An SaaS offering with APM roots that positions itself as an observability platform for DevOps, security, and business. It is native to OpenTelemetry; sports over 400 integrations; and supports traces, metrics, and logs.

- *SolarWinds (https://www.solarwinds.com/solarwinds-observability)*—Integrates an impressive range of observability solutions from acquisitions in the past decade, including, but not limited to, Pingdom, Librato, Papertrail, LogicNow, Loggly, VividCortex, and SentryOne.

- *Splunk (https://www.splunk.com/)*—One of the big players in the observability ISV space. Nowadays, it is available as an SaaS and for on-prem deployments; it has been around for a while (all the way back to 2003). Splunk is often used for logs but supports metrics and traces as well, with an extensive array of functionality, including analytics, dashboarding, and business diagnostics. Splunk is heavily invested in and contributes to OpenTelemetry, and hence, it comes as no surprise that it provides first-class support for it in its products.

- *Sumo Logic (https://www.sumologic.com/)*—An SaaS offering integrated with all major cloud providers. It comes with many integrations, supporting a range of use cases with monitoring and security-related functionality and supports Open-Telemetry as well.

With that, we've reached the end of the all-in-one offerings and now move on to considerations when selecting one.

6.3 Selecting frontends and all-in-ones

Given the sheer number of options for frontends and all-in-ones you've seen in this chapter, you could imagine it's not an easy task to pick one (or more). If you can, work backward from the value you want to deliver to your internal customers, developers, and business stakeholders. Consider the following questions: Are you looking for a solution to support the acceleration of shipping features and fixing bugs? Are you interested in a product that allows you to reduce the time to fix an issue in prod? Do you want to increase developer productivity?

Depending on the answers, you first want to make a decision on the following: build or buy. In general, unless you've identified this as a competitive advantage, you want to outsource as much as possible. In other words, buy. There are several big enterprises, however, that have a strategic interest in minimizing their dependence on vendors and/or a cloud provider. In this context, using open source (components) and basing the work on open standards makes a lot of sense. In other words, build.

Your mileage may vary, but here a couple of considerations when you evaluate and select offerings in this space:

- Can you determine the costs? Costs of frontends are typically on a per-user basis (viewer and editor) in a hosted offering and relatively predictable. All-in-ones typically have backend-like cost plans (and may have seat-based pricing). For self-hosted setups, make sure you take into account the operational costs of patching, scaling, on-call hours, security-related requirements and work, as well as keeping up with upstream. There may also be costs associated with data storage, ingestion, and query, as we discussed in chapter 5 in greater detail.
- All-in-ones are typically the closest you can get for a single pane of glass, and if you make sure open standards, such as OpenTelemetry, are supported, minimizing vendor lock-in, they are an excellent choice.
- For all open source offerings, make sure you understand who is behind the project (i.e., a single vendor open source versus a community, usually hosted by CNCF or ASF), the licensing (which can potentially change), and the health of the open source project. Concerning the last point, simply looking at how many

GitHub stars it has is not sufficient (this is purely a popularity indicator). You need to invest the time to look at the release cadence (you should be able to accommodate the pace), how many contributors (ideally, multiple, from different places) and users (ideally, in different industry verticals) it has, the documentation available, how many issues and pull or merge requests there are (and how quickly they get addressed), and a strategy for support (i.e., in-house or community-based), as support is key to enterprise usage.

- One of the increasingly more relevant and requested features that helps you more efficiently use your tool of choice is correlation (https://www.youtube.com/watch?v=qVITI34ZFuk). Make sure you check what kind of correlation (time-based, exemplars, etc.; see also chapter 11) is available and how much manual work is required to go from one signal type to another, assuming the tool you're evaluating, indeed, supports more than one signal type, which is the basis for correlation to work.

TIP Given the very nature of the frontends and all-in-ones, being the visible part end users interact with, make sure you bring all stakeholders on board. Selecting a tool purely based on a price tag or because of how polished it is may turn out to be challenging.

Now, that was a lot of new information! I hope you can use it to your advantage when selecting tooling in this space. It's a fast-moving and exciting space, so it makes sense to revisit your choices on a regular basis.

Summary

- Frontends allow you to interact with the observability datasets stored in backends.
- You use a frontend to find answers to your (ad hoc) questions in various graphical and textual manners.
- There are many open source frontends (Grafana, Kibana, Metabase, etc.) available, and when you build your own in-house observability solution, consider these rather than building something from scratch.
- All-in-ones are an excellent choice if you manage to avoid too much vendor lock-in; they allow you to outsource most of the operational burden and typically provide you with a range of functionality, for a premium.
- What used to be APM is now, by and large, rebranded as distributed tracing.
- Selecting tools in this space can be tricky, but make sure you understand costs associated with it well and have a clear idea of the value you want to deliver (and to whom).
- Picking open source tooling is a great way to be interoperable and vendor agnostic; however, make sure you understand the dynamics of the open source project and have a clear strategy for getting support.

- The more open standards like OpenTelemetry a tool supports, the more likely you are not locked in and are able to move on to another tool if it doesn't fit your needs anymore.
- Frontends are typically where correlation happens; that is, you would expect that the UI supports operations and visualizations to easily switch from one telemetry signal type to another.

Cloud operations

So far in this book, we have focused on the happy path of our cloud-native setup, covering the signal sources, telemetry, and destinations to store, query, visualize, and interact with the signals to understand and influence the system. In this chapter, we will discuss an aspect of cloud-native solutions I call *cloud operations*, which spans several topics you will likely come across, especially in an operations role.

We start off with incidents: how to detect when something is not working the way that it should, react to abnormal behavior, and learn from previous mistakes. Then, we focus on alerts, or alarms (I'm using these terms interchangeably here, though an alert can be a triggered condition, and alarms can potentially cover multiple alerts)—that is, the automated process to check for a condition and inform someone responsible for a service or a piece of infrastructure about it. In the final part of this chapter, we talk about usage tracking, be that what your internal or external users access or the costs of the resources you're using to provide a cloud-native app.

Why can cloud operations be tricky? Well, in the context of cloud-native solutions, be that a workload running on Kubernetes or a bunch of lambda functions, what all of them have in common is many moving parts with potentially many different owners. So when end users of your cloud-native app are impacted—for example, by slower-than-usual response times or (partial) failures—the murder mystery starts: Which of the services along the request path contributed to the problem? Who owns it and, hence, should be notified to fix it?

Remember that for the end user, the fact that you're running, say, hundreds of microservices is unknown and, frankly, shouldn't matter. What they perceive is that something is not working, and it's your organization's responsibility to make sure you detect such issues—ideally, before you learn of them from your users—and have strategies in place not only to fix the issues as fast as you can but also learn from an issue to make sure it doesn't happen again. In this context, we can consider tracking the customer experience (not always clear who owns this) versus infrastructure tracking (usually clearly defined ownership). Let's start with incidents and how to detect and respond to them in a structured manner.

7.1 Incident management

In the context of this book, we'll consider two incidents: unexpected behavior of services or the platform that negatively affects its function or performance, and a repeat of unexpected behavior that is yet to have the learnings applied. For the latter case, the repeated unexpected behavior, it can be helpful to have a runbook of how previous incidents were resolved for handling the repeat situation.

Generally, it is best to have an incident response process in place. This incident response process is typically a set of procedures that define how you go about resolving and learning from an incident. You can think of it in terms of three phases:

1 First, you need to be able to detect that something is going wrong (health and performance monitoring).

2 Then, you need to be able to react to and handle an incident in a structured manner.

3 Last but not least, you need to learn from an incident. You want to avoid repeating a similar occurrence in the future (what action items should be completed to not have repeat occurrence of the same problem). We'll start by covering detecting an issue.

7.1.1 Health and performance monitoring

We previously discussed that the first step in resolving an incident is to be able to understand that something is broken in the first place. This may sound simple, but in a cloud-native system with many components, it is a nontrivial issue. In other words, manual approaches, such as visiting your website in a browser and checking if everything looks good, are not something you want to consider. Instead, aim to automate as many of the checks against your services and the "outside view"—that is, customer experience (CX) as possible. In this context, it's crucial to emphasize this outside view; imagine a situation in which all your services report they are healthy and working as expected, but your end users can't access the app due to, say, a DNS issue.

The actual mechanisms you need to use to perform health and performance monitoring are really a spectrum, including the following:

- *Reachability monitoring*—Perform a simple call (ICMP, TCP, HTTP) to check for reachability or to ensure an endpoint returns a predefined status code.
- *Synthetic monitoring*—Execute scripts to simulate typical end user actions. These simulated end users are sometimes called *canaries* (a reference to the original use case, in which those little birds were used to detect gas leaks in mines). Several open source and commercial offerings allow you to perform synthetic monitoring—for example, Datadog (https://docs.datadoghq.com/synthetics/, Elastic (http://mng.bz/5wDO), New Relic (http://mng.bz/6Dle), and Amazon CloudWatch (http://mng.bz/o17Z). See figure 7.1 for an example.

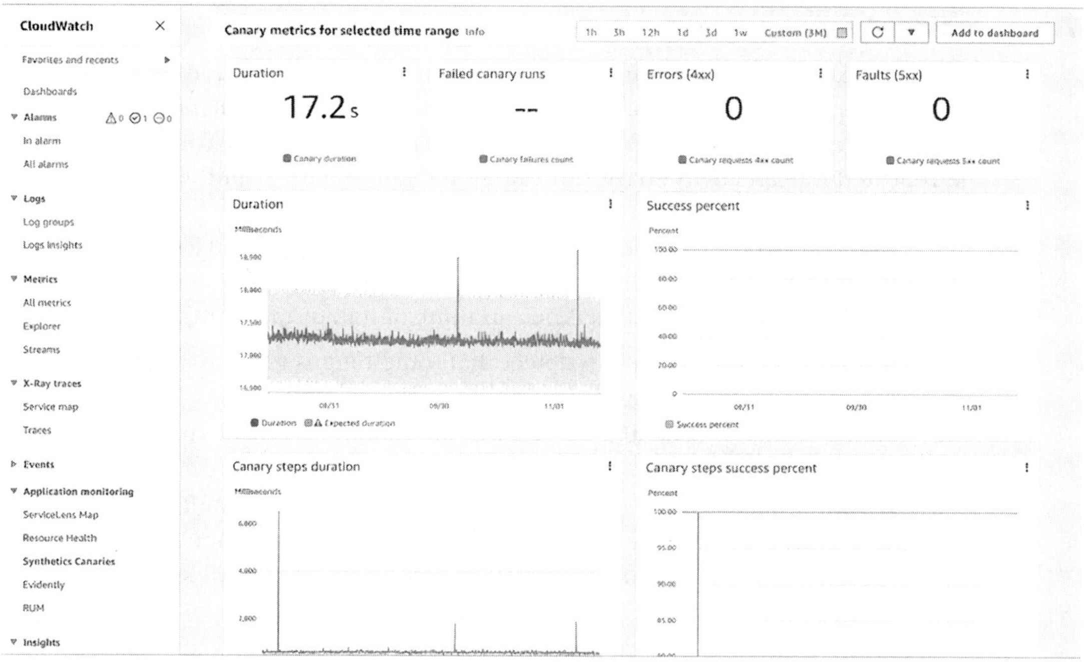

Figure 7.1   CloudWatch, an example of synthetic monitoring, tracking the availability of a website

You typically want to automate the process of checking for a condition and inform someone responsible about it, which is also known as *alerting* or *alarming*. There is a nice high-level article, "When to Alert on What?" (https://ali.sattari.me/posts/2023/when-to-alert-on-what/), which is a useful article for getting started on the topic, ranging from manual to working with service-level objectives (which we cover in detail in chapter 10).

On a related note, how do you know if something is out of the normal? You need a baseline. You can determine the baseline (i.e., "How does the service or system look when everything is healthy?") manually by observing and noting things or by employing more sophisticated techniques, usually referred to as *anomaly detection* (https://www.reddit.com/r/sre/comments/zxdd2y/anomaly_detection/). With the detection basics out of the way, we now focus on how to deal with the incident after learning about it.

7.1.2 Handling the incident

Now that we're in a position to detect when something goes sideways in our cloud-native app by having health and performance monitoring in place, we move on to the question of how to handle an incident. Let's first discuss the "who" and then move on to the "what" and "how." In general, a human needs to be in the loop, assigned to handle the incident. This is oftentimes done via an on-call mechanism. For a certain time period, ranging from hours to a week or maybe even more, the person on call is notified by the monitoring system and needs to get on top of things as quickly as possible.

> **TIP** There are some offerings, sometimes called *AIOps*, that attempt to optimize the human-in-the-loop experience (e.g., Shoreline, https://www.shoreline.io/).

Nowadays, this notification is usually delivered via an app (and in parallel via email, Slack, MS Teams ping, phone call, etc.) and can come at any time of the day or night. You can probably imagine that if such a notification (or page) reaches you at, say, 2 a.m. and you have, say, 15 minutes to check in, you want to make sure you have a structured approach.

There are several things to consider when talking about on-call roles and models:

- *Traditional vs. on call*—In a traditional setting, where development and operations are strictly separated, the operations (ops) team is on call (technical responder). This can cause issues, since not only is the on-call setting demanding, but also, the person most familiar with a certain service is certainly not the ops person on call. Alternatively, one can establish a model where development and on-call are combined. For example, this is how AWS service teams work. This provides incentives for developers to properly instrument their code, enabling on-call to resolve issues as fast as possible.

- *Engineering and communication*—It goes without saying that to fix a technical issue, you need engineers on call. There is, however, another role that may be separated out: communication (incident manager or commander). On one hand, that can be internal communication (keeping stakeholders up to date), and on the other hand, it can refer to communication of the issue to customers. Someone needs to determine if customers are, indeed, impacted (versus canaries); how many customers are impacted; and where they are impacted (if we're talking about a global system). Depending on the outcome, you might see an update on a more personalized level, such as the AWS Personal Health Dashboard (http://mng.bz/nW75), or a global view, relevant for all users, as with the GitHub Status (https://www.githubstatus.com/) page.

Regarding the *what* and *how*, the most important thing to remember is to stop the bleeding— that is, try to fix the problem and, ideally, gather data points along the way. The analysis (why it went wrong) comes later; don't let analysis slow down your efforts to stop the bleeding.

To support the person on call, the organization usually develops playbooks and runbooks (http://mng.bz/vn7p) that describe what to check during an incident and documents dependencies to understand downstream effects or possible sources of upstream trouble. Also, some teams practice the processes or material available (including coverage of runbooks) in something usually called a *game day* (http://mng .bz/4DNR).

7.1.3   *Learning from the incident after the fact*

Let's assume the on-call team did a good job and fixed the problem. That isn't the end of the story. You want to have a process in place that looks at the incident and allows you to achieve two things: understand what the underlying issue was and ensure you don't repeat the same mistake.

I recommend following the path of a blameless postmortem (http://mng.bz/ QPO6); in AWS, we call these *corrections of error* (COE; https://wa.aws.amazon.com/ wat.concept.coe.en.html). These sessions help you to determine what caused an issue and how to avoid it in the future, typically employing the five whys technique (https:// www.lucidchart.com/blog/5-whys-analysis). You may also come across the term *root cause analysis* (RCA; https://www.techtarget.com/searchitoperations/definition/root-cause-analysis), which refers to testing various theories about what originally caused the problem with empirical data.

After this theory-heavy section, let's move on to how to handle notifications for on-call roles—in other words, *alerting*.

7.2   Alerting

In this section, we start by looking at alerting in the Prometheus ecosystem. We then move on to alerting with Grafana, and finally, we discuss alerting offerings of the cloud providers and beyond.

7.2.1   *Prometheus alerting*

We talked about Prometheus and saw it in action in previous chapters (e.g., in chapters 2 and 5). Now that we have a more complete picture in terms of instrumentation and backends, let's see how Prometheus handles alerting.

In the context of Prometheus, alerting comprises two distinct parts:

- *Prometheus itself*—You define what an alert is. This effectively means you define conditions using PromQL, and Prometheus evaluates them periodically. Once a condition is met, Prometheus considers this to be the alert "firing" and sends it to the Alertmanager API.
- *Alertmanager API*—This provides an API that enables clients (typically Prometheus) to send in alerts and takes care of the notifications. For example, you could define a policy that sends a notification for certain types of alerts via email or implement a policy such as *during work hours, send the notification to Slack; after work, send a text message.* But that's not the only thing the Alertmanager does: it deduplicates alerts and allows you to group and suppress notifications to reduce alert fatigue and lessen alert storms.

Figure 7.2 shows how Prometheus and Alertmanager work together to handle alerts. As we discussed in chapter 4, the scrape targets (e.g., your instrumented applications or Prometheus exporters, such as the Node exporter) expose metrics in the Prometheus exposition format, which Prometheus scrapes (in other words, it calls the endpoints, which are by default expected to be at /metrics). If you have alerting rules defined in Prometheus, Prometheus continuously evaluates them and calls the Alertmanager in case the defined threshold is reached. The Alertmanager, in turn, processes alerts with the goal of sending out as few and concise notifications as possible. Via the configured receivers in the Alertmanager, it delivers a notification to one or more destinations, where the operator (a human) finally consumes the notification and acts upon it accordingly.

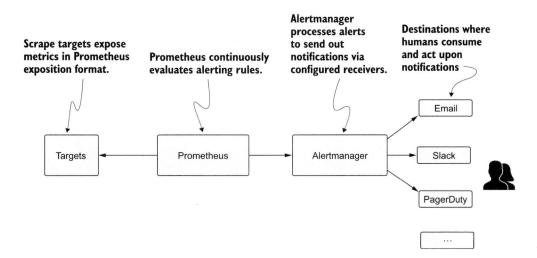

Figure 7.2   Prometheus and the Alertmanager

The separation of Prometheus and the Alertmanager, as shown in figure 7.2, allows for flexibility and scalability. For example, you can scale or restart either of the tools without interrupting the other.

> **TIP** From an operations perspective, at the end of the day, you want to avoid alert fatigue (https://en.wikipedia.org/wiki/Alarm_fatigue). That is, you want to minimize the notifications to act on while making sure you don't miss something substantial. Imagine the case in which you're responsible for a Kubernetes cluster with multiple namespaces. If there are data plane problems with the nodes not being reachable or rebooting, you only want to get one notification, rather than, say, one notification for every single pod in the cluster.

Now, let's dive deeper into how alerting rules and the Alertmanager work.

PROMETHEUS ALERTING RULES

Starting with Prometheus, we now work our way through defining and handling alerts. In the Prometheus configuration, you define the alerts using alerting rules (http://mng.bz/XNj9). An alerting rule defines the condition you want Prometheus to evaluate. A concrete example looks as follows (adapted from the excellent reference site Awesome Prometheus Alerts (https://awesome-prometheus-alerts.grep.to/), which provides a large collection of curated alert examples you can use):

The name of the alert. The convention is CamelCase.

The condition to evaluate—a PromQL expression Prometheus executes

Optionally, you can specify for how long the condition needs to be met before sending the alert to the Alertmanager.

```
- alert: PrometheusAllTargetsMissing
  expr: sum by (job) (up) == 0
  for: 0m
  labels:
    severity: critical
  annotations:
    summary: Prometheus all targets missing {{ $labels.instance }}
    description: "A Prometheus job has no alive targets.\n
                 VALUE = {{ $value }}\n  LABELS = {{ $labels }}"
```

Key–value metadata for filtering and routing in the Alertmanager

Key–value context for direct human consumption (content of the notification) using templating

While the `for` field is optional, you should consider setting it. The reason is that, in cloud-native systems, you're dealing with a lot of ephemeral components, network connectivity issues, and timeouts or retries. You don't want a trigger-happy alert spamming you while, really, it was just a temporary issue with the telemetry, for example. Let's say we would have chosen `for: 3m` in the preceding example. In this case, Prometheus initially considers the alert in the pending state when the condition is met for the first time. The alert is considered to be in the firing state and sent to the Alertmanager if the condition persists for 3 minutes. In the preceding snippet, we used `for: 0m`, and because of this, the alert went directly to firing.

Concerning the `annotations` field, you want to provide rich context for the human operator receiving a notification based on the alert. Consider that the notification may reach the person on call at an early hour, and the last thing you want in this situation is to start digging for references, wasting valuable time to stop the bleeding, while still trying to wake up. For example, you could, in addition to the `summary` and `description` fields we defined in the preceding example, add the following:

- A link to a dashboard that shows the time series for the relevant time frame
- An assessment of who or what is impacted (whether these are real customers or canaries)
- A link to a runbook, for known issues and contributing factors. If you can follow these links from your phone without having to log in to, say, eight systems to get them to render, you've done a good job.

Now that we know what alerting rules are and how to define them, let's see how to set up Prometheus to include the alerting rules and establish the connection to an Alertmanager. This is done as follows in the Prometheus configuration file prometheus.yml:

```
global:
  scrape_interval: 30s
  external_labels:          ⊲┐  Adds external labels to
    environment: dev            provide context for the
    region: us-west-1           Prometheus instance
rule_files:
  - alert.rules           ⊲┘  Points to the file where the
alerting:                     alerting rules are defined
  alertmanagers:        ⊲┐  Configures the Alertmanager
  - static_configs:         Prometheus should use
    - targets: ["alertmanager.local:9093"]
scrape_configs:
  ...
```

ALERTMANAGER

Let's now move on to the Alertmanager (http://mng.bz/yQ7p). First, we have a look at how the Alertmanager processes alerts. This is done in the so-called notification pipeline, consisting of the following phases:

1 *Inhibition*—Suppress notifications for alerts if other (related) alerts are already firing. For example, think of the preceding case, where you don't want pod-level notifications when you're already notified of a cluster data plane issue.

2 *Silencing*—Suppress notifications ad hoc, in a proactive manner. For example, if you're upgrading nodes in an Kubernetes cluster, you already know in advance that nodes will go down temporarily, so you don't want to get a notification for this.

3 *Routing*—Decide who gets a notification.

4 *Grouping and throttling*—Ensure you get one notification per event.

5 *Notification*—Using so-called receivers, define how the notification should be delivered, such as via email, Slack, PagerDuty, or Amazon Simple Notification Service (SNS; https://aws.amazon.com/sns/).

An example config (http://mng.bz/MBaQ) for the Alertmanager should give you some idea of how you can configure the notification pipeline, but let's have a look at a concrete end-to-end example to fully appreciate how things work.

In this example, we implement a simple Prometheus self-monitoring case. The goal is to receive a notification once a certain number of Prometheus API calls is exceeded.

As usual, we need to stand up a Prometheus and an Alertmanager instance using the Docker Compose file in listing 7.1, which you launch (from `ch07/prometheus/`) with the following command:

```
docker-compose -f docker-compose.yaml up
```

In the Docker Compose file, we pass on the environment variables and the configuration files.

Listing 7.1   The Docker Compose configuration for the Prometheus alerting setup

```
version: "3.5"
services:                          Configures Prometheus
                                   with alerts and
  prometheus:              ◁────   Alertmanager
    image: prom/prometheus:latest
    ports:
    - "9090:9090"
    volumes:
    - ./prom-config.yaml:/etc/prometheus/prometheus.yml
    - ./alerting.yaml:/etc/prometheus/alert.rules

  alertmanager:              ◁───  Configures Alertmanager with
    image: prom/alertmanager:latest   grouping and notification
    volumes:
    - ./am-config.yaml:/etc/alertmanager/alertmanager.yml
    ports:
    - "9093:9093"
                                    Sets up a generic webhook
  webhook:              ◁────       the Alertmanager can call
    image: kennethreitz/httpbin
    ports:
    - "9999:80"
```

The next listing shows the complete Prometheus configuration in prometheus.yml, defining where to find alerts and connecting to the Alertmanager.

Listing 7.2   The Prometheus config

```
global:
  scrape_interval: 5s
```

```
    external_labels:
      env: "docker"                    References where the
rule_files:                    ◁────   alerting rule is defined
- alert.rules
alerting:                      ◁────
  alertmanagers:                       Configures the
  - static_configs:                    Alertmanager
    - targets:
      - "alertmanager:9093"        Defines what to scrape
scrape_configs:                ◁──   (in this case, Prometheus
  - job_name: "prometheus"           self-scrape)
    static_configs:
    - targets: ["localhost:9090"]
```

Our alert is defined in alert.rules, shown in the following listing. We want to fire the alert once the total number of HTTP requests Prometheus sees exceeds a certain number (40, in our example).

Listing 7.3 Alerting rule

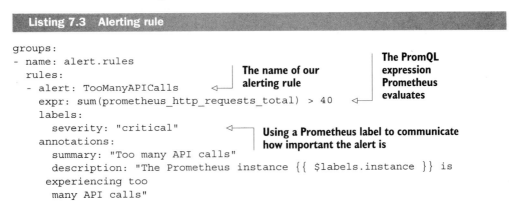

```
groups:
- name: alert.rules
  rules:                                                    The name of our
  - alert: TooManyAPICalls                ◁────             alerting rule
    expr: sum(prometheus_http_requests_total) > 40    ◁────
    labels:
      severity: "critical"          ◁────
    annotations:                            Using a Prometheus label to communicate
      summary: "Too many API calls"         how important the alert is
      description: "The Prometheus instance {{ $labels.instance }} is
    experiencing too
    many API calls"
```

The name of our alerting rule

The PromQL expression Prometheus evaluates

The Alertmanager config alertmanager.yml is depicted next.

Listing 7.4 Alertmanager configuration

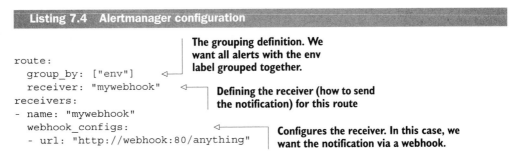

```
                              The grouping definition. We
                              want all alerts with the env
route:                        label grouped together.
  group_by: ["env"]     ◁────
  receiver: "mywebhook"   ◁──    Defining the receiver (how to send
receivers:                       the notification) for this route
- name: "mywebhook"
  webhook_configs:               ◁──   Configures the receiver. In this case, we
  - url: "http://webhook:80/anything"   want the notification via a webhook.
```

If you go to http://localhost:9090, you should see the Prometheus UI. You can find the alerting rules and their status, as shown in figure 7.3, via the top-level Alerts menu item. If you want to speed up things, you need to perform a few queries (e.g., using the PromQL query `sum(prometheus_http_requests_total)`) or, otherwise, wait a few minutes until you see the alert firing.

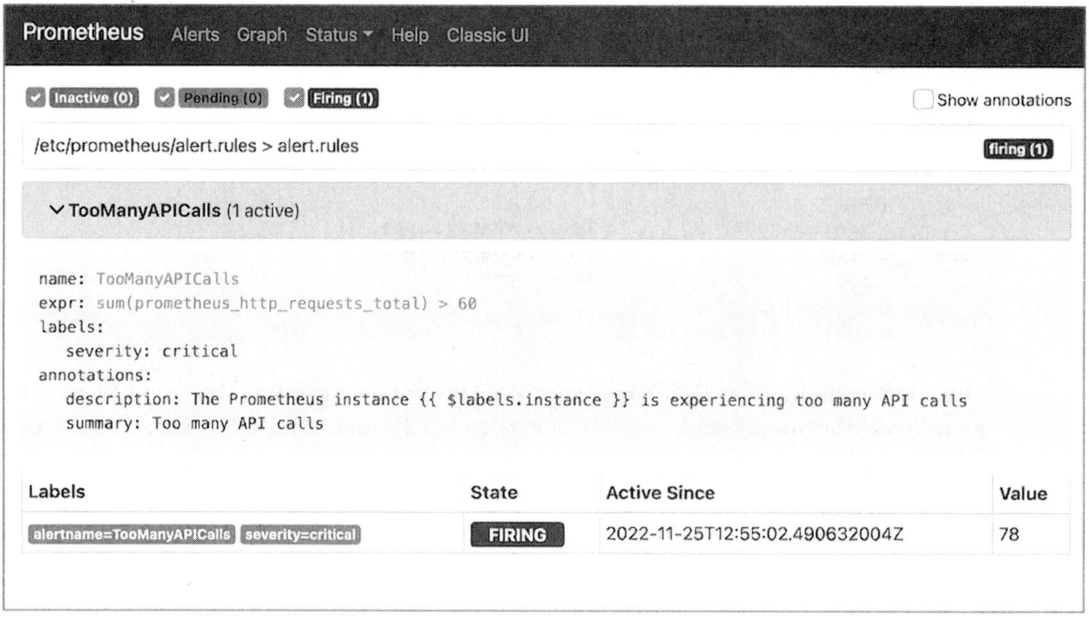

Figure 7.3   Screenshot of firing alert in Prometheus

Now, you should see in Prometheus that our alert is firing; hence, the Alertmanager is invoked. So once you see the alert `TooManyAPICalls` firing in Prometheus, head over to http://localhost:9093, where you should see the alert (figure 7.4) once you filter by `env=docker`.

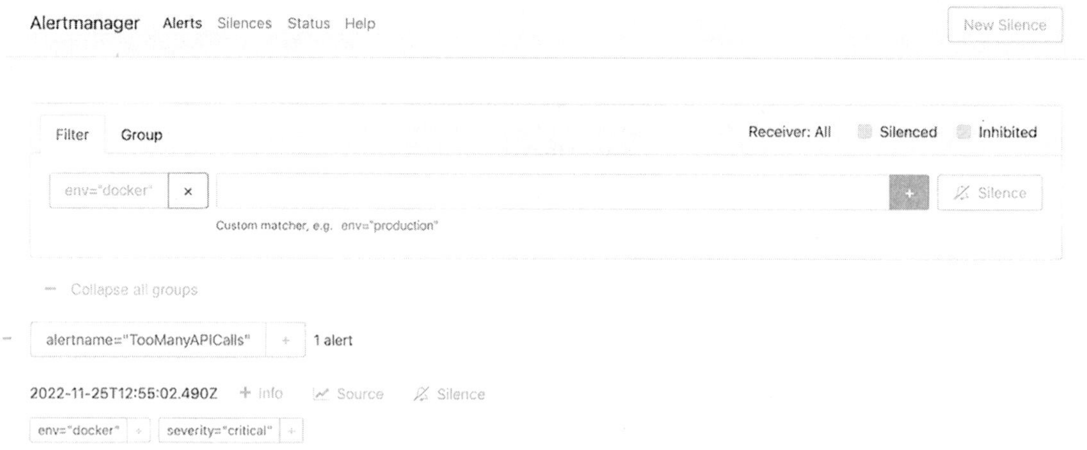

Figure 7.4   Screenshot of an alert being processed in Alertmanager

Figure 7.5 shows the notification you would have received if you had configured an email receiver rather than the generic webhook. It contains the labels as defined in the alerting rule and the external label `env`.

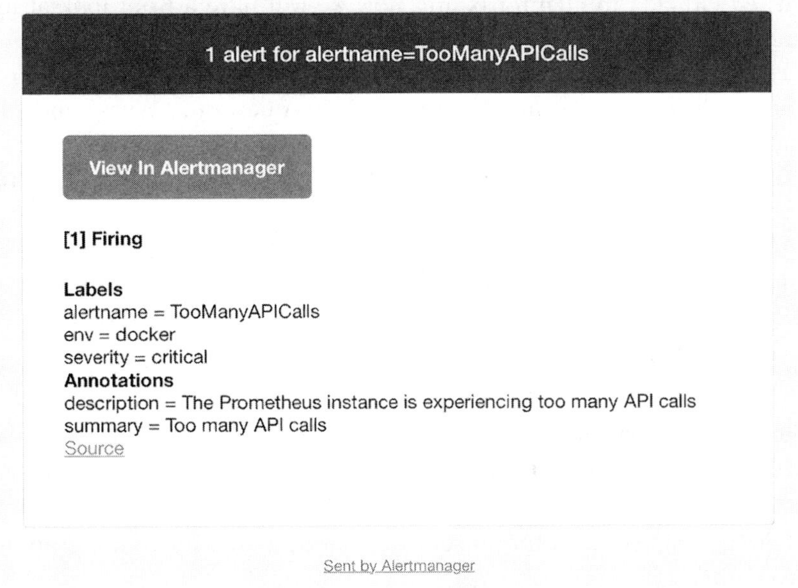

1 alert for alertname=TooManyAPICalls

View In Alertmanager

[1] Firing

Labels
alertname = TooManyAPICalls
env = docker
severity = critical
Annotations
description = The Prometheus instance is experiencing too many API calls
summary = Too many API calls
Source

Sent by Alertmanager

Figure 7.5 Screenshot of the notification email

> **TIP** The Alertmanager offers a number of excellent customizations that you can use to make your notifications more actionable and helpful (e.g., notification templates, http://mng.bz/a1rj).

With this, we've completed the Prometheus alerting end-to-end example. The concepts discussed here also apply to other tooling in the Prometheus ecosystem, such as the CNCF projects Cortex (http://mng.bz/gB2e) and Thanos (http://mng.bz/e1Z9); both support Alertmanager-compatible alerting rules. This makes it easy to migrate to a federated setup, effectively allowing you to reuse all the configuration.

If you want to dive deeper into the topic of alerting with Prometheus, here are a few resources I can recommend:

- *Prometheus Up and Running* by Brian Brazil (2018, O'Reilly, http://mng.bz/OxeK)
- "Improved Alerting With Prometheus and Alertmanager" by Julien Pivotto (2019, PromCon talk, http://mng.bz/Y1Wo)
- "Life of an Alert" by Stuart Nelson (2018, PromCon talk, https://www.youtube.com/watch?v=PUdjca23Qa4)

Next, we will have a quick look at alerting with Grafana, enabling you to manage alerts and notifications beyond Prometheus.

7.2.2   *Using Grafana for alerting*

We discussed Grafana in chapter 6, and now we will have a brief look at its alerting capabilities. Up until version 8, Grafana supported a dashboard-centric alerting model. This means an alert was confined to a dashboard, making it hard to manage notification policies. For example, answering the question, "What sends alarms via PagerDuty to a certain destination?" would require manually checking all dashboards. We will focus on unified alerting (http://mng.bz/GyvM), available from Grafana version 9 and beyond.

First off, why would you want to use Grafana for alerting? In general, your use case covers multiple backends (chapter 5). That is, imagine you are using Prometheus to store metrics and OpenSearch to store logs and traces and want to define alerts across these backends in a central place.

With unified alerting, Grafana now supports these use cases with the following:

- There is support for a range of data sources, including Amazon CloudWatch, Azure Monitor, Google Cloud Monitoring, InfluxDB, Jaeger, and Prometheus.
- You can organize alerts by group (similar to what we've seen in Prometheus).
- There is support for different Alertmanagers, including an integration with the Prometheus one.
- For notifications (http://mng.bz/zX7w), you use so-called contact points, supporting a wide array of types (https://grafana.com/docs/grafana/v9.5/alerting/fundamentals/contact-points/), including Discord, Email, Kafka, PagerDuty, Slack, Telegram, and WebHook.
- You can suppress notifications using silences. Note that the alert rule still gets evaluated by Grafana, causing potential costs for calling the backend, but the notification does not get created.

Now, let's move on to alerting solutions from cloud providers.

7.2.3   *Cloud providers*

Every major cloud provider offers an alerting solution, typically deeply integrated with its offerings. These offerings are a great baseline you should always consider, since they cover the cloud provider's APIs. These include

- Amazon CloudWatch alarms (http://mng.bz/0Kjp), which uses Amazon SNS to send email or SMS notifications
- Azure Monitor Alerts (http://mng.bz/KeyP), which supports email, SMS, and push notifications
- Google cloud alerting (https://cloud.google.com/monitoring/alerts/), supporting a range of notification types, from email to Pub/Sub

As previously mentioned, you could use these alerting solutions also from Grafana (which has a CloudWatch data source available if you want to control alerts from that pane), providing a single pane of glass. We're switching gears now for a quick look at end user tracking as well as resource usage tracking.

7.3 Usage tracking

Alerting is by and large a reactive process. This means something is happening, and based on this, someone gets notified, reacting to the event. In this section, we cover a different cloud operations technique that you can use for a variety of cases, from troubleshooting to security to planning. I'm talking about tracking users and what they access. Let's start with end users of your cloud-native app.

7.3.1 Users

To understand how your end users use your app, you need to have a way to track their activity within your app. This allows you to identify popular features and potential UX issues. Over the years, the term *real user monitoring* (RUM; https://github.com/open-telemetry/oteps/issues/169) has been popularized for this. For example, there is, for web applications, the widely used Google Analytics (https://analytics.google.com/analytics/web/), and you can use CloudWatch RUM (http://mng.bz/9Drx) in AWS. All these offerings require the up-front embedding of some small JavaScript snippet in your web pages to see the usage information (demographics, region, device types, usage paths, etc.) in a dedicated place. If you'd like to dive deeper into the topic, I recommend perusing the excellent article, "An Introduction to Real User Monitoring (RUM): Monitoring and Observability," by Chinmay Gaikwad (http://mng.bz/jPJz).

> **NOTE** One thing to be aware of with RUM is the rise of single-page application (SPA; https://en.wikipedia.org/wiki/Single-page_application) websites. In the context of SPAs, the traditional metrics, such as page load time, no longer matter (or make sense), since the page only loads once, at the beginning of a session, and the UI updates are effectively local renderings. For more on this topic, check out episode 60 of the O11ycast, "Customer-Centric Observability With Todd Gardner and Winston Hearn" (http://mng.bz/Wz94), as well as the article, "Observable Frontends: the State of OpenTelemetry in the Browser," by Jessica Kerr (http://mng.bz/8rdZ).

RUM is also something the CNCF OpenTelemetry project considers; the OpenTelemetry Enhancement Proposal OTEP 169 (http://mng.bz/EQoo) covers this by proposing a new data model and semantics, supporting the collection and export of RUM telemetry, a new signal type, alongside traces, metrics, logs, and profiles. While still in its early days, you can expect more development in this space, especially since the logs signal type stabilized in June 2023 (meaning you can use OpenTelemetry to handle logs in prod).

While RUM focuses on end users, there is another user-tracking category: internal users, including developers and operators. For example, you might want to have a record of the actions taken by a user or a service account for compliance or risk auditing reasons. An example of this kind of service is AWS CloudTrail (http://mng.bz/N2gN), supporting a long list of services, including Amazon API Gateway, AWS CloudFormation, Amazon CloudWatch, Amazon EKS, AWS Lambda, and AWS Systems Manager.

You can also set up alarms from the aforementioned internal-user audit logs. With that said, let's now move on to costs.

7.3.2 Costs

A totally different category of tracking access to resources is cost tracking. No matter if you want to educate internal users about costs and usage (showback) or offer services that require charging certain tenets (chargeback), you want to have an idea of what the actual costs are on as fine-grained a level as possible. We can distinguish between metering, which is counting the access (e.g., API endpoint XYZ was called 3,478 times in the last 15 minutes), and the actual charges that can depend on many things, from upfront commitments to special deals you may be able to negotiate based on the volume you are consuming.

Cloud providers typically offer services that allow you to (interactively) explore your usage (e.g., AWS Cost and Usage Reports [CUR], http://mng.bz/D46n). In addition to these native offerings, you may wish to opt into using solutions that provide for cost allocation and resource usage monitoring down to single units of execution, like OpenCost (https://www.opencost.io/) does for Kubernetes environments.

With this high-level discussion of user and usage tracking and reporting, we've reached the end of the cloud operations chapters. While most of the topics we've discussed are primarily important to understand and owned by folks in operator roles, with cloud-native systems, it's crucial that the people in every role involved, from developers to testers to release managers, have a solid grasp of the concepts. This can, in the case of a fully serverless environment, mean that, indeed, developers themselves are on call (http://mng.bz/lW76).

Summary

- To successfully operate cloud-native applications, you need to have a structured approach to detecting, handling, and learning from incidents.
- Health and performance monitoring allows you to have a system-external view and learn that something is not working as expected.
- If you're on call for a service and an incident happens, focus on stopping the bleeding; the analysis of what went wrong comes later, ideally in a blameless postmortem.
- The goal of alerting is for a human to automatically be notified of an event impacting the system.

- You want to avoid alert fatigue and, hence, need policies in place that allow you to receive a meaningful number of notifications (but not too many).
- Prometheus allows you to define alerting rules, and the grouping, filtering, suppression, and notification is handled by a separate component: the Alertmanager.
- If you want to centrally manage alerts across various backends, you can use Grafana.
- Usage tracking means capturing end user interactions in the app or capturing access to system resources as well as costs.

Distributed tracing

8

This chapter covers

- What distributed tracing is and why it's important
- Seeing distributed tracing in action for troubleshooting
- Considerations on how and where to use distributed tracing
- How to go about selecting a distributed tracing solution

In the "good old days," when running a monolithic application, things were sort of convenient, from an observability perspective; you had a web server as the frontend tier, your application server (like a Java-based app), and a database such as MySQL. In this setup, it was not too hard to figure out which of the components caused an issue. The logs from these components would cover both the *where* and *what*. In addition, you may capture some metrics, indicating overall health and performance.

With the rise of cloud-native systems and microservices, from the end user perspective, nothing should change, or better put, they should not notice a difference in terms of the user experience, compared to a monolith. From a developer and operations perspective, we expect to benefit from microservices. This includes

158

feature velocity (different parts of the application can be written and deployed independently), partial availability (while certain parts of the application might not be available to the end user, the overall application might still be working), as well as enabling us to use the best-fitting programming languages and data stores for a certain functionality (e.g., JavaScript for a frontend or an in-memory key–value store, like Redis, for a shopping basket).

> **NOTE** We previously covered feature velocity as an advantage of microservices-based architectures. Diving deeper here, the cause of increased feature velocity is that smaller units make for an increase in the deployment velocity. In other words, if your deployment units are smaller, they are easier to test, upgrade, and fix. It's worth noting that some enterprises have achieved increased development velocity even with what would be considered a monolith, when applying the "small units" idea to strictly decoupled modules in the monolith.

On the flipside, microservices are, indeed, distributed systems, and as such, they are more complex to operate than monolithic apps. Observability is not optional anymore. Part of the problem is determining where something happened. You don't have to be eBay, Netflix, or Uber, dealing with hundreds of microservices, to face this problem. Even if you "only" have a couple dozen services making up your cloud-native app, figuring out exactly which of the services along the request path caused an error or contributed to a slower-than-usual response can be tricky.

So how can you get an overview of how all your services play together and spot services that don't work as expected? Perhaps, you could drill down into a specific service to examine how it is performing.

> **NOTE** One challenge with distributed systems is that (potentially) services are running on different machines. The logs of these services may come with timestamps that are not 100% aligned (http://mng.bz/Bmp0), which is tricky to handle, since it ruins log ordering across services, hence, breaking the cause–effect analysis. Even when ingesting the logs into a central place, the dynamics of the execution would usually need to be manually restored, based on tags or labels. So while it's possible to use logs alone in the context of microservices, it is not the most effective use of your time and may require more skill on the part of the analyst than the solution we discuss in this chapter.

In this chapter, we have a closer look at a solution to the aforementioned challenge: distributed tracing. We discussed the topic on a high level in chapter 2, but now, it's time to dive deeper. I will first provide an overall introduction to this relatively new concept in the observability space, and then we will see distributed tracing in action in the context of a concrete use case. Finally, we will close out the chapter with practical considerations around selecting and using distributed tracing solutions.

8.1   *Intro and terminology*

In this subsection, I will first walk you through a motivational example, showing the power of distributed tracing. Then, I will define terminology used throughout the chapter.

8.1.1   *Motivational example*

To set the scene, let's start off by having a look at a concrete example of a microservices-based application that serves as a motivation. Figure 8.1 shows such an example app. It's a simplified version of an e-commerce app that allows end users to browse and search for items, order them, and have them shipped. To be a little more concrete, imagine you're building an e-commerce app that allows you to shop telescopes, akin to the walk-through example we will cover in the appendix.

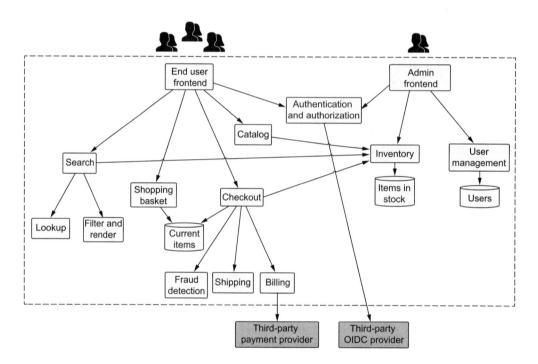

Figure 8.1   An example microservices-based e-commerce app (within the dotted box)

In our e-commerce example app, we have two logical parts, with some of the functionality, such as the payment details, provided by external (third-party) services and some (authentication) shared between these logical blocks (with the dotted box being our web app).

   The left-hand side of figure 8.1 shows the end user–serving (customer) part, implementing features like searching for an item and allowing end users to add items to a shopping basket. The right-hand side of the figure shows the admin-serving part, allowing shop admins to maintain the inventory and manage customers.

Let's drill down into one of the request paths in the end user–serving part of our e-commerce app (see figure 8.2). This describes the various components that process requests after a consumer clicks the Purchase button; also note that for the rest of this section, we will focus on the end user–serving part, not the admin part. So after a customer has put an item, say, a pair of binoculars, into the shopping basket, they want to check out to pay for the item and have it shipped.

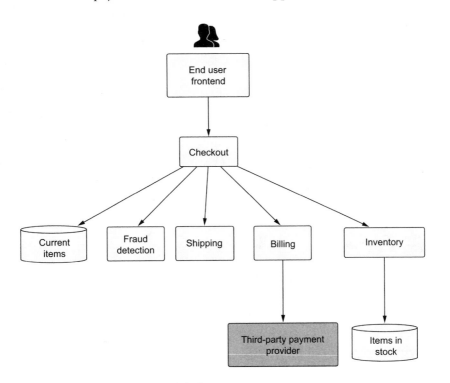

Figure 8.2 A single request path in the app

So what happens after the end user has entered all the necessary info, such as shipping address and payment details? As depicted in figure 8.2, the request path for this case looks as follows: the end user frontend calls the checkout service, which, in turn, has a couple of phases to complete, some of which may terminate the request (e.g., due to wrong user input or timeout of an external dependency):

- The checkout service queries the current items data store.
- A fraud detection service is invoked, checking if there are any reasons not to proceed.
- The shipping info from the shipping service is used to determine the shipping costs.

- The `billing` service gathers all the payment info and calls out to a third-party provider to handle the payment.
- Last but not least, if everything is in order, the checkout service invokes the `inventory` service to update what is in stock.

The representation of the microservices in figure 8.2 has different names in observability frontends, such as *service map* or *dependency graph*. This service map provides a nice overview of the architecture and shows the flow of information. However, it does not capture the temporal aspects. In other words, we need a way to visualize the service execution along a time axis, typically called a *waterfall visualization*. Figure 8.3 shows one such alternative way to represent the invocations the checkout service does based on time elapsing.

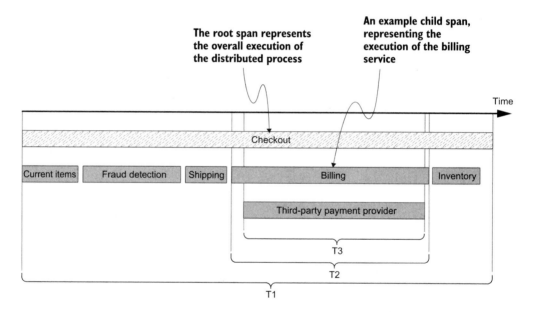

Figure 8.3   A single request path in the app, as a temporal (waterfall) visualization

The entire unit depicted in figure 8.3 is called a *trace* and represents the end-to-end processing of the catalog request in a waterfall visualization. Each service invocation, such as the `checkout` service calling the `billing` service, is a span (compare our discussion in chapter 2):

- The root span is the overall execution of the `checkout` service and takes the time T1 to execute end to end.
- Examples of child spans are the execution of the `billing` service (which takes T2 to complete) and the execution of the third-party payment provider call (which takes T3 to complete). Besides some setup time that our billing service has to do, it seems most of the time is taken up by invoking that external service.

One advantage of the waterfall visualization is that we can tell, simply by visually inspecting all the spans in the trace, where most of the time is spent (in our case, in figure 8.3, the checkout service spends around half of the time in the billing phase). With this concrete motivational example of a microservices-based e-commerce app established, let's move on to a more formal definition of terms you will come across in the distributed tracing space.

8.1.2 Terminology

While there are differences in terminology across vendors, the following are terms that are usually well defined and understood across offerings. I'm following mostly the OpenTelemetry nomenclature (http://mng.bz/d1QN), especially where there is no consensus among distributed tracing solutions:

- A *span* represents a unit of work and, with it, captures a part of the execution of the request (compare with figure 8.2). This can happen within the scope of a service, such as the execution of a function in a service or across services. A special kind of span in a trace is the *root span*, which is created when the request enters the app. A span has an ID, and typically, it stores the ID of the trace it belongs to and the root span it was triggered from as well as payload-including metadata (think timestamps, tags, etc.). Note that in AWS X-Ray, this unit is called a segment.
- A *trace* is the end-to-end processing of a request in a distributed system, consisting of a group of spans that are temporally ordered. It has an ID and metadata.
- In the context of cross-service calls, the *trace context* captures all unique identifiers for individual traces and requests. This enables a trace to exist beyond a single service via a process called *context propagation*, where this trace context is forwarded in a network call. The calling service (parent) attaches all necessary data for the trace context to the request to the downstream (child) service, such as was the case in our example e-commerce app (figure 8.2) between the billing service and the third-party payment provider. Nowadays, with OpenTelemetry establishing itself as the standard, this propagation is usually done based on the Trace Context (https://www.w3.org/TR/trace-context/) W3C Recommendation (the standard way to use HTTP headers to propagate the context).
- To reduce the volume of data (number of traces and spans), you can make use of a technique called *sampling*. This allows you to selectively drop traces based on a characteristic including a fixed percentage or based on the nature of a trace—for example, if an error is present in one of the services, and with it we see that error fagged in the span representing the service.

Now that we have a basic understanding of distributed tracing terms and what they mean, let's look at some use cases.

8.1.3   Use cases

Distributed tracing can be useful not just in distributed systems where services call others over the network but also for monolithic apps. In general, you can benefit from it in the following cases:

- *Monitoring microservices-based applications*—These allow you to acquire an end-to-end overview of the actual architecture of your app, including call dependencies. Rather than relying on static architecture diagrams of how the app is supposed to work, you get a visual representation of how the app actually works. You can determine error states (what services error out) and performance issues (latency graphs of service invocations) of services, usually with a single glance at a service map.
- *Optimization*—This is used to determine where along the request path most of the time is spent. You can pinpoint the slowest service and start the latency optimization there, promising the most yield in terms of investment.
- *Release management*—When rolling out a new version of a service, you can assess the impact on the overall request paths the service is part of, comparing before and after the new version.
- *Troubleshooting*—In the case of an incident, as we discussed in chapter 7, you can use the distributed tracing solution to figure out which services contribute to the issue and can roll them back to a known good state to stop the bleeding. We will see this common use case in action in the next subsection of this chapter.

OK, that was more than enough theory! Let's get our hands dirty with distributed tracing, focusing on the troubleshooting use case.

8.2   Using distributed tracing in a microservices app

In this section, you will use distributed tracing in the context of a simple example microservices app. The goal is to understand how the services work together and, once we start simulating errors, use distributed tracing to identify which services cause issues and what kind of errors you encounter.

8.2.1   Example app overview

Our example app (to be set up later) consists of four services, as depicted in figure 8.4. We have a frontend service as the entry point, which calls two services: service A and service B; in turn, service B calls two other services (B0 and B1). Some of the services also call out to static assets on the web to simulate calls to external third-party APIs. Note that our example app doesn't do anything useful; all of the services use the holly (http://mng.bz/rWxg) synthetic signal generator to generate traces, and we can configure it to simulate certain failure modes.

Our example app stack contains the five services making up the microservices app as well as the OpenTelemetry collector to ingest the spans generated from the four

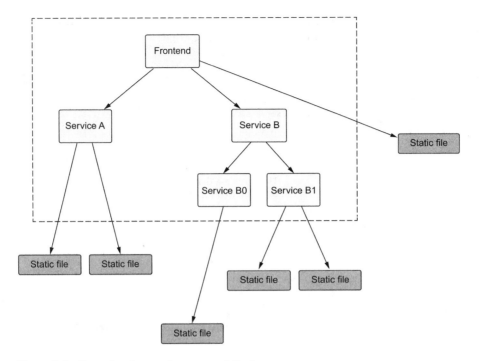

Figure 8.4 Example microservices app architecture

services into the distributed tracing tool (CNCF Jaeger). The setup is based on what you already saw in chapter 6.

8.2.2 Implementing the example app

To stand up our example app stack, using the Docker Compose file shown in listing 8.1, execute the following command from within the ch08/jaeger/ directory:

```
docker-compose -f docker-compose.yaml up
```

> **NOTE** The holly synthetic signal generator has several configuration options that are defined via environment variables. With HOllY_PORT, you can define on which port holly should be listening for service requests, and with DOWNSTREAM0 to DOWNSTREAM4, you can define URLs that the holly instance should call (and, hence, allow you to wire up and simulate arbitrary complex microservices). To simulate dropping requests, we will use the HOllY_INJECT_FAILURE environment variable, which causes the holly instance to return some 4xx or 5xx HTTP status codes in half of the cases, rather than returning a 200 HTTP status code. Finally, to simulate another kind failure mode (throttling of the upstream service), we will use the HOllY_CUTOFF_TPS environment variable to define a cutoff point, beyond which holly will return a 429 HTTP status code (https://httpstatuscodes.org/429/).

Listing 8.1 shows the relevant snippets (focusing on the wiring and configuration of our microservices app) of the Docker Compose file.

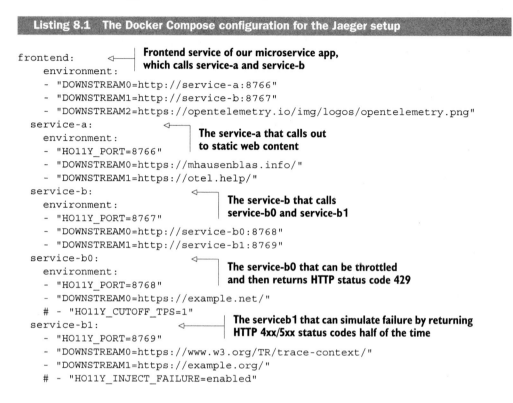

Listing 8.1   The Docker Compose configuration for the Jaeger setup

```
frontend:                    ←──┐  Frontend service of our microservice app,
    environment:                 │  which calls service-a and service-b
    - "DOWNSTREAM0=http://service-a:8766"
    - "DOWNSTREAM1=http://service-b:8767"
    - "DOWNSTREAM2=https://opentelemetry.io/img/logos/opentelemetry.png"
  service-a:                 ←──┐  The service-a that calls out
    environment:                 │  to static web content
    - "HO11Y_PORT=8766"
    - "DOWNSTREAM0=https://mhausenblas.info/"
    - "DOWNSTREAM1=https://otel.help/"
  service-b:                 ←──┐  The service-b that calls
    environment:                 │  service-b0 and service-b1
    - "HO11Y_PORT=8767"
    - "DOWNSTREAM0=http://service-b0:8768"
    - "DOWNSTREAM1=http://service-b1:8769"
  service-b0:                ←──┐  The service-b0 that can be throttled
    environment:                 │  and then returns HTTP status code 429
    - "HO11Y_PORT=8768"
    - "DOWNSTREAM0=https://example.net/"
    # - "HO11Y_CUTOFF_TPS=1"   ←──┐  The serviceb1 that can simulate failure by returning
  service-b1:                ←──┘  HTTP 4xx/5xx status codes half of the time
    - "HO11Y_PORT=8769"
    - "DOWNSTREAM0=https://www.w3.org/TR/trace-context/"
    - "DOWNSTREAM1=https://example.org/"
    # - "HO11Y_INJECT_FAILURE=enabled"
```

The OpenTelemetry collector config shown in the next listing is essentially the same that we used in chapter 6, with a single trace pipeline to ingest spans into Jaeger.

Listing 8.2   Collector config for collecting traces in OTLP and ingesting into Jaeger

```
receivers:
  otlp:
    protocols:
      grpc:
        endpoint: 0.0.0.0:4317
processors:
  batch:                    ←──┐  The batch size is intentionally
    timeout: 1s                  │  small for demonstration purposes.
    send_batch_size: 10
exporters:
  jaeger:
    endpoint: jaeger:14250
    tls:
      insecure: true
service:
  pipelines:
```

```
traces:
    receivers: [ otlp ]      ⊲────
    processors: [ batch ]    ⊲────
    exporters: [ jaeger ]    ⊲────
```

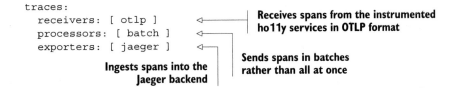

**Receives spans from the instrumented
ho11y services in OTLP format**

**Sends spans in batches
rather than all at once**

**Ingests spans into the
Jaeger backend**

Note that, compared to the setup in chapter 6, I have removed the debug-level logging config for the collector here, since we don't need it and it makes it more distracting to follow along.

8.2.3 The "happy path"

Now, it's time to head over to http://localhost:16686/ to open the Jaeger UI, where we will first have a look at the "happy path" (see figure 8.5), meaning everything works as expected, and no errors are present. This gives us the baseline for what we would expect, in terms of how services should work (e.g., execution time duration).

As the initial step to explore and understand our distributed system, let's create the service map showing the (dynamically generated) overall app architecture. For that, select frontend in the left-hand-side box labeled Search, and then click the Find Traces button at the bottom. Now, you should see a graph of execution durations over time on the right-hand side, and if you now click the Deep Dependency Graph button right below it, you should see something akin to figure 8.5. Also, note what we don't see: the external services or calls to services are not represented as spans.

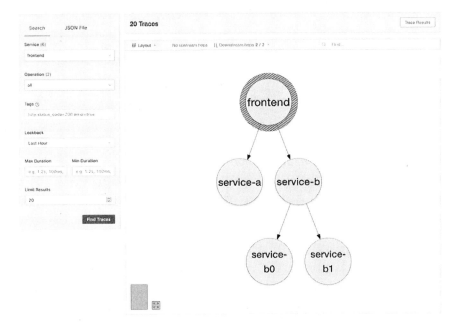

Figure 8.5   Troubleshooting demo microservices app: the happy path dependency graph

Next, we want to see the waterfall model. This means we want to visualize the temporal rendering of the service execution as all four of the services work together to serve a request. For that, click the Trace Results button in the upper-right corner of the dependency graph, and then select a trace (it doesn't matter which one; simply pick the top one in the list). You should then see something along the lines of figure 8.6. This screenshot shows an expanded single span that looks at the invocation of the service B0. From this, we can tell it took some 135 ms to execute, and of that, it spent more than 129 ms in the call to an external resource. Now that we've seen the happy path, let's simulate some failure and use Jaeger to figure out what's going on.

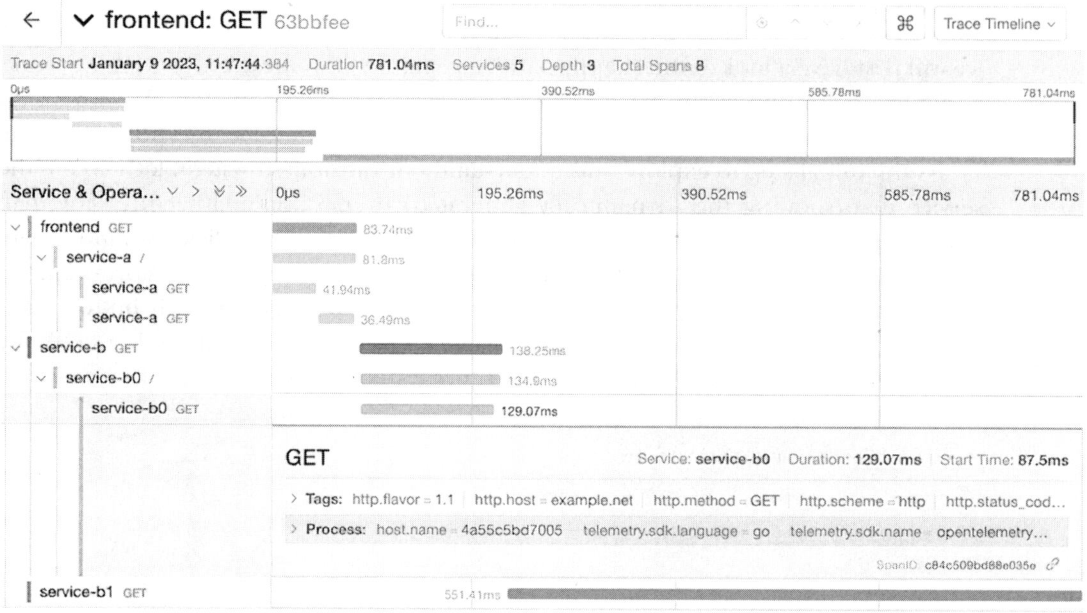

Figure 8.6   Troubleshooting a demo microservices app: a happy path example trace with its spans

8.2.4   *Exploring a failure in the example app*

To begin our failure example, stop the Docker Compose stack with CTRL-C, and to reset the app, also execute `docker-compose -f docker-compose.yaml down` so that all containers are removed. Now, go to the `ch08/jaeger/` directory and open the docker-compose.yaml file in your editor of choice, removing the comments (the #) in front of `HOllY_CUTOFF_TPS` in line 62, as well as line 76 in front of `HOllY_INJECT_FAILURE`. This causes services B0 and B1 to show errors.

Once you've saved your changes in the editor, do a `docker-compose -f docker-compose.yaml up` to bring up the stack, and go back to the Jaeger UI in your web browser of choice. There, again, select `frontend` in the left-hand-side box labeled Search, and then click the Find Traces button at the bottom.

If you now look at failure spans by filtering for the HTTP status code (in the `tags` input field, add, for example, `501` or filter by `error=true`) or clicking on one of the spans that shows an error (you should see a red exclamation mark on that span), you should see something like what is shown in figure 8.7. What does this mean? Jaeger provided us with a visual rendering of failures and allowed us to drill down into services that show errors. By clicking on a span, you can explore the service and compare things like execution time duration with the baseline you have from the happy path as well as see what the error code is. This means you can pinpoint services that cause issues very quickly and then focus on those to troubleshoot.

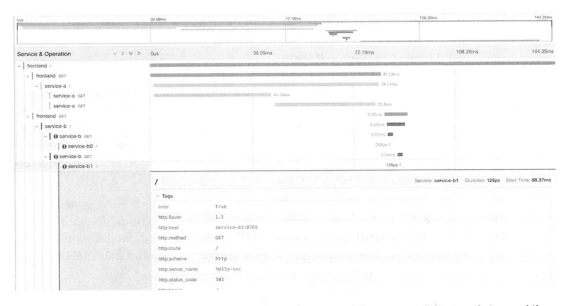

Figure 8.7　Troubleshooting the demo microservices app: an example failure trace and the span that caused the failure

This hands-on exercise using distributed tracing for troubleshooting a microservices-based app is now complete. Next, we will discuss how to benefit from our new app in a practical setup.

8.3 *Practical considerations*

Now that you know the basics of distributed tracing and have seen it in action in the context of a concrete use case, let's talk a little bit more about things to consider when going all in with distributed tracing. On a high level, it's important to understand that not every span of a trace has the same information value. For example, if 99 out of 100 times you see a span with an HTTP status code of `200`, what does this tell you? In contrast, the one span that carries a `500` HTTP status code indicates that the service that emitted the span likely had some kind of issue you may wish to research deeper.

Further, since a trace is made up of a collection of spans, you would expect that when looking at a trace, you will see all the spans that make up the trace. This sounds obvious, but it can be more difficult in practice. Several challenges, with the following being the most prominent, can cause broken and partial traces:

- *Context propagation*—To see all spans, every service needs to propagate the trace information (root span and metadata). What if one of the services (you don't own) doesn't participate in distributed tracing? What if you're using a cloud provider API that is not instrumented and, hence, doesn't propagate? How about the case in which an API supports a different trace header than what you use (e.g., proprietary versus W3C trace header)? To address this, you may need to upgrade your API integration (supporting a new header type); use a middleware or translation layer to translate header types; and, potentially, lobby with your provider to support tracing.
- *Dropped spans*—This can be due to a faulty or starved agent (e.g., an OpenTelemetry collector's in-memory queue overflows and may even be OOMed—that is, the Linux kernel kills the process, due to not enough memory being available) or some intermediary being configured to filter certain spans (e.g., a Gateway deployment in OpenTelemetry; https://opentelemetry.io/docs/collector/deployment/), where collectors used at the edge send spans to a central collector, unbeknownst to you.

The investment you're making with distributed tracing comprises the generation of the spans (ideally, via auto-instrumentation); the collection (think, for example, an OpenTelemetry collector); the ingestion and storage costs; and, last but not least, the query or usage in the frontend (e.g., for the purpose of graphing traces in a waterfall diagram or to provide service maps and other aggregates).

Let us zoom in on the topic of how to select spans that are worth being collected and ingested into backends: in other words, sampling.

8.3.1 Sampling

Distributed tracing means that in production environments you regularly see large volumes of data being generated. Given its natural alignment with distributed systems (microservices), it's not uncommon to be faced with dozens of billions of spans, representing a TB of data per day. The question is then as follows: How can we select relevant spans to collect and store? The term we're using here for the selection process is *sampling*. Mind you, there are some innate limitations to sampling (https://research.swtch.com/sample), but ignoring that for now, the following high-level strategies are available:

- *No sampling*—You ingest all spans, which could be useful for dev/test environments, to evaluate a tool, or if you have a tool that doesn't charge on a volume basis. Caching can help a lot for the query path when you're investigating traces, but the span ingestion path is still challenging.

- *Head-based sampling*—In this case, you decide which span to emit at the beginning of the request (the root span). It's simple to implement, but given that you likely don't know if there will be any issues downstream (nodes and leaves of the tree), you risk missing out on interesting or valuable spans. In addition, given that the sampling decision is made at the start, the decision needs to be globally propagated.
- *Tail-based sampling*—In a sense, it's the opposite of head-based sampling, since the decision is made when the request is completed. That's great, since you know for certain which spans are relevant, but it has the challenge of being, in practice, hard to know when the request is actually completed. For example, one or more services along the request path may time out. How long will you wait until you declare the request completed?

If you're interested in further details on sampling, I highly recommend the book *Cloud-Native Observability With OpenTelemetry* by Alex Boten (Packt, 2022; http://mng .bz/rW9B). With that, let us move on to the topic of resources.

8.3.2 *Observability tax*

We touched on resource usage a little bit when we talked about dropped spans, at the start of the subsection. Let's step back a bit and look at what I like to call the "observability tax"—that is, costs you will encounter in the context of distributed tracing (though they are not necessarily unique to it—some, if not most, of which you will also see with metrics and logs—but the controls may differ):

- *Instrumentation costs*—Cover everything that has to do with generating spans, including the manual work you have to put into emitting spans from your application, the costs of finding and fixing bugs related to instrumentation, the additional resource usage your app has due to instrumentation (e.g., even in the best case, auto-instrumentation will consume CPU cycles and occupy RAM you have to pay for).
- *Transport and ingestion costs*—Break down into the network ingress, at least in the context of cloud provider accounting (where you typically need to pay for network usage); and sending spans from your environment (that could be on-prem) into the backend, where you may have to deal with costs of double-digit dollars or euros per TB. In addition, your distributed tracing may charge per GB or amount of spans ingested.
- *Storage costs*—Typically, not the highest line item you'd find in your provider bill, since storage is optimized for efficiency and, oftentimes, even offered for free. You usually have limited or fixed retention periods (e.g., AWS X-Ray has 30 days, and Datadog has 15 days).
- *Query costs*—Represent all lookups and API calls to retrieve a range of traces for the purpose of viewing them or presenting them in an aggregate form, including histograms (http://mng.bz/V1AP); service maps (http://mng.bz/x4DW);

and advanced visualizations, such as Honeycomb's BubbleUp (https://www
.honeycomb.io/bubbleup).

Practically speaking, this is a very simplified view of the potential costs involved, and
you should work with your vendor of choice to come to a better understanding of the
costs in your specific case, including appropriate discounts, where applicable. While
there *are* costs, don't forget that at the end of the day, the return you get from distributed tracing is that you're not flying blind anymore with your microservices app and
can expect a decrease in mean time to repair/recover (MTTR) and an increase in
developer productivity.

8.3.3   *Traces vs. metrics vs. logs*

Keep in mind that one signal type alone can't usually answer all the questions you may
have to arrive at actionable insights. We will dive deep into that topic in chapter 11.

Independent of correlation, you can sometimes derive signals from each other.
For example, you can create metrics based on observed spans, such as with Open-
Telemetry's span metrics connector (http://mng.bz/Aoez). The distributed tracing
space is evolving quickly, and various vendors and communities are experimenting
and iterating (https://keyval.dev/distributed-tracing-2025/) to improve both its performance and usability, including automation of collection and compression of telemetry signals.

Summary

- Distributed tracing provides you with the *where* and *what* concerning visibility
  into distributed systems.
- An execution is distributed over microservices, and to get the overall picture,
  the various moving parts must be stitched together via context propagation.
- A trace is the end-to-end processing of a request in a distributed system, with a
  span representing a unit of work, such as the invocation of a single service or a
  call to a database.
- There is a long list of possible use cases for distributed tracing, from monitoring
  microservices-based applications to latency optimization to troubleshooting.
- There are several costs involved with distributed tracing, including instrumentation costs to transport and ingestion costs to query costs.
- You will have to work backward from your use case to determine the return on
  investment (see chapter 2 for a definition), making sure your stakeholders
  understand the value, be that MTTR reduction or, indeed, an increase in developer productivity.
- A signal type, such as metrics or logs, alone can't usually produce actionable
  insights; hence, support for signal correlation is a critical factor in selecting a
  distributed tracing solution.

- Distributed tracing is still a relatively young domain, and a lot of innovation is happening, which means building on standards such as OpenTelemetry should help reduce the risk of investments and make your solutions more portable if and when you want to switch backends.

Developer observability 9

This chapter covers

- What developer observability means
- What continuous profiling is and why you should care
- How cloud and developer observability drive developer productivity
- What tooling is available in the developer observability space

In chapter 1, we talked about different observability use cases and target audiences. In the past couple of chapters, we often had a rather operations-biased view—that is, the topics focused on cloud-native applications running in production. Now, we are changing gears to focus in this chapter on developers as the main audience for observability. We will talk about their natural habitats (IDEs and the command line) and how observability for developers is useful. So this chapter is about observability for developers, not observability on or about developers (such as time tracking or commits created or LOC produced per day).

Before we get to the core of the challenge, we will first define a concept pertinent to our conversation: *shift left*. This concept started out in the context of testing

(http://mng.bz/Zq1P) and CI/CD and then was extended to security (http://mng
.bz/RxdK). Nowadays, this term is also something marketing departments like to
apply in the context of observability.

The concept of shift left (see figure 9.1) is to enable developers to do things that
were traditionally testers' or operation folks' tasks and responsibilities. In the "good
old days," and in rather conventional environments, developers still mainly focus on
one thing: writing code—maybe with a bit of unit testing as well. At the end of the
day, developers "throw their work over the wall" to be tested; packaged (e.g., into a
WAR file); and, finally, deployed and operated. All of these steps are carried out by
roles other than developers, such as release engineers, QA testers, or operators. If
you think about the software development and operations process as a continuum,
with the leftmost side representing developers churning out source code and the
rightmost side representing operators deploying a binary, you can picture what *shift
left* means.

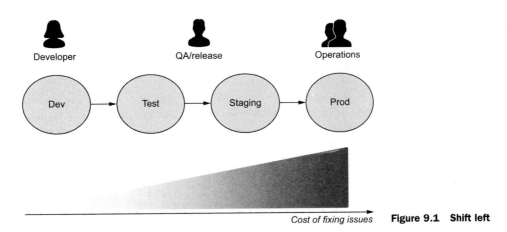

Cost of fixing issues **Figure 9.1   Shift left**

Applying the concept of shift left to observability, *developer observability* means using
telemetry signals to equip developers with actionable insights to accelerate development, debug code, or understand the impact of a new feature in terms of resource
usage. This results in shortening the feedback loop, resulting in lower overall costs to
identify and fix issues. For example, rather than a developer needing to wait four
weeks to find out if the code passes a test suite or crashes in the prod environment,
they can, and oftentimes now must, run the test suite themselves in the process of
sending in a pull or merge request.

In this chapter, we will first discuss a specific developer observability method called
continuous profiling and how it can help you understand the resource usage (e.g., CPU
and memory) of the code you write, even across different versions of your source
code. Then, we will have a look at developer productivity based on observability tooling deeply integrated into editors and IDEs that give you, as a developer, insights into

how changes you introduced impact your service, far beyond the traditional "all green" of testing. In the last subsection of the chapter, we will discuss how you can go about getting started in the developer observability space and what to watch out for. With that, let's jump right into the first topic: continuous profiling—what it is and when you can benefit from it.

9.1   *Continuous profiling*

In this subsection, we will have a look at continuous profiling, its use cases, and tooling available to you. First, we will look at its origins in the context of operating systems, and then we will review common techniques and tooling available to you. Finally, we will apply that knowledge in the context of an end-to-end walk-through example.

As usual, we will be covering open source tooling as well as commercial offerings. The open source tooling allows you to explore this space without needing to invest money for licenses or the like. After you've validated this technology, you can determine your return on investment (ROI), with it potentially paying for one of the offerings.

So what is *continuous profiling* (CP)? There are two words in this term; let's focus on the latter (profiling) first and return to what we mean by the former (continuous) later in the section. Before we get into any of the details, let's define what we mean by the term on a high level:

> *Continuous profiling enables you to understand your operating system's and services' resource usage (such as CPU or main memory and function execution times), over time. You can benefit from it in troubleshooting and performance optimization scenarios.*

You can use continuous profiling not only to understand the current performance and resource usage of your service but also to compare it with previous iterations. Think of the following use case: you add a new feature to your service and want to assess what the tradeoffs are now. On the one hand, your service is more powerful and useful now, but on the other hand, it may consume much more resources in terms of CPU or memory than you expected.

> **NOTE**   In a sense, continuous profiling is related to logging, since you're operating in the context of a service, in contrast to the cross-service execution of distributed tracing. As with logging, with profiling, you're interested in certain function calls in the context of your service. However, you're interested in numerical answers, such as the time it took to execute a function or CPU utilization or the amount of main memory used in a certain code path rather than the event emitted by a log line. Continuous profiling is, from a symbols perspective (function names, data types, etc.), also related to debugging; however, in contrast to debugging, you're looking holistically at the execution, rather than stepping through single steps.

At the end of the day, whether the new functionality justifies the increased resource usage is a business decision. However, you can now, with continuous profiling, get the raw data to make that decision.

9.1.1 The humble beginnings

Where and how did continuous profiling start, and what is the *continuous* in the term referring to? Let's step back a bit. Profiling has been around for decades, with GNU gprof (https://ftp.gnu.org/old-gnu/Manuals/gprof-2.9.1/html_mono/gprof.html) and Sun/Solaris DTrace (https://brendangregg.com/dtrace.html) as early examples, further developing in the context of Linux. It was typically considered in the context of performance analysis and often on the (operating) system level.

Now, what is a *profile*, and how does a profile look in practice? We will use an application that emits profiles in the following code. Have a look at this Go code (available in full via ch09/cp/main.go—here, we focus on the relevant bits only) using pprof (https://go.dev/blog/pprof):

```
import (
    _ "net/http/pprof"        ◁─┐ The Go package that automatically
)                                collects and exposes profiles for us

func quickTask() (result string) {   ◁─┐ A function that relatively quickly
}                                        completes (10% or less overall CPU time)

func slowTask() (result string) {   ◁─┐ A function that relatively is slow
}                                       (80% or more overall CPU time)

func main() {                    ◁─┐ A simple web server
    go func() {                      exposing the profiling info
        http.ListenAndServe("localhost:6060", nil)
    }()

    for true {
        result := quickTask()
        fmt.Printf("Quick task result is %s\n", result)
        result = slowTask()
        fmt.Printf("Slow task result is %s\n", result)
    }
}
```

Note that the functions slowTask() and quickTask() don't do anything useful other than using the CPU so that we can see something in the profiler. You can now run the Go program in a terminal session like so:

```
$ go run .
Quick task result is 692530d563c476aea00dd73067d7e146edbece4c17bff4c
Slow task result is 692530d563c476aea00dd73067d7e146edbece4c17bff4c9
...
```

If you navigate to http://localhost:6060/debug/pprof/, you will now see the web server output of the net/http/pprof Go package. Looking at the output here shows you various types of profiles offered, including details on goroutines, heap allocations, and so forth.

Next (and you will need to have the `graphviz dot` [https://graphviz.org/docs/layouts/dot/] command installed), you can generate an image to, for example, render the goroutine call graphs, using

```
$ go tool pprof -png http://localhost:6060/debug/pprof/goroutine > gr.png

Fetching profile over HTTP from http://localhost:6060/debug/pprof/goroutine
Saved profile in ~/tmp/pprof/pprof.goroutine.002.pb.gz
```

OK, that web view or the image may or may not be insightful, but there is another (more popular) way to use `pprof`: the interactive mode (think shell). Let's do that (gathering CPU profiles for 30 seconds, so you will need to wait a little bit):

```
$ go tool pprof "http://localhost:6060/debug/pprof/profile?seconds=30"

Fetching profile over HTTP from
http://localhost:6060/debug/pprof/profile?seconds=30
Saved profile in ~/pprof/pprof.samples.cpu.002.pb.gz
Type: cpu
Time: Mar 8, 2023 at 07:01am (GMT)
Duration: 30.13s, Total samples = 29.55s (98.09%)
Entering interactive mode (type "help" for commands, "o" for options)
...
```

At this point, you're in the `pprof` interactive shell, and you can list the top 50 functions (called *nodes* here) and use the cumulative focus with the `top 50 cum` command like so (edited to show the most important bits):

```
(pprof) top 50 cum
Active filters:
   focus=cum
Showing nodes accounting for 15.54s, 52.59% of 29.55s total
Dropped 47 nodes (cum <= 0.15s)
      flat  flat%   sum%        cum   cum%
     3.72s 12.59% 12.59%      3.73s 12.62%  fmt.(*fmt).fmtSbx
     2.12s  7.17% 19.76%      4.15s 14.04%  runtime.mallocgc
     1.44s  4.87% 24.64%      1.44s  4.87%  crypto/sha256.sha256block
      ...
     0.12s  0.41% 50.19%     14.59s 49.37%  main.slowTask
      ...
         0     0% 52.59%      1.73s  5.85%  main.quickTask
```

From the output of the `top` command in `pprof`, you can tell that the `slowTask()` function (over the 30-second sampling period) took up almost 50% of the runtime and the `quickTask()` function in the same time took up less than 6%. I won't go into further detail here, since the purpose of this exercise is not to teach you Go's `pprof` tooling but to give you an idea of the effort involved.

So let us recap what we had to do to see something at all:

1 We had to instrument our code by including net/http/pprof.

2 We had to include a web server to expose the profiles (alternatively, we could have written out the data to a file).

3 We had to use a browser or `curl` (and other dependencies, such as `dot`) to get a "point in time" result and, hence, an answer to our resource usage question.

4 We had to wait 30 seconds for `pprof` to gather profiles we were then able to query interactively.

NOTE Truth to be told, I've been using Go as an example here, since it comes with a powerful profiler already built into its tool chain and standard library. The same exercise for other programming languages would likely mean even more effort.

For example, here are a few language-specific approaches to collect profiles:

- Java has async-profiler (https://github.com/jvm-profiling-tools/async-profiler)
- .NET has dotTrace (https://www.jetbrains.com/profiler/)
- PHP has phpspy (https://github.com/adsr/phpspy)
- Python has `cProfile` (https://docs.python.org/3/library/profile.html)
- Ruby has `rbspy` (https://rbspy.github.io/)
- Rust has `pprof-rs` (https://github.com/tikv/pprof-rs)

Don't get me wrong; as you can see in the Go example, profiling is possible but requires specialized knowledge, just like using containers before around 2015 (when Docker became available) was doable but required intimate knowledge of Linux kernel features, including cgroups and namespaces. Nowadays, running a container is a mere `docker run` away for anyone.

But then, in 2010, something happened: a bunch of Google engineers published the seminal paper "Google-Wide Profiling: A Continuous Profiling Infrastructure for Data Centers" by Gang Ren, Eric Tune, Tipp Moseley, Yixin Shi, Silvius Rus, and Robert Hundt (2010, IEEE Micro, https://research.google/pubs/pub36575/). In this paper, the authors described the idea of continuously capturing CPU and memory usage and associating this data (the profiles) with the source code so that it enables engineers to locate slow or buggy lines of code as well as shared lessons learned using their continuous profiling system at scale. This paper influenced the community, and in the following years, we witnessed a number of commercial offerings growing in said space. In conclusion, profiling is doable using the primitives, but creating and consuming profiles on that level is complicated and, hence, it didn't go mainstream.

The tradeoff that continuous profiling takes is to profile at relatively low frequency and gather statistical significance over time. This is in contrast to traditional profiling, where we profile at very high frequency because we want to reach statistical significance over a short period of time—say, 10 seconds. Now, before we get into continuous profiling tooling, let us first step back and discuss some common techniques and technologies widely used in this space.

9.1.2 Common technologies

There are three technologies that you will find in many, if not all, continuous profiling tools. Before we get to the tooling itself, let us quickly discuss these common technologies.

PPROF

We already saw `pprof` in action in the introduction of this section, but let's zoom out a bit. `pprof` (https://github.com/google/pprof) is a visualization and analysis tool for profiling data, developed by Google. It is well integrated into Go, but more importantly for our discussion, it defines a data format to represent profiles. This `pprof` format is based on a protocol buffers (protobuf) schema (https://protobuf.dev/) defined in profile.proto (see the following site for the fully documented protobuf file and the following text for a description of the most important parts: https://github.com/google/pprof/blob/main/proto/profile.proto):

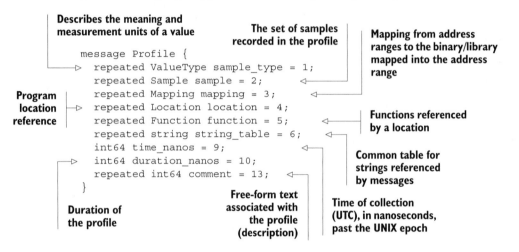

The `Profile` message uses several other messages (again, edited to the most important parts; see profile.proto for the details), including the following:

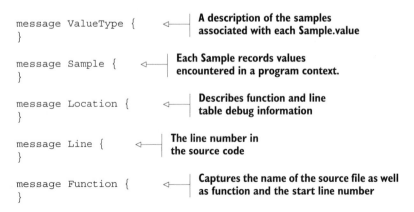

While there is no industry standard yet regarding how to represent profiles on the wire or at rest (say, as a file in your file system), the `pprof` format is the closest we have to such a standard, and many of the tools available can read or generate it.

`pprof` as a format is highly efficient, as it's based on Protocol Buffers, but that also means it can be hard to work with compared to a setup where you get JSON from an HTTP API (and can use `curl` and `jq` to filter for any value). There is some tooling available to deal with `protobuf`, such as

- *Protoc (https://grpc.io/docs/protoc-installation/)*—Short for *protocol buffer compiler*, which you can use to compile .proto files but also to decode or deserialize them (useful for debugging)
- *Buf (https://github.com/bufbuild/buf)*—A powerful CLI tool for working with protobuf
- *Protoman (https://github.com/spluxx/Protoman)*—A Postman-like API client for protobuf-based messages
- *Postman (https://github.com/postmanlabs/postman-app-support/issues/2801#issuecomment-1002247567)*—A popular tool that has added (indirect) support for it via a new gRPC API type

What does debugging a protobuf file look like?

Let's use `protoc` for that. First, we need to get a `pprof` protobuf formatted file. We, indeed, already produced a couple of those in our previous example, where we used `go tool pprof` for profiling. Note that your setup may have a different path configured; look at the output of the `go tool pprof` command, where it says Saved Profile In … (mine is in ~/pprof). Execute the following in the `ch09/cp/` directory:

```
$ cp ~/pprof/pprof.samples.cpu.001.pb.gz \
    ./pprof.gz && gzip -d pprof.gz
```

Now that we have the `pprof` protobuf file, we can use `protoc` to deserialize it:

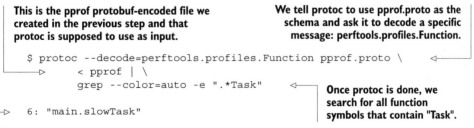

This is the pprof protobuf-encoded file we created in the previous step and that protoc is supposed to use as input.

We tell protoc to use pprof.proto as the schema and ask it to decode a specific message: perftools.profiles.Function.

```
$ protoc --decode=perftools.profiles.Function pprof.proto \
    < pprof | \
    grep --color=auto -e ".*Task"
6: "main.slowTask"
```

Once protoc is done, we search for all function symbols that contain "Task".

As expected, we found at least one function mentioned in the pprof file, and that happens to be slowTask() in my case.

With that, we're done for now with `pprof`, but we will certainly see it again in action later in the chapter.

FLAME AND ICICLE GRAPHS

Brendan Gregg, performance maestro of Netflix fame, invented flame graphs (https:// www.brendangregg.com/flamegraphs.html) when, while working on a MySQL performance issue, he needed to understand CPU usage. Brendan released them in late 2011, and the core idea of this visualization (figure 9.2) is as follows:

- The stack profiles are located on the x-axis. Note that the x-axis *does not* represent time but the collection of stack traces. Each rectangle represents a stack trace (compare call stacks in programming languages) or, put more simply, a call to a function or operating system syscall. The width of the rectangle represents the number of times the function was called or how much time it spent running. For example, we see in figure 9.2 that `slowTask()` spent much more time on CPU than `quickTask()`.

- The y-axis shows the stack depth, counting from zero (function call entry point). The rectangle at the top represents the function call that is on-CPU (that is, actually running) at the point of stack trace collection. In our example, we can see that `slowTask()` was called from `main()`.

- Originally, Brendan used random colors to help differentiate stack frames; however, they could be used to convey additional information. In other words, the colors do not have semantics, per se, and are only meant to help you navigate the flame graph.

Figure 9.2 An flame graph using our `pprof` Go example

While flame graphs for resources were originally focused on CPU usage, they have grown into covering a wider set of resources, including main memory (RAM) or network I/O as well as runtime and the operating system level (e.g., garbage collection in a Java virtual machine or Go).

Having said that, don't think of flame graphs as being restricted to system-level tasks. In fact, being able to see both what your operating system (or JVM) does as well as how your application is performing with respect to execution time or CPU and memory usage is the real sweet spot. You may also come across the term *icicle charts*, which simply refers to upside-down flame graphs (as an icicle would grow from the top to the bottom). If you want to dive deeper into the topic, I recommend reading Polar Signal's article, "Ice and Fire: How to Read Icicle and Flame Graphs" (http:// mng.bz/2DP0).

eBPF

Another piece of technology that many (open source) continuous profiling tools use is the Linux kernel feature eBPF. Nowadays, it is used as a term in itself, but originally, the term derives from *Berkeley Packet Filter* (BPF).

Linux kernel v3.18 (released on December 7, 2014) introduced support for eBPF. This kernel version requirement and the fact that you need good support for debug symbols to meaningfully use it means eBPF is, at least at the time of writing in early 2023, still restricted to certain environments, including dev/test (where you have full control over the Linux version used, in contrast to production environments, where using debug symbols slows down execution).

> **NOTE** You might wonder why I'm saying that eBPF is restricted to certain environments when looking at the kernel version in which it was introduced. At time of writing, it has been almost 10 years since that happened; however, cloud providers and large enterprises take a little longer to move their default Linux versions to "newer" kernels, due to distributions or otherwise. Ask your platform team if you can use eBPF in prod, but don't be surprised if the answer is, "We're working on it."

Now, why do we need eBPF, and how does it work? It enables you to safely and efficiently extend the Linux kernel by adding new functionality as you see fit. It is exposed to the Linux user space via the `bpf(2)` syscall (see also the man page [https://man7.org/linux/man-pages/man2/bpf.2.html] for further details) and implemented in the kernel as a virtual machine (VM) that defines a custom 64-bit RISC instruction set. Figure 9.3 shows a high-level overview of how eBPF works, from the book *BPF Performance Tools* by Brendan Gregg (2019, Addison-Wesley, http://mng.bz/1q1j). If you want to learn more about eBPF, I highly recommend reading *What Is eBPF?* by Liz Rice (2022, O'Reilly, http://mng.bz/Pzln).

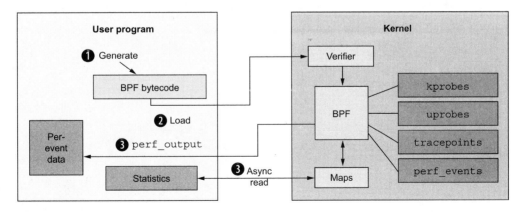

Figure 9.3 The eBPF call flow in the Linux kernel at a conceptual level (Source: Brendan Gregg. Licensed under CC BY 4.0)

9.1.3   *Open source CP tooling*

Let us first have a look at open source tooling in the continuous profiling space. This is a domain that exploded around 2020, and we see increasing interest in it to the extent that OpenTelemetry kicked off an activity in September 2022 (see also OTEP 139, http://mng.bz/JgjV) to explore how to support profiles as a signal type. In alphabetical order, we will now have a look at popular OSS tooling for continuous profiling.

PARCA

Parca (https://www.parca.dev/) is a Prometheus-inspired open source continuous profiling tool that specifically focuses on zero-instrumentation using eBPF, so you don't have to change anything about your application or drop any libraries into your code to make it work. It uses Prometheus service discovery to find profile sources. Parca supports a long list of programming languages (https://www.parca.dev/docs/parca-agent-language-support), including C, C++, Rust, Haskell, Java, Python, .NET, and WebAssembly.

You can install it and try it out yourself or use the zero-install online environment at demo.parca.dev (https://demo.parca.dev/) to give it a try. Figure 9.4 shows a CPU profile of a Kubernetes application in Parca, and at the end of this section, we will use Parca in an end-to-end walk-through.

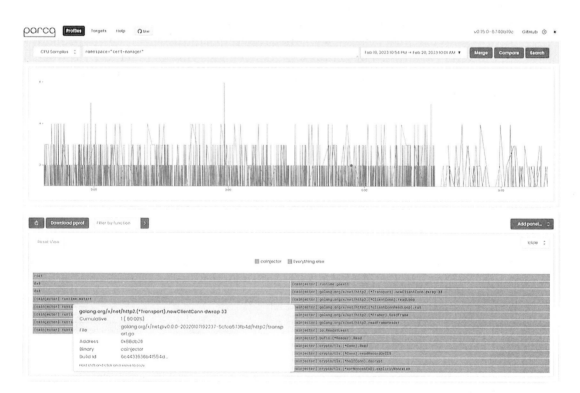

Figure 9.4   Screenshot of the Parca demo environment

PIXIE

Pixie (https://px.dev/) is a CNCF project focusing on Kubernetes clusters, which we covered in chapter 6. It's not just about continuous profiling; Pixie also offers full-body requests (e.g., a JSON blob return value from an HTTP API) and resource and network metrics, among other useful items.

Because Pixie collects so much rich data, the telemetry data in Pixie is kept in memory and local to the Kubernetes cluster. To put it succinctly, you can think of Pixie as the "What is going on in my Kubernetes cluster right now?" tool. In terms of resource usage, Pixie claims to use less than 5% of cluster CPU at the maximum. Pixie can help you see your application profiles in a specific pod, across a node, and more, all without requiring you to make any code changes or redeploy your app. At the time of writing, Pixie supports continuous profiling for compiled languages such as Go, Rust, and Java.

PYROSCOPE

Pyroscope (https://pyroscope.io/) is an open source continuous profiling tool that comes with a rich client-side collection mechanism for several programming languages, including Go, Python, Java, Ruby, Rust, PHP, .NET, and Node.js, as well as eBPF support. In June 2023, Pyroscope was acquired by Grafana Labs (http://mng .bz/wvNP) and is, going forward, the foundation of the continuous profiling offering in Grafana Cloud.

The makers of Pyroscope recommend a hybrid approach for profile collection: that is, to use eBPF to profile the system (e.g., the VM or Kubernetes node) in combination with the specific language instrumentation per service. Additionally, Pyroscope sports FlameQL, a query language that enables you to explore profiling data. You can use the zero-install online environment at https://demo.pyroscope.io/ to try out Pyroscope or install it locally if you like.

Figure 9.5 shows an overview (and an overlay with a zoom into the baseline flame graph) of the Pyroscope UI. In the upper part of the figure, the time-based visualization of the profiles is displayed, and when you click any of the profiles, you can generate and zoom in on specific profiles (in this case, memory usage).

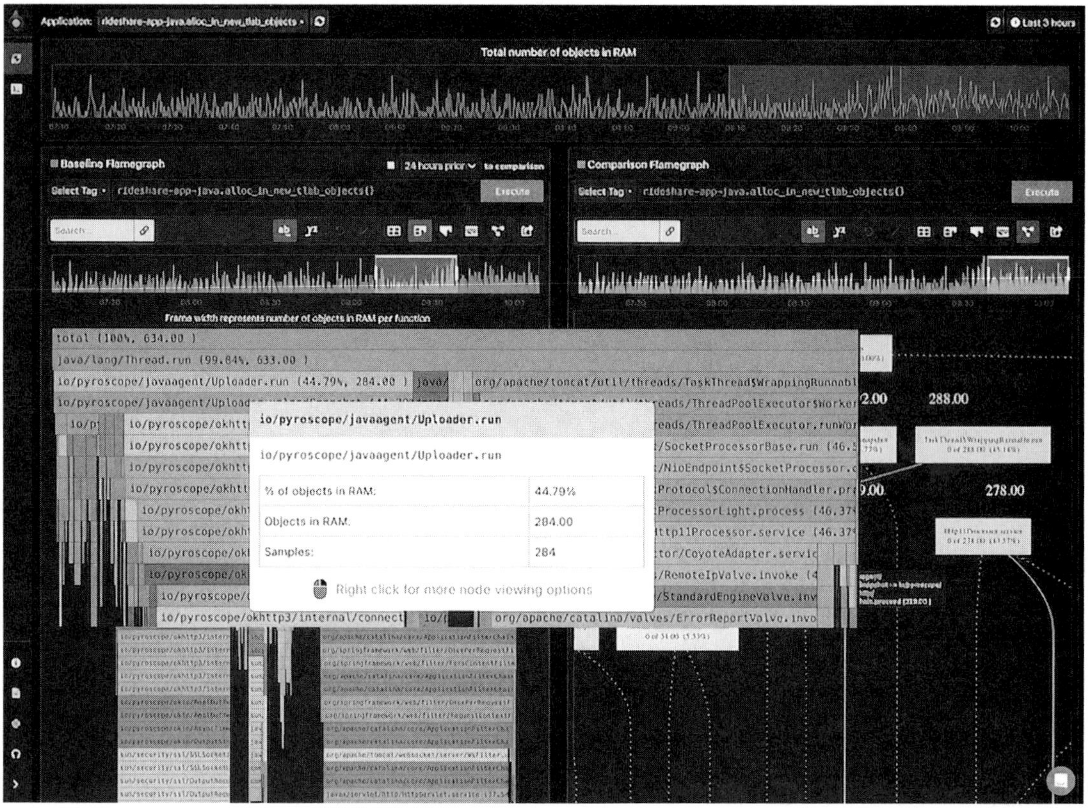

Figure 9.5   Screenshot of the Pyroscope demo environment

9.1.4   *Commercial continuous profiling offerings*

There are plenty of commercial offerings in the continuous profiling space, starting with cloud providers:

- AWS offers the Amazon CodeGuru Profiler (http://mng.bz/qrKr), optimized to fine-tune your app performance. It provides machine learning algorithms to find your most expensive lines of code and beyond that offer ways to improve efficiency.

- Azure offers Application Insights Profiler (http://mng.bz/7Dov), which enables you to view performance traces for your apps. It captures median, fastest, and slowest response times for each request and helps you identify hot code path spending for a particular request, supporting .NET and Java.

- Google pioneered the space with its Cloud Profiler (http://mng.bz/mVYa). It is a sampling profiler with low overhead and is, hence, suitable for production environments. Cloud Profiler supports common languages and environments (e.g., Go, Java, Node.js, and Python) and a range of profile types, including CPU time, heap, and threads.

Then, there are several ISVs that either bundle profiling or have standalone offerings. Some have been released in a source-available manner, including but not limited to the following:

- The Datadog profiler (https://docs.datadoghq.com/profiler/), part of the overall offering, enables you to find CPU, memory, and I/O bottlenecks; the profiles are broken down by function, class name, and line number in your code.
- Dynatrace's offering (http://mng.bz/5w5O), part of their overall suite, allows you to do CPU profiling, including drilling down to the function level, memory dump analysis, and process crashes.
- g:Profiler (https://granulate.io/continuous-profiling/) is an SaaS offering (but also available as open source) supporting AWS, Azure, and Google Cloud environments. It supports an array of languages (Clojure, Scala, C/C++, Ruby, Java, Python, JavaScript, PHP, and Go), uses eBPF, and claims a less-than-1% utilization penalty.
- New Relic has a feature called Real-time profiling for Java (http://mng.bz/OP6n) that supports flame graphs as well as the Thread profiler tool https://docs.newrelic.com/docs/apm/apm-ui-pages/events/thread-profiler-tool/ that you can use for Java, .NET, Python, and Ruby.
- Prodfiler (https://prodfiler.com/) touts itself as the distributed lightweight continuous whole-system profiler, enabling you to get insights into CPU usage, supporting flame, requiring Linux Kernel with version 4.15 or above, and available in platforms such as Kubernetes and AWS ECS.
- Splunk offers the AlwaysOn (http://mng.bz/5w5O) profiler.

A great overview and lookup for the continuous profiling space is Mark Hansen's Profilerpedia (https://profilerpedia.markhansen.co.nz/), a catalog of tools and profiler data formats. If you want to dive deeper into the topic, consider checking out *The Busy Developer's Guide to Go Profiling, Tracing and Observability* (https://github.com/DataDog/go-profiler-notes/tree/main/guide) from Datadog.

9.1.5 *Using continuous profiling to assess continuous profiling*

In this subsection, we will cover using continuous profiling to measure resource usage of an OpenTelemetry collector. I'm using the OpenTelemetry collector here as an example CP source, since it readily exposes `pprof`-formatted profiles, but you could really plug in any other HTTP API offering profiles (e.g., our Go example from the beginning of the chapter).

To generate profiles, we will set up a signal source (as usual, we will use `holly` with a load generator) that sends traces to an OpenTelemetry collector, and then we will use Parca to receive and query profiles from the collector. All the sources are in ch09/parca, so change to that directory. First off, to see profiles from the OpenTelemetry collector, you need to have the pprof extension (http://mng.bz/6D6e) configured in the collector (see the otel-config.yaml file below for details). So let's bring up the Docker Compose stack in the usual form:

```
docker-compose -f docker-compose.yaml up
```

The following listing shows the snippets of the Compose file pertinent to our conversation.

Listing 9.1   The relevant snippets of the Docker Compose configuration for the Parca setup

```
otel-collector:
    image: otel/opentelemetry-collector-contrib:0.68.0
    command: [
      "--config=/conf/otel-collector-config.yaml"
    ]
    volumes:
    - ./otel-config.yaml:/conf/otel-collector-config.yaml
    ports:
    - "4317:4317"
    - "1777:1777"        ⟵  We expose the pprof extension on this
                             port in the OpenTelemetry collector.

  parca:                       ⟵        Parca, as the server,
      image: ghcr.io/parca-dev/parca:v0.15.0    providing service
      command: /parca --config-path=/opt/parca.yaml   discovery and UI.
      ports:
      - "7070:7070"
      volumes:                       The Parca
      - "./parca.yaml:/opt/parca.yaml"  ⟵  configuration file
```

The OpenTelemetry collector config in otel-config.yaml shown in the following listing configures a simple trace pipeline to send traces to stdout of the collector via the logging exporter.

Listing 9.2   The OpenTelemetry collector configuration for producing profiles

```
receivers:
  otlp:
    protocols:
      grpc:
        endpoint: 0.0.0.0:4317

exporters:
  logging:
    loglevel: debug        The pprof extension for
                           collector self-telemetry
extensions:           ⟵   profile generation
  pprof:
    endpoint: "otel-collector:1777"
```

```
service:
  pipelines:
    traces:
      receivers: [ otlp ]
      exporters: [ logging ]
```

A simple traces pipeline, to have some load

Effectively means log to stdout and no ingestion into a backend

Note that the details of the pipeline in listing 9.2 do not matter to us, since we are focusing on the `pprof` extension and, with it, the overall collector, not a specific pipeline.

Next, we need to make sure Parca knows where to get the profiles from. Akin to Prometheus, we define a scrape config (in parca.yaml), as shown in the following listing.

Listing 9.3   Parca configuration for collecting profiles from the OpenTelemetry collector

```
object_storage:
  bucket:
    type: "FILESYSTEM"
    config:
      directory: "./tmp"

scrape_configs:
  - job_name: "default"
    scrape_interval: "2s"
    static_configs:
      - targets: ["127.0.0.1:7070"]
```

Tells Parca that we are only using local storage

The source of our profiles (the collector's pprof extension)

Now, you should be able to open localhost:7070 in your browser and, after a few minutes (to give Parca enough time to scrape some profiles), see something like figure 9.6. Make sure you select a profile (I chose Memory In-Use Bytes) and press the Search button on the far-right-hand side. To see a flame graph, which Parca calls an Icicle Graph, click the line graph.

OK, that was quite a lot to digest, but I hope you've not only seen but experienced the power of CP and how you can harness it to solve concrete problems—in our case, troubleshooting. So with this walk-through completed, let us move on to the wider topic of developer productivity, in which you can consider CP a special case—or sometimes even a feature. And now, we'll shift left to developer productivity and observability in action.

TIP You can also use CP in production environments; however, the impact on resources and potential disruption of the workloads is less understood. See also my InfoQ talk, "Profiles, the Missing Pillar: Continuous Profiling in Practice" (http://mng.bz/o1zZ), for more details.

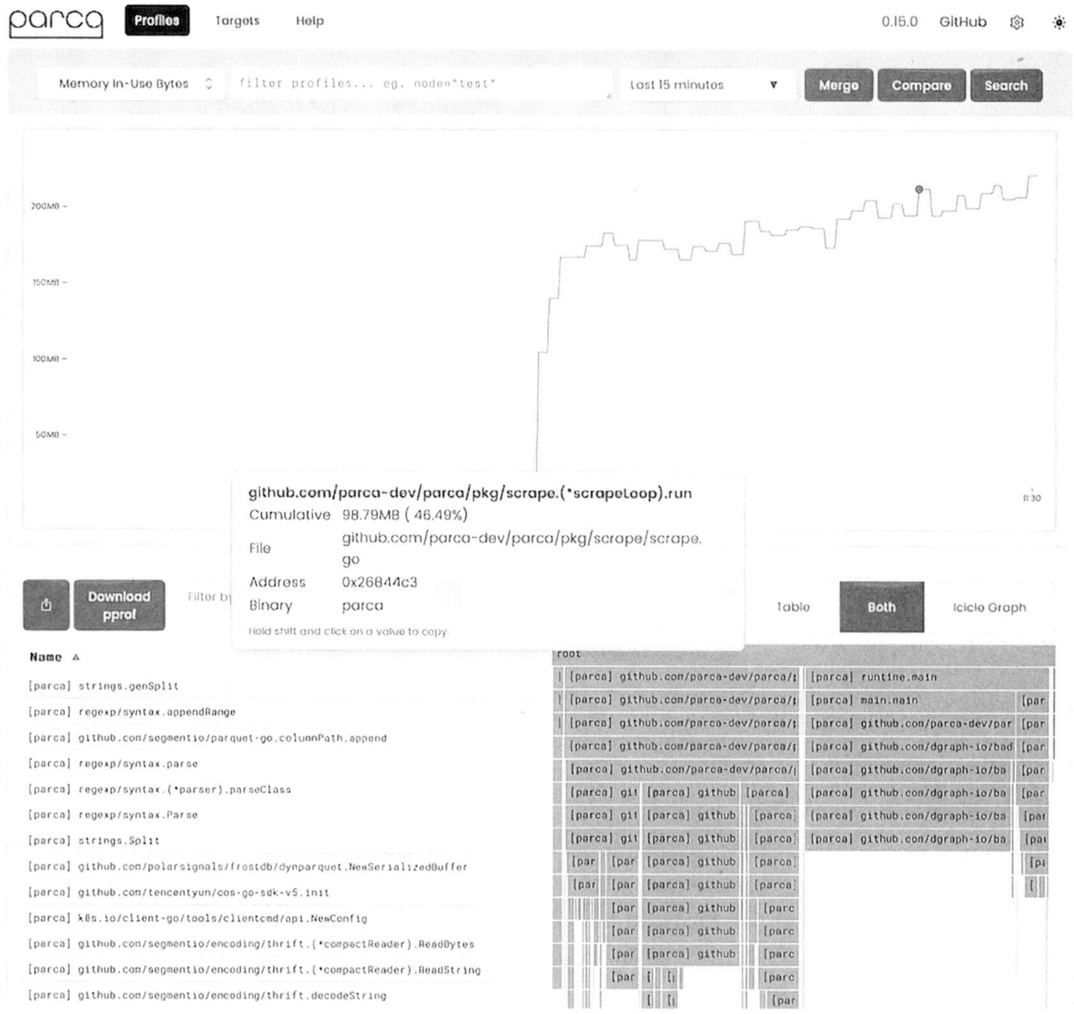

Figure 9.6   Screenshot of Parca profiling the OpenTelemetry collector

9.2   *Developer productivity*

We are witnessing the rise of a set of tooling that aims at increasing developer productivity by providing insights for developers, following the shift-left trend. In this section, we will have a look at the tools in this space and describe how they relate to continuous profiling.

9.2.1   *Challenges*

What are the actionable insights developers are seeking to increase productivity? That is, how can we add new features or fix bugs faster and, at the same time, in a safe manner? The challenges roughly break down into the following categories:

- *Volume of data*—The source code you write as a developer and all the libraries, packages, and modules you build your service on top of make up a large part of the data. Then, there are contextual datasets, including issue trackers (GitHub, GitLab, etc.) as well as road maps and user input and feedback, such as interviews or recordings. Then, there is documentation, both related to the source code and standalone project or product docs, and APIs, with their actions and data types based on a schema. All of that data serves as input, and as developers, we tend to try to keep all of these connections between the various artifacts in our heads. This is increasingly challenging, the more layers of abstractions we use.

- *Testing*—Many things changed with the introduction of cloud offerings, and I don't necessarily mean cloud-based IDEs; instead, I mean where and how software is tested. Now, we will keep doing unit testing (depending on the programming language, that's a more or less important aspect of reliable and maintainable code), but where should we do integration and end-to-end tests? One hypothesis is to test in production and mitigate impact via canaries, A/B testing, and feature flags (as offered by LaunchDarkly [https://launchdarkly .com/]) or Amazon CloudWatch Evidently (https://aws.amazon.com/blogs/ aws/cloudwatch-evidently/).

- *Distributed systems*—Microservices are distributed systems and, as such, rely on network communication. No matter whether you're using HTTP, gRPC, or WebSockets, you need to understand the communication behavior, the payload (encoding, format, etc.), and how to explore what a remote API does when it experiences load. This means being forced to, on the one hand, deal with leaky abstractions (implementation details shining through an abstraction layer) and, on the other hand, detect and handle timeouts, retries, and throttling. Remember that your network(s) are likely not reliable or secure (https:// architecturenotes.co/fallacies-of-distributed-systems/).

9.2.2 Tooling

The developer productivity tools we will have a closer look at in the following subsections are generally based on or use OpenTelemetry and provide deep IDE integrations, typically into VS Code. Increasingly, companies have begun to open source their (usually OpenTelemetry-based) developer productivity–related tooling, including eBay, which made an interesting framework called *flow telemetry* (https://github.com/ eBay/flow-telemetry) available. Note that the tools discussed in this section are rapidly evolving, and you can expect changes in the functionality or consolidations with other tools or platforms.

DIGMA

Digma (https://digma.ai/) is positioned as a *continuous feedback pipeline* (which seems to be a marketing term, as I haven't found a formal definition), with an analysis backend and IDE plug-in. Its goal is to continually analyze observability sources and provide you, as a developer, feedback. The plug-in generates code-level insights related to performance, errors and usage, provided to you as you edit your code. Digma generates these insights from your OpenTelemetry traces and metrics, which are collected and analyzed by the Digma backend. Figure 9.7 (on the left-hand side) shows the plug-in in action in VS Code.

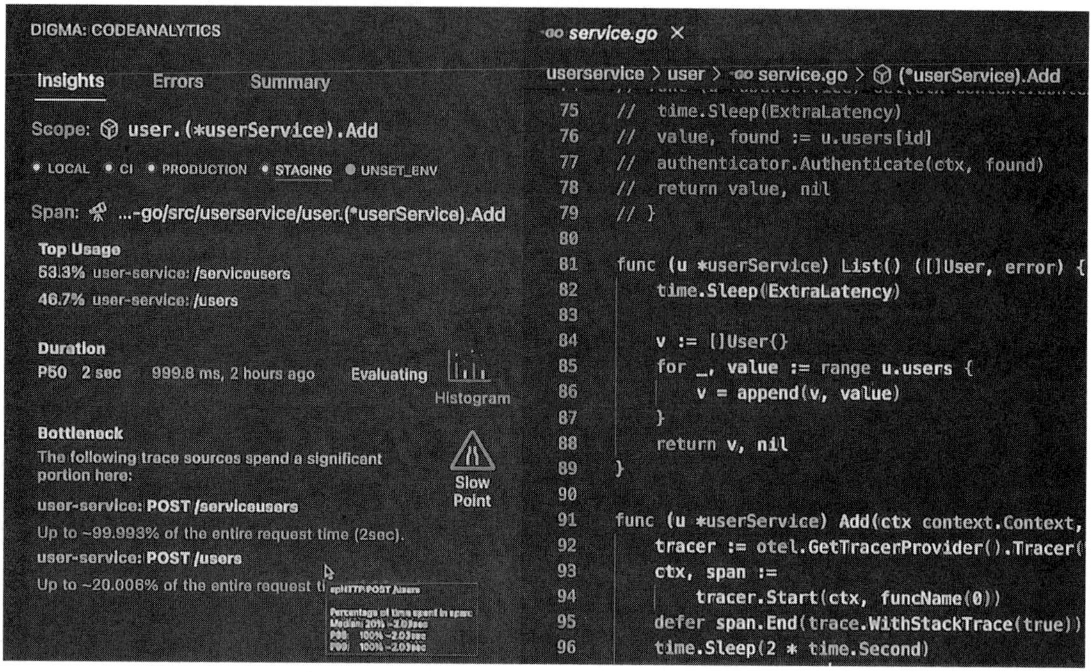

Figure 9.7   Screenshot of Digma

SPRKL

Sprkl (https://sprkl.dev/) touts itself as the "personal observability platform," providing personalized feedback on your code changes while coding in the IDE. It uses OpenTelemetry to instrument code and allows you to explore code changes upon execution. You get code-level traces, insights into how your code change plays with other entities in the system, as well as code performance reports.

Currently, Sprkl focuses on Node.js code, with partial support for Java, C#, and Python via Kubernetes. Sprkl requires Docker locally and focuses on VS Code (available there as an extension) as the IDE. Once you've set up Sprkl in VS Code and have Docker running, a good starting point to explore its features is the sample app sprkl-dev/use-sprkl (https://github.com/sprkl-dev/use-sprkl).

TRACETEST

Tracetest (https://tracetest.io/) is a bit different than the previous two tools. It focuses on enabling you to build integration and end-to-end tests, driven by OpenTelemetry traces. This means you need a distributed tracing backend and to point Tracetest to it or, alternatively, directly send spans to Tracetest, using an OpenTelemetry collector, for example. You can use it to define tests and assertions against services along a request path and define assertions against both the response and trace data. In addition, you can run the tests manually or via CI build jobs. Figure 9.8 shows Tracetest test results, rendering the requests in a waterfall manner.

Figure 9.8 Screenshot of the Tracetest UI (results view)

You can install Tracetest (http://mng.bz/nWG5) via Docker Compose or a Helm chart and a number of example integrations, such as with AWS X-Ray (http://mng .bz/vnEp) or Grafana Tempo (http://mng.bz/4DwR).

ROOKOUT

Rookout (https://www.rookout.com/) calls itself the "developer-first observability tool." It captures live debugging data across your stack, supporting Java, .NET, Node.js, Python, Ruby, and Go. Rookout allows you to live debug in a range of environments as well as view traces alongside available breakpoints.

AUTOMETRICS

Autometrics (https://autometrics.dev/) is built on top of Prometheus and Open-Telemetry client libraries. It makes it easy to instrument functions in your code (currently for Rust, Go, Python, Typescript, and C#) with common metrics, including request rate, error rate, and latency, and generates PromQL queries for you.

With this, we've completed the tools review. Now, let's discuss what to consider when adopting tooling in the space.

9.3 Tooling considerations

We have examined continuous profiling and, more generally, developer productivity tooling in this chapter, and you may by now be excited to jump into the deep end. Before you get too far, I'd like to share a few thoughts and words of caution in the following subsections. While I'm personally super bullish and supportive, we have to recognize sharp edges and set expectations correctly.

Developer observability is a relatively young field, with many of the contenders having been on the market for less than a year. The following is a discussion of challenges that CP tooling faces specifically.

9.3.1 Symbolization

By *symbolization*, we mean the process of translating machine addresses to human-readable (symbolic) names. For example, if you look at a profile and it contains stack frame labels, such as `0x8c6fff910`, you would not really know what that memory address signifies. On the other hand, if you were to see something like `/some/path/file.go:42` or `calculateSummary()`, that would be meaningful.

The challenge now is to determine the location of symbolic information. For compiled languages, such as C/C++ or Go, the symbol table (containing symbols used) is usually part of the binary, and for interpreted languages, including Python, Ruby, or JavaScript, the symbols are typically part of the program.

For further reading on this topic, see also these blog posts:

- "Fantastic Symbols and Where to Find Them" by Kemal Akkoyun (http://mng .bz/QPB6)
- "BPF binaries: BTF, CO-RE, and the Future of BPF Perf tools" by Brendan Gregg (http://mng.bz/XNR9)
- "BPF CO-RE (Compile Once – Run Everywhere)" by Andrii Nakryiko (https:// nakryiko.com/posts/bpf-portability-and-co-re/)

Once we have the symbols, we're not done yet; we still need to store the profiles. But how can we do that in an efficient and budget-friendly manner?

9.3.2 Storing profiles

In-memory storage of profiles is sufficient for certain use cases when you are examining what is happening in the moment. However, in cases when you want to compare longer time ranges or different versions of your service, you need to be able to deal with the volume of the profiles and store them somewhere in a persistent manner.

Two common techniques found in continuous profiling tools are

- *To efficiently store and query profiles, columnar storage is used (see also chapter 5, where we discussed the design and properties of columnar data stores). For example, in the* context of Parca, the team decided to develop FrostDB (https://github.com/polarsignals/frostdb), a dedicated columnar database for profiles, written in Go. You can embed FrostDB, and it features semistructured schemas (where some or all of the schema fields and or types are unknown or undefined) using Apache Parquet for storage and Apache Arrow for querying.

■ *To minimize the storage footprint for the timestamps, continuous profiling backends typically use XOR compression.* Think of it as a delta-of-delta encoding for timestamps. This technique was first described by a team of Facebook engineers in "Gorilla: A Fast, Scalable, In-Memory Time Series Database" by Tuomas Pelkonen et al. (2015, Proceedings of the VLDB Endowment; http://www.vldb.org/pvldb/vol8/p1816-teller.pdf). If you want to learn more about compression in this domain, check out "Time-Series Compression Algorithms, Explained" by Joshua Lockerman and Ajay Kulkarni (https://www.timescale.com/blog/time-series-compression-algorithms-explained/).

Once stored efficiently, you will want to query profiles. So what's the challenge here?

9.3.3 Querying profiles

Ideally, we would be able to support expressive queries for profiles. Currently, mostly simple, label-based query languages, such as in Parca (https://www.parca.dev/docs/querying-parca) and Pyroscope's FlameQL (https://pyroscope.io/docs/flameql/), exist. This is not a bad thing, per se, since the widely used and popular query language for Prometheus, PromQL, is also a label-based query language. The question here, however, is if and when an (open) standard will emerge as well as whether it will be an SQL-related or a DSL-related format.

9.3.4 Correlation

One of the key challenges, as well as promises, in the developer observability space is correlation. Naturally, one would expect to jump from other signal types, such as a distributed trace or metric, to profiles (be that label-based or via frontend support, as with a Grafana plug-in). This is an area of active research, and we can expect more to happen here. We will cover the topic in greater detail in chapter 11.

9.3.5 Standards

We already discussed standards a couple of times; the gist is that you want to make sure the tools you are using to achieve developer observability are built atop and use open standards, including OpenTelemetry, for signals on the wire, as well as up-and-coming standards, like `pprof`, for representing profiles on the wire.

9.3.6 Using tooling in production

You can use continuous profiling in development environments as well as in production environments. There, you will need to come up with a strategy concerning the impact on live traffic versus usefulness to understand what is going on. The challenge here is twofold:

- To get meaningful insights, you need to load debug symbols, which can and will change the execution times and cause higher resource usage.
- Then, there is the overhead of tracking, ingesting, and storing the profiles (e.g., in `pprof` format). For that, you will need another backend that is able to store profiles efficiently and allows you to query them or one of your existing backends to introduce support for profile handling.

What we see in real life so far is that CP is validated in prod, but there are few best practices to share. Therefore, you would need to decide on a case-by-case basis whether the returns from CP outweigh the investments required (in terms of storage, ingestion, latency impact, etc.).

Summary

- Developer observability means using telemetry signals to equip developers with actionable insights to accelerate development; debug code; or understand the impact of a new feature, in terms of runtime or resource usage.
- You can use continuous profiling to understand the current performance and resource usage of your service as well as compare resource usage with previous versions of your service.
- The protobuf-encoded `pprof` format is the closest we have to a standard for representing profiles on the wire or at rest.
- Flame graphs render call stacks in a visual manner, and eBPF is a Linux kernel extension mechanism used for profile collection across many continuous profiling tools.
- To automate the collection of profiles from either your app code or the operating system, you can use eBPF, increasingly gaining traction.
- Open source continuous profiling tools are a relatively recent development and include Parca, Pixie, and Pyroscope.
- Cloud providers and observability vendors alike provide commercial offerings in the continuous profiling space.
- Developer productivity tools, usually based on OpenTelemetry, provide developers with insights on code changes from a performance and resource usage view.
- There are a few challenges, including a lack of interoperability and the risk of small players being acquired or discontinuing an offer; however, the overall benefit of developer productivity tooling is clear and will likely go mainstream.
- You can benefit from continuous profiling not only in dev environments but also in prod, if you know the impact on the system.
- Support for open standards is crucial. You will have to do your due diligence to make sure your vendor (or open source project) of choice is fully committed to supporting their offering.

Service level objectives 10

This chapter covers
- What we mean by service level objectives
- How to implement service level objectives
- The tooling available in the SLO space
- Considerations for implementing SLOs

At this point in the book, you should have a good idea about what *ROI-driven observability* means. There is, however, an operations topic we haven't discussed yet and that is needed to complete the picture: how satisfied is the consumer of a service, and how do we know whether the consumer is satisfied, based on data? The consumer doesn't have to be an external customer, especially in larger organizations, where consumers could be different business units. Now, don't get me wrong—there's nothing more motivating than a snarky tweet or a thoughtful comment on the orange site (aka Hacker News). However, wouldn't it be nice if we could automate the whole process?

If you step back, you will find that DevOps and site reliability engineering (SRE) took off in the past decade, with the former being more bottom up and the latter clearly being driven by Google. The core concepts and ideas in this chapter are, indeed, a Google invention, and if you want to study every last detail, including best

practices, I encourage you to head over to the Google SRE books site (https://sre
.google/books/) and read everything. In this chapter, we will take a more practical
approach, covering the fundamentals quickly and then showing how to use them.

The main objective is to make the availability of a service measurable and compare
the metrics derived from services with goals. Once you have the goals agreed upon
and you are in a position to automatically measure them, you can do a lot more:

- You can draw nice charts and look at them, which is good for usage in frontends.
- You can alert if you're at risk of breaching a goal (see also our conversations in
  chapter 7 on cloud operations).
- You can use these metrics as an input in a contract with your customer to promise something, and in case you are not able to deliver what you promised, you
  can commit to a financial compensation (possibly credits or even penalty pay-
  ments). This means you're earning trust from your customer in a quantifiable
  and systematic manner.
- You can drive compliance (e.g., in the financial or health care domain).

> **Note**
> There is a parallel to the ideas we discuss in this chapter in real life: when one of our
> kids and I agree there will be a reward for, say, a clean room, we first need to define
> and agree on what *clean* means (that would be the contractual piece). I might say,
> for example, that over a month's time, I expect to only find three pieces of dirty
> clothes on the floor (that's the goal the child needs to reach to qualify for the reward).
> Then, I would randomly inspect the room and note how many dirty clothes I find on
> the floor (the measurement) and, at the end of the month, compare with the goal. If
> I were to find three or fewer pieces of clothes on the floor, I would declare the goal
> successfully completed, and the child would get their reward.
>
> At any point in time, the child could look at my list and see how many pieces of
> clothes (in the measurement period here, which is one month) I found. With that, they
> could determine how close they were to breaching the agreed-upon goal or, in other
> words, how much wiggle room they had left (you could call that a *budget*, and indeed,
> that is the official term for it: an *error budget*).

In this chapter, we will first tackle service level objectives on a theoretical level; however, I'm afraid there is a bit of terminology we need to untangle first. Then, we will
shift gears and have a look at tooling available in this space, and you will complete a
hands-on session of implementing availability metrics and comparing with the goals
you defined. In the last section, we will discuss some important considerations and
provide further reading.

10.1 *The fundamentals of SLOs*

In this chapter, we differentiate between three similar-sounding but entirely different
terms: service level agreements (SLAs), service level objectives (SLOs), and service

level indicators (SLIs). In this first section, we will dive deep into how these three terms interplay and for whom (role-wise) one or more of these terms are relevant.

Figure 10.1 shows how SLAs, SLOs, and SLIs interact, on a high level. We have four personas at work here in two buckets:

- The *service consumer*, or *customer*, typically external to the team, who owns the service (the service boundary line)
- The *service provider*, comprising
  - The *sales team*, who could be on the business side of things, solution engineers, customer success engineers/support people, or a point of contact for the service
  - The *product owner*, who is the person who owns the road map and works with both the sales team and engineering
  - The *engineering team*, who own the service from a feature development and, potentially, operations perspective (though there may be dedicated roles, such as SRE, for that task available in the organization)

It's perfectly possible for the service customer to be within the organization (internal customer); however, that doesn't change the expectations or commitments to them, only the potential flow of money. If the costs of a service are attributed to an internal customer, we call it a *chargeback*. A slightly less extreme form (no actual charges, just cost and usage awareness) of a chargeback is a *showback*, where costs are displayed to internal customers. For our discussion, what matters is that the service customer is outside of the boundaries of the service team.

OK, but what does all of that really mean? What really are SLAs, SLOs, and SLIs, and how should you go about defining and implementing them? Let's start at the bottom of figure 10.1 and work our merry way up. First, let's define what we mean by *service*.

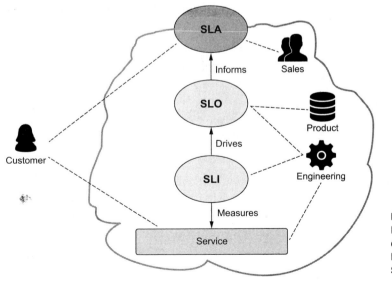

**Figure 10.1
Interaction and
dependencies
between SLAs,
SLOs, and SLIs**

10.1.1 *Types of services*

I will be using the terms *service* and *API* interchangeably in this chapter. What I really mean in either case is the API of a synchronous service, asynchronous services, or *sui generis* (unique) service types. Let's have a closer look at the types of services now:

- *Synchronous services*, generally request–response-based systems, such as long-running RESTful web services, WebSocket-based systems, and RPC-based (gRPC or SOAP) systems but also data pipelines (e.g., ETL)
- *Asynchronous services*, including event buses, queues, and Pub/Sub systems in which there is no obvious causal relation between a publishing action, such as *put event X on a queue with topic Z*, and a consuming action, like *read the most recent event from queue with topic Z*
- *Sui generis services*, including
  - Batch jobs triggered by a certain event, run for a certain time, and expected to terminate
  - Storage, such as POSIX-compliant local or remote file systems (including ext4 and NFS) or object storage, like Amazon S3
  - Databases and datastores, including relational databases, such as PostgreSQL, and NoSQL datastores, like AWS DynamoDB or MongoDB

Depending on the type of service, there are different ways to measure how the service customer perceives the service. Enter SLIs.

10.1.2 *Service level indicator*

The service level indicator (SLI) is a quantitative means to determine how your service is doing. In short, all SLIs are metrics, but not all metrics are SLIs. The purpose of an SLI is to allow you to measure how the service customer is experiencing your service, based on a numerical value. You can aggregate this value and do fancy math, like percentiles, on it. But at the end of the day, SLIs really are only service metrics, such as

- Uptime, availability, or reachability of a service
- Error rate (e.g., errors to total requests) of a synchronous service
- Duration, or latency, such as how long a synchronous service took to respond to a request
- Successfully completed or failed jobs for an asynchronous service
- Throughput, or how many transactions per second (TPS) a service is able to sustain

If you're interested in details on what kind of metrics (for synchronous services) to consider, I recommend reading "The RED Method: A New Approach to Monitoring Microservices" by Joab Jackson (http://mng.bz/a1nj). Now that you know what an SLI is on a high level, a service metric that you, as an engineer, define and track, let's move on to setting goals—or SLOs.

10.1.3 *Service level objective*

SLOs are system-external goals, and you can use one or more of them in the context of informing SLAs. Having multiple SLOs for a service enables you to combine them for a comprehensive pass/fail test. In contrast to SLAs, the audience for SLOs is not your service customer; it's your service team. You, as a product owner, define SLOs together with your engineers in cooperation with sales to determine which errors are acceptable to the users of a service. For example, you may agree that for a specific service, you want to reach 90% availability over the time period of a month. Then, at the end of the month, you may compare the SLIs with the SLOs to determine whether you met the goal.

The balancing act of setting SLO thresholds is made between the competing demands of availability and velocity. Think of the extreme case of an SLO that states 0% availability. This is easy to achieve; the service can be down any time and you can ship new code into production at will. That's great from a developer's perspective, since developers can push new features or bug fixes at any time. From a service customer point of view, it is less great; it means they cannot rely on the service at all. The other end of the spectrum would be 100% availability, meaning that, effectively, no changes are allowed and no bugs or other factors bring down your service. Clearly, neither extreme is desirable or realistic.

> **NOTE** In some respects, SLOs are a bit like the speed of light: the closer you want to get to it, the more energy you have to invest. Setting an SLO of 99% versus 99.9% may only look like 0.9% more, from a goal perspective, but consider the work that has to go into achieving it. Also, remember that the weakest link in the request path determines what you can achieve, overall. For example, if you have three services—A, B, and C—where A is calling B; B is calling C; and, let's say, A and B have an SLO of 99.9% and C has an SLO of 90%, you can not expect to promise 99.9% overall, since C will not support this. See Steve McGhee's SLOconf 2021 talk, "SLO Math," (https://www.youtube .com/watch?v=lHPDx90Ppg) for more information.

There is more terminology related to SLOs, such as the *error budget*, which defines how much wiggle room you have left for an SLO with respect to the SLIs in a time period, and *burn rate*, which defines how quickly you are using up your error budget. While the terminology can be a bit dense, in a nutshell, error budgets allow you to significantly improve alert accuracy, reduce noisy alerts, and improve practice leading indicators. I was told by Nobl9 representatives that there are case studies with customers that show a 90%+ reduction in false positive alerts after implementing SLOs.

We will not go into further details here. If you are interested in learning more about the advanced terminology (which is not widely adopted outside of Google), check out the freely available SRE books (https://sre.google/books/). To learn more about where SLOs originally stem from, I recommend "The Origin of Service Level Objectives" by Akshay Chugh and Piyush Verma (http://mng.bz/gBMe).

From a practical perspective, there is also tooling available, such as the SLI Analyzer (https://docs.nobl9.com/slocademy/SLI_Analyzer/) by Nobl9, enabling you to generate SLOs based on (historical) SLIs. Now that we have an idea what SLOs are (goals) and how to measure to what extent we meet them (SLIs), let's move up the stack to the contract between the service provider and the service customer.

10.1.4 Service level agreement

An SLA is what you, as a service provider, promise to your (service) customer, which is mostly a contractual topic. A more tongue in cheek way to say that is, "SLOs are written in engineer, and SLAs are written in lawyer" (kudos to Jamie!). This is mostly between the sales folks and the customers, based on and informed by the SLO that product and engineering commit to.

For example, if product and engineering commit to an SLO that states that an API is available for 99% of the quarter and, after a quarter, you were only able to make the API available for, say, 98% of the time, then you have violated the availability SLA. This may result in consequences, such as a refund or even paying a penalty, depending on the type of service you operate or kind of relationship you have with the customer.

10.2 Implementing SLOs

Now that you know about the terminology, let us discuss how to go about implementing hypothetical SLAs, SLOs, and SLIs. We will start off with an example conversation between sales, product, and engineering and then have a look at a concrete example of how to implement SLOs within the Prometheus ecosystem.

10.2.1 High-level example

Imagine the following: your service team plans to launch a new API for a conversational chat bot called Chat2Much. The hypothetical conversation goes something like the following:

Sales → Product: Yo, I hear Chat2Much is soon ready to launch. I'm working on the SLA and wanted to understand what we can promise to customers about an API availability rate over the month as well as the request failure rate.

Product → Sales: Sure thing, let me get back to you on this.

Product → Engineering: I'd like to establish an SLO that sales can use as a basis for the Chat2Much SLA.

Engineering → Product: What SLO did you have in mind for Chat2Much?

Product → Engineering: I was thinking of committing to 99% API availability over a period of a month—what do you think? Also, can we do request count and errors?

Engineering → Product: That sounds reasonable, I believe we can achieve 99.9% with the current head count and technology stack. We will implement the service metrics A, B, and C, which you can use as SLIs to track the SLO.

Product → Engineering: OK, thanks—sounds good. I will work with Sales on the details.

Product → Sales: Alright, we can commit to 99% availability over the time period of a month for the Chat2Much API, and there is some wiggle room on our end already baked in with it. We are using SLIs A, B, and C to track this SLO.

Sales → Product: Perfect, thanks! I will use this and attach the financial implications—that is, the credits that a customer receives in the case we fail to meet the SLO.

TIP   To arrive at an availability percentage, you can work backward from how many errors you want to tolerate at most. Let's say you've observed that your service in load testing has received 1,000,000 requests in a period of time and that in the same time period, there were 6,942 failed requests. To implement some headroom, you can round up, so make this 7,000. Therefore, you can commit to 99% availability, realistically.

Continuing the example, the Chat2Much API then goes into production, and engineering is using dashboards and alerts to track the SLIs A, B, and C. They report on a monthly basis how the SLO is met and if not, by how much. The customer knows the availability from the SLA and can see how the API is performing against the contractually agreed upon goals on their own dashboards. Everyone is happy—end of story.

If you want to dive deeper into this topic, I recommend the following resources:

- *Implementing Service Level Objectives* by Alex Hidalgo (2020, O'Reilly Addison-Wesley, http://mng.bz/5w5q)
- "From Critical User Journey to SLO/SLIs" by Adam Roberts (http://mng .bz/6D65)
- "The SLO Development Lifecycle" (SLODLC; https://www .slodlc.com/)
- "Effective SLOs and You" (http://mng.bz/o1zj)
- "A Practical Guide for Implementing SLO" by Prathamesh Sonpatki and Saurabh Hirani (http://mng.bz/nWG8)

Let's now shift gears and look at a concrete domain: Prometheus. We'll also look at how to implement SLOs in the context of this ecosystem.

10.2.2 Using Prometheus to implement SLOs

After our theoretical treatment on what SLAs, SLOs, and SLIs are and how to implement them conceptually, we will now have a closer look at how to specifically implement SLOs and SLIs with open source tooling from and in the Prometheus ecosystem. As with all other chapters in the book, the idea is that you can try out and evaluate things without costs or (license) commitments involved, and the steps should be applicable more or less to any provider in this space.

PYRRA

Pyrra (https://github.com/pyrra-dev/pyrra) is an open source tool that aims to make SLOs with Prometheus easy to use. Pyrra focuses on Prometheus as the source of the

SLIs, which turns out to be a big advantage, since Prometheus is so widely adopted in a cloud-native context. From an architectural point of view, it comprises the following components:

- As the operator, you use (YAML) documents to define the SLOs and, with it, SLIs.
- A backend watches for `ServiceLevelObjective` resources (either from the local file system or the Kubernetes API) and creates Prometheus recording rules, based on this input.
- The Pyrra API gathers SLIs from a backend, such as Kubernetes.
- The Pyrra UI uses the Pyrra API to display SLOs, SLIs, error budgets, and more.

TIP   If you don't want to invest the time needed to set up the Docker-based example here, you can, alternatively, play around with the online environment at demo.pyrra.dev (https://demo.pyrra.dev/).

To stand up the stack using the Docker Compose file shown in listing 10.1, execute the following command from within the `ch10/pyrra/` directory:

```
docker-compose -f docker-compose.yaml up
```

The following listing shows the relevant snippets of the Docker Compose file we use for this exercise, focusing on the configuration of Prometheus and Pyrra.

Listing 10.1   Snippets of the Docker Compose configuration for the Pyrra setup

```
prometheus:
    image: prom/prometheus:v2.40.0
    restart: always
    ports:
    - "9090:9090"
    command:
    - --config.file=/etc/prometheus/prometheus.yml
    - --storage.tsdb.path=/prometheus
    - --storage.tsdb.retention.time=33d
    volumes:
    - ./prometheus/prometheus.yaml:/etc/prometheus/prometheus.yml:ro
    - ./prometheus_pyrra:/etc/prometheus/pyrra        ◁─┐ Tells Prometheus
                                                          where the rule files
                                                          are stored locally
  pyrra-api:
    image: ghcr.io/pyrra-dev/pyrra:v0.5.5
    restart: always          ┌─ Configures Pyrra with
    command:        ◁────────┤  the Prometheus info
    - api
    - --prometheus-url=http://prometheus:9090
    - --prometheus-external-url=http://localhost:9090
    - --api-url=http://pyrra-filesystem:9444
    ports:
    - "9099:9099"                      ┌─ Sets up Pyrra's local file
                                          system provider (to store
  pyrra-filesystem:        ◁───────────┘  generated rules)
    image: ghcr.io/pyrra-dev/pyrra:v0.5.0
```

```
  restart: always
  command:
    - filesystem
    - --prometheus-url=http://prometheus:9090
  volumes:
    - ./pyrra:/etc/pyrra
    - ./prometheus_pyrra:/etc/prometheus/pyrra
```

The following listing shows the Prometheus config (prometheus/prometheus.yaml).

Listing 10.2   Prometheus config

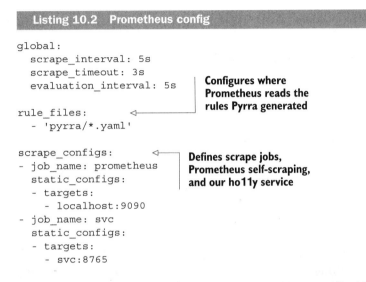

```
global:
  scrape_interval: 5s
  scrape_timeout: 3s
  evaluation_interval: 5s          Configures where
                                   Prometheus reads the
                                   rules Pyrra generated
rule_files:
  - 'pyrra/*.yaml'


scrape_configs:               Defines scrape jobs,
- job_name: prometheus        Prometheus self-scraping,
  static_configs:             and our ho11y service
  - targets:
    - localhost:9090
- job_name: svc
  static_configs:
  - targets:
    - svc:8765
```

The next listing is the content of the YAML file pyrra/ho11y-http.yaml with the SLO definition of our `ho11y` service. We set the target to 75% overall.

Listing 10.3   Pyrra SLO definition

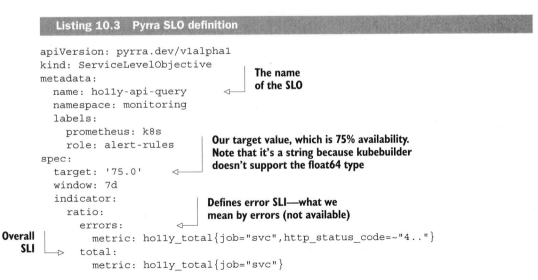

```
apiVersion: pyrra.dev/v1alpha1
kind: ServiceLevelObjective      The name
metadata:                        of the SLO
  name: ho11y-api-query
  namespace: monitoring
  labels:
    prometheus: k8s
    role: alert-rules            Our target value, which is 75% availability.
spec:                            Note that it's a string because kubebuilder
  target: '75.0'                 doesn't support the float64 type
  window: 7d
  indicator:                Defines error SLI—what we
    ratio:                  mean by errors (not available)
      errors:
Overall      metric: ho11y_total{job="svc",http_status_code=~"4.."}
  SLI   total:
        metric: ho11y_total{job="svc"}
```

We mentioned earlier that Pyrra effectively converts `ServiceLevelObjective` resources into Prometheus recording rules. How does that look? If you take listing 10.3 as an input, the respective output (which you will also find on your local drive in the `prometheus_pyrra/` directory), is shown in the following listing (note that this file has some 94 lines overall, so we only show the first rule here).

Listing 10.4   Prometheus recording rules derived from `ServiceLevelObjective`

```
groups:
- interval: 1m
  name: holly-api-query-increase
  rules:
  - expr: sum by(http_status_code) (increase(holly_total{job="svc"}[1w]))
    labels:
      job: svc
      slo: holly-api-query
    record: holly:increase1w
  - alert: SLOMetricAbsent
    expr: absent(holly_total{job="svc"}) == 1
    for: 1m
    labels:
      job: svc
      severity: critical
      slo: holly-api-query
...
```

Now, let's see it in action. Head over to http://localhost:9099/ in your browser, and you should see something like figure 10.2, the Pyrra landing page, providing an overview of all SLOs.

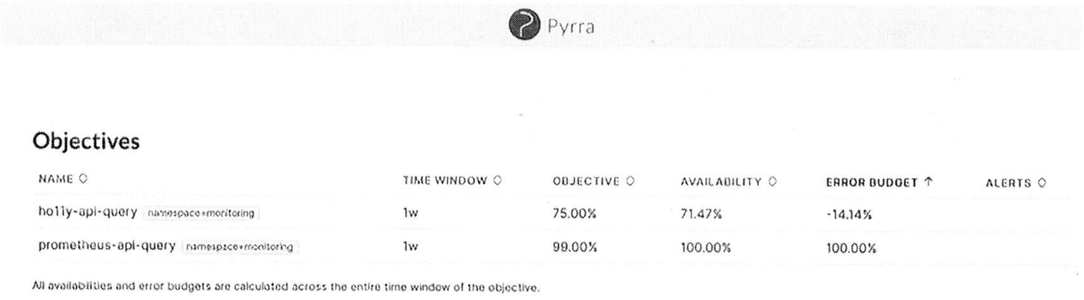

Objectives

NAME	TIME WINDOW	OBJECTIVE	AVAILABILITY	ERROR BUDGET ↑	ALERTS
holly-api-query namespace=monitoring	1w	75.00%	71.47%	-14.14%	
prometheus-api-query namespace=monitoring	1w	99.00%	100.00%	100.00%	

All availabilities and error budgets are calculated across the entire time window of the objective.

Figure 10.2   Pyrra landing page (SLO list)

Figure 10.3 depicts the Prometheus SLO. You can see that we're in compliance (the SLO is met).

Objectives > **prometheus-api-query**   🔵 Pyrra

prometheus-api-query
namespace=monitoring

Objective
99.000% in 1w

Availability
100.000%
Errors: 0
Total: 305

Error Budget
100.000%

Figure 10.3   Prometheus SLO in Pyrra (SLO details)

Figures 10.4 and 10.5 show the SLO for `holly` in Pyrra and (as configured and, hence, expected) we see the SLO of 75% breached.

Objectives > **ho11y-api-query**   🔵 Pyrra

ho11y-api-query
namespace=monitoring

Objective
75.000% in 1w

Availability
71.465%
Errors: 777
Total: 2,725

Error Budget
-14.140%

4w   1w   1d   12h   **1h**   **10s**

Error Budget   ⬀ Prometheus
What percentage of the error budget is left over time?

-8.00%

-10.00%

-12.00%

Figure 10.4   The `holly` service SLO in Pyrra (overview)

If you would like to learn more about Pyrra, check out the excellent KubeCon 2022 talk "SLO-Based Observability for All Kubernetes Cluster Components" with Pyrra

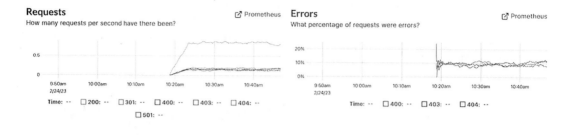

Requests
How many requests per second have there been?   ⤤ Prometheus

0.5	
0	

Time: -- ☐ 200: -- ☐ 301: -- ☐ 400: -- ☐ 403: -- ☐ 404: --
☐ 501: --

Errors
What percentage of requests were errors?   ⤤ Prometheus

Time: -- ☐ 400: -- ☐ 403: -- ☐ 404: --

Multi Burn Rate Alerts

STATE	SEVERITY	EXHAUSTION	THRESHOLD		SHORT BURN		LONG BURN	FOR	PROMETHEUS
inactive	critical	12h	3.500	>	0.253 (1m)	and	0.286 (15m)		⤤
inactive	critical	1d	1.750	>	0.305 (8m)	and	0.284 (1h30m)		⤤
inactive	warning	3d12h	0.500	>	0.284 (30m)	and	0.284 (6h)		⤤
pending	warning	1w	0.250	>	0.284 (1h30m)	and	0.286 (1d)		⤤

Figure 10.5   The `holly` service SLO in Pyrra (details)

lead maintainers, Matthias Loibl and Nadine Vehling (https://www.youtube.com/watch?v=AC38JtXXE50).

SLOTH

Sloth (https://sloth.dev) also uses Prometheus to generate SLOs. In a nutshell, it generates three rule groups per SLO, containing recording and alert rules for SLIs, informative metrics, and alerts. In addition, it features so-called SLI plug-ins (https://sloth.dev/sli-plugins/coredns-availability/), allowing you to abstract and extend SLIs, including plug-ins for CoreDNS, Istio, and Traefik. Like Pyrra, it comes with support for error budgets (how much wiggle room you have for an SLO) and burn rates (how quickly you're using up the budget).

Given the similarities and substantial overlap with Pyrra, we won't dive into how Sloth works. Simply pick the tool that fits your requirements better in this space. Next up, we'll cover commercial SLO and SLI tooling.

10.2.3 *Commercial SLO offerings*

As SLOs are going mainstream at time of writing, you can expect more and more commercial offerings. The following are some of the notable offerings available today:

- Nobl9 (https://www.nobl9.com/) is a complete SLO solution. It has the deepest integration and breadth of coverage, and if you're serious about SLOs, you will want to evaluate it.
- From a cloud-provider perspective, Google Cloud offers support for SLOs via its operations suite (http://mng.bz/vnEq).

- The Service Level Objectives status page (http://mng.bz/4Dwg) and the SLO Summary widget are both part of Datadog's alerting offerings.
- Honeycomb (https://www.honeycomb.io/slos) offers a trace-based SLO offering as part of their suite.
- Dynatrace allows you to define SLOs (http://mng.bz/QPBe) in their offering.
- New Relic provides a service level management feature (http://mng.bz/XNRM).
- Splunk offers SLO and SLI monitoring (http://mng.bz/yQmE) support.

The SLO commercial offering space is rapidly evolving, and you can expect an increasing number of cloud providers and ISVs to support SLOs natively going forward.

10.3 Considerations

As usual, open standards rule. In this space, OpenSLO (https://openslo.com) is the relevant (emerging) open specification for defining SLOs to enable vendor-agnostic tracking and interfacing with SLOs.

For example, in OpenSLO, you would represent the Pyrra walk-through example from earlier in the chapter (compare with listing 10.3) as follows:

```
apiVersion: openslo/v1
kind: SLO                          ◁──── We are defining an
metadata:                                OpenSLO SLO object.
  name: ho11y-api-query
  labels:
    prometheus: k8s
    role: alert-rules              ──── The reference to the
spec:                                   targeted service for
  service: ho11y          ◁────         this SLO
  indicator:
    metadata:
      name: ho11y-error
      displayName: ho11y error
    spec:
      ratioMetric:                 ──── In contrast to Pyrra, where we
        counter: true                   defined errors, here, we define
        good:             ◁────         what the "happy path" looks like.
          metricSource:
            metricSourceRef: prometheus-datasource
            type: Prometheus
            spec:
              query: ho11y_total{job="svc",http_status_code~="2.."})
        total:
          metricSource:
            metricSourceRef: prometheus-datasource
            type: Prometheus
            spec:
              query: ho11y_total{job="svc"}
  objectives:                              ──── The goal that this SLO
    - displayName: ho11y total errors           tracks: 75% availability
      target: 0.75          ◁────               (or non-error responses)
```

Usually, systems define SLOs and SLIs, such as with Kubernetes. See "Kubernetes scalability and performance SLIs/SLOs" (http://mng.bz/MBEm) for an example. Last but not least, if you want to start contributing in the space or just learn more, consider having a look at the excellent SLOconf (https://www.nobl9.com/community/sloconf) event, an annual gathering of the SRE community to exchange SLO-related updates and learnings.

Summary

- Reliability regulations are on the horizon, like security was 15 years ago.
- Using SLOs to measure and report reliability for compliance is becoming a hot topic in finance, communications, and aeronautics and will likely spread to other industries.
- To make contractual promises in SLAs quantifiable and automated, define SLIs to drive the goals (SLOs).
- SLAs are contractual constructs between a service provider and a service consumer.
- SLOs are goals your organization defines and can be used to inform SLAs.
- SLIs are the actual measurement or metric (depending on the service type) to verify to what extent a goal (the SLO) was fulfilled.
- There is open source tooling (Pyrra and Sloth) available to implement SLOs/SLIs for the Prometheus ecosystem.
- There are some commercial offerings for SLOs, especially Nobl9's tool.
- You don't have to go all in with SLOs (e.g., error budgets or burn rate); in fact, not many folks in the wild do so (yet), but defining service metrics (SLIs) and tracking them against established goals (SLOs) helps you and your customer.
- SLOs can be used as a means of improving alert accuracy—early warning systems (nonemergency) that reduce false positives and the number of one-off rules used to suppress alerts and improve trend-based early warnings that can be tied to runbooks and automated remediation.
- Make sure to build on open specifications—OpenSLO, in this space.

Signal correlation

This chapter covers

- What we mean by signal correlation
- Why you need correlation
- How to implement correlation
- Challenges implementing correlation

Cloud-native systems are *distributed systems*, which refers to many services working together to handle a request. When many services are working together, it turns out it's not always clear which service contributes to a failure or causes latency issues.

The four fundamental observability signal types (logs, metrics, traces, and profiles) each provide insights on their own; however, they typically can't answer all of your questions. Remember, the goal of observability is to derive actionable insights from the signals. So what should you do if a single signal type doesn't yield the insights you hoped for? Use more than one signal type—combine them.

Where might correlation come in handy? Glad you asked:

- *Incident response*—Imagine you're on call for a microservices-based app. You get paged, and the alert contains a link to a Grafana dashboard. From the

211

dashboard, you see an increased error rate in the app, and to figure out which services contribute to the error, you use metrics–traces correlation to find traces of services causing errors.

- *Root cause analysis*—Suppose there was a recent incident, and you want to figure out what caused it. Metrics telemetry provides you with information about the compute environment (e.g., region), and you can gather version information (e.g., about the libraries used, the service itself, etc.) from logs. To figure out what the causes of an outage were, you can use metrics–logs correlation to determine whether the problem is relevant for certain machine types, service versions, regions.
- *Service performance improvements*—Let's assume you're a developer working on a ticket that calls out a certain number of customers reporting slower execution for an endpoint. The service graph provided by distributed tracing allows you to pinpoint services that, together, handle the request path for said endpoint. To determine which services to improve, you use traces–profiles correlation and compare profiles of service versions you can optimize.

While it's possible to use multiple signal types together based on manual correlation, it's not an effective use of your time. By *manual signal correlation*, I mean starting with a signal type, such as traces, and, based on the time range covered, trying to find, for example, log lines of the services that contribute to the trace and hoping they are somewhat relevant. Hope is not a strategy. We will first discuss signal correlation on a conceptual level in this final chapter. Then, we will see correlation in action, using tooling you are already familiar with. Finally, we will wrap up with some considerations for implementing signal correlation.

11.1   *Correlation fundamentals*

Let's first define what we mean by *signal correlation* and then look at how it works conceptually. I've based the signal correlation definition on Bartek Płotka's thoughts in "Correlating Signals Efficiently in Modern Observability" (https://www.bwplotka.dev/ 2021/correlations-exemplars/). I've not only referenced Płotka's work because I know and trust him but also because he served as a tech lead in the CNCF TAG Observability.

> **DEFINITION**   *Signal correlation* is the metadata-driven process of connecting different signal types, with the goal of gaining actionable insights faster and/or more accurately. The metadata enables automation of multisignal observability. A correlation path is the transitioning from one signal type to a correlated one.

The correlation stack, shown in figure 11.1, shows the conceptual layers of how signal correlation can be achieved. Remember that we want to automate as much as possible, so the better the layers are integrated, the closer we may come to full automation.

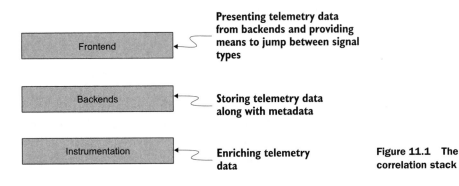

Figure 11.1 The correlation stack

The correlation stack, from bottom to top, consists of the following:

- *The instrumentation layer*—This layer comprises your code and the telemetry agent, enriching the telemetry data and ingesting it into backends. We covered this in detail in chapters 3 and 4. Note that without the support of this layer, the higher layers are challenging to implement. Many of the sources-related metadata pieces (e.g., which lambda function or pod in which namespace in which Kubernetes cluster emitted a, say, span) are only available at collection time, and it is hard to provide comprehensive correlation without said information.
- *The backends layer*—Telemetry data is stored along with metadata in this layer. This may consist of separate backends per signal type or backends with several signal types, such as OpenSearch. See also chapter 5, where we covered this topic in greater detail. This layer is mostly concerned with driving the next layer, offering the raw data that is then presented to the user for choosing a concrete correlation path.
- *The frontend layer*—Sometimes also referred to as the *presentation layer* (see chapter 6, where we covered the topic, including tooling), this layer is where signals are presented and can be used to consume correlated telemetry data. Various visualizations and renderings can help you quickly select, filter, and jump between signal types.

The metadata necessary to drive correlation can either be standardized after the fact (e.g., when using the Prometheus relabeling feature discussed in chapter 4) or up front. The latter approach, establishing defined semantics, is what OpenTelemetry does with its semantic conventions. Let's have a closer look at that now.

11.1.1 Correlation with OpenTelemetry

With semantic conventions (https://opentelemetry.io/docs/concepts/semantic-conventions/), OpenTelemetry defines a metadata scheme, including common names and sometimes common values for different kinds of telemetry data. More specifically, OpenTelemetry supports the following metadata to enable signal correlation in backends:

- *Resource attributes (http://mng.bz/a1nY)*—Capture information about the entity for which telemetry data is recorded. They may capture an entire hierarchy of entity identification. You can use them to describe, for example, a Kubernetes node in a specific cluster in a specified cloud region or a specific container in a pod running an application you care about.
- Signal attributes are specific to a signal type, including
  - *Traces (http://mng.bz/gBMn)*—Semantic conventions, including for HTTP client and server spans, for remote procedure calls, such as gRPC (https://grpc.io/) spans, messaging system (Apache Kafka, RabbitMQ, etc.) spans, exceptions associated with a span, and many others.
  - *Metrics (http://mng.bz/e1XZ)*—Semantic conventions for HTTP client and server metrics; RPC client and server metrics; standard system metrics, like CPU usage or disk I/O; hardware; and a whole list of other metrics.
  - *Log (http://mng.bz/pP00)*—Attribute semantic conventions are, at the time of publication, still experimental in nature. Only two are defined: one for log media (describing the source of a log, such as the file name or I/O stream) and an event attribute that can, for example, describe the business context (e.g., browser or device).

What would a concrete example of a resource and signal attribute look like? Let us assume we are running an app that consists of certain services. Assume one of them is `svc-wow`, in a namespace called `boom`, in an EKS cluster called `prod-42`, in the `eu-west-1` region, and that service exposes HTTP metrics.

This scenario would be represented in OpenTelemetry with the pod as the signal source, so we would use these resource attributes:

- For the EKS cluster the service is located in, we would use the `cloud.region` (http://mng.bz/OxDO) attribute with a value of `eu-west-1` and the AWS-specific `aws.eks.cluster.arn` (http://mng.bz/Y12Q) attribute with a value such as `arn:aws:ecs:eu-west-1:123456789123:cluster/prod-42`.
- For the Kubernetes namespace the service is located in, we would use the generic resource attribute (http://mng.bz/GyQ8) `service.namespace` with a value of `boom` and `service.name` with a value of `svc-wow`.
- The signal type we're looking at here is metrics, which means we are using signal attributes to provide metadata on the metrics emitted. Let's say the `svc-wow` service exposes an HTTP API, and we want to report on the inbound request duration. We would use the `http.server.duration` (http://mng.bz/zXYg) metric with attributes such as `http.method`, `http.status_code`, and `net.host.name`. Coincidentally, the `http_status_code` attribute is an example of an attribute where not only the name is standardized but also its values—that is, the official list of HTTP response status codes (https://www.rfc-editor.org/rfc/rfc7231#section-6), as defined in RFC 7231.

Table 11.1 provides an overview of possible combinations and transitions from one signal type to another, with traces representing the cross-services execution, metrics representing the numerical aggregates (e.g., percentage of errors), and logs as the signal type representing a single service along the request path. Note that these transitions are not specific to a format, such as OpenTelemetry.

Table 11.1 Overview of signal correlations

From/To	Traces	Metrics	Logs
Traces	Related spans	Trace to representative metrics	Trace to log lines from services
Metrics	Metrics to representative spans	Related metrics	Metrics to logs from services
Logs	Logs to spans from services	Logs to relevant metrics	Related logs

The term *correlation path* in the following subsections refers to the transitioning from one signal type to another, correlated one. This may include more than one transition. Let's dissect table 11.1 now, discussing specific correlations by signal type.

11.1.2 Correlating traces

In this first case, the starting points of correlation paths are traces, representing cross-service execution, covering synchronous services along the request path and, potentially, async services, such as message brokers. From here, we will transition to specific correlations.

To TRACES

Traces–traces correlation refers to finding related spans by environment or service. For example, you can use the Span Links feature (http://mng.bz/0KNW) in OpenTelemetry, which allows you to associate a span with one or more other spans, defining a causal relationship for asynchronous fire-and-forget workloads, where a parent span doesn't wait for its children to close before it closes itself. This is particularly useful for async services such as message buses and message queues, including Apache Kafka (https://kafka.apache.org/) and Amazon EventBridge (https://aws.amazon.com/eventbridge/).

To METRICS

Traces–metrics correlation means the input is a trace representing cross-service execution and the output consists of relevant metrics from services contributing to the spans of the input trace.

To LOGS

Traces–logs correlation means the input is a trace representing cross-service execution and the output consists of log lines from services contributing to the spans of the input trace. Correlation support in AWS X-Ray SDK for Java (http://mng.bz/KeaE) is an example.

11.1.3 Correlating metrics

The starting point of correlation paths in this case are time series of metrics—numerical aggregated values. From here we can transition to specific correlations.

TO TRACES

Metrics–traces correlation means you have a metric as input (e.g., graphed on a dashboard or from an alert), and the expected output consists of representative spans from services contributing to said time series. We will have a concrete look at such a correlation case in the next subsection, where we will use Prometheus, Jaeger, and Grafana to implement exemplar-based correlation between a metric and spans.

TO METRICS

Metrics–metrics correlation means related metrics (by type or service) (e.g., client-side and server-side errors).

TO LOGS

Metrics–logs correlation means the input is a metric (e.g., from a dashboard) and the output consists of log lines from services contributing to the aggregate value.

11.1.4 Correlating logs

The starting points of correlation paths in this case are logs from one or more services. From here we can transition to specific correlations.

TO TRACES

Logs–traces correlation means we have log lines of a service as an input and seek corresponding spans emitted from the service that wrote the log lines.

TO METRICS

Logs–metrics correlation uses log lines of a service as an input and outputs relevant metrics from said and related services (e.g., along the request path).

TO LOGS

Logs–logs correlation attempts to find related logs by service, environment, or severity. For example, you could ask for all ERROR logs from services along the request path.

11.1.5 Correlating profiles

We discussed the nature and use cases of profiles in chapter 9; they are somewhat comparable to log lines, as their scope is a single service. Profiles can be emitted automatically (via eBPF or language-specific means) or manually. In contrast to logs, profiles are numerical. So while many of the preceding to–from correlation observations apply, take into account that profiles are numerical values, at the end of the day (so in a sense, they behave like metrics, from a correlation point of view).

11.2 Using Prometheus, Jaeger, and Grafana for correlation

Now that you know what correlation is on a conceptual level, let's examine how to implement it. To do so, we will use a concrete example that shows how to do metrics–traces correlation based on exemplars. In the case of metrics–traces correlation, this means embedding a link from the metrics representation to a trace. This is done by inserting a trace ID so that when the metric is rendered in a time series graph, you can click on exemplars and jump directly to a representative trace and navigate its spans. Conceptually, this "embedding of the trace ID in a metric" would look something like the following (using the Prometheus exposition format or, to be more precise, Open-Metrics, since this feature only exists there):

```
a_counter 42.0 # {traceID="a6427ef2021cce03"}
```

Now, we'll move on to our example correlation setup.

11.2.1 Metrics–traces correlation example setup

We will be using Prometheus and Jaeger as backends and Grafana as the frontend. The example service in this example is based on the `echo` service we used in chapter 2. It emits spans that an OpenTelemetry collector routes to Jaeger, and at the same time, the collector scrapes the service `/metrics` endpoint for metrics with embedded trace IDs and makes them available to a Prometheus backend for scraping. You should already know all of these tools and how to configure them, so I will keep it brief here.

All the sources shown are in chapter 11, so change to that directory. First off, the `echo` service, written in Go, emits spans and exposes metrics. In addition, it now also supports OpenMetrics exemplars (http://mng.bz/9DZ0). The source code is in the echo/main.go file; we will only focus on the additions related to how to emit exemplars, and we will only cover the happy path (the error case looks more or less the same, but it returns a `500` code in 40% of the cases, rather than a `200`):

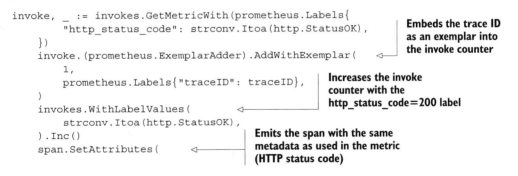

```
invoke, _ := invokes.GetMetricWith(prometheus.Labels{
        "http_status_code": strconv.Itoa(http.StatusOK),
    })
    invoke.(prometheus.ExemplarAdder).AddWithExemplar(
        1,
        prometheus.Labels{"traceID": traceID},
    )
invokes.WithLabelValues(
    strconv.Itoa(http.StatusOK),
).Inc()
span.SetAttributes(
```

Embeds the trace ID as an exemplar into the invoke counter

Increases the invoke counter with the http_status_code=200 label

Emits the span with the same metadata as used in the metric (HTTP status code)

Besides emitting spans and metrics, with embedded exemplars, there's only one other thing to pay attention to in main.go: the configuration of the Prometheus metrics exposition. We need to make sure we're using the OpenMetrics format, which is done like so:

```
http.Handle("/metrics", promhttp.HandlerFor(
        registry,
        promhttp.HandlerOpts{
            EnableOpenMetrics: true,
        },
    ))
```

Now, we need to pull in all the dependencies, so (assuming you have Go version 1.20 or above installed) do the following:

```
go mod vendor
```

You should now see a subdirectory, vendor/, which has all the necessary packages available locally.

Next, let's go back to the main directory, ch11/metrics-traces, and bring up the Docker Compose stack defined in docker-compose.yaml:

```
docker-compose -f docker-compose.yaml up
```

The following listing shows the relevant snippets of the Docker Compose file we are using for the metrics–traces example.

Listing 11.1 The relevant snippets of the Docker Compose file for the correlation setup

```
prometheus:
    image: prom/prometheus:v2.33.4
    ports:
    - "9090:9090"
    volumes:
    - ./prometheus.yml:/etc/prometheus/prometheus.yml
    command:
    - "--config.file=/etc/prometheus/prometheus.yml"
    - "--storage.tsdb.path=/prometheus"
    - "--enable-feature=exemplar-storage"      ◁─┐  Need to configure
grafana:                                          Prometheus to support
    image: grafana/grafana:latest                 exemplars (in-memory)
    ports:
    - "3000:3000"
    volumes:                                ◁─┐  Used for automatically configuring
    - ./grafana-storage:/var/lib/grafana        the Prometheus and Jaeger data
    - ./grafana:/etc/grafana/provisioning       sources as well as the dashboard
    - ./grafana/dashboards:/var/lib/grafana/dashboards
```

Let us move on to the OpenTelemetry collector configuration shown in the following listing—the otel-config.yaml file.

Listing 11.2 The OpenTelemetry collector configuration for the correlation setup

```
exporters:
  prometheus:
    endpoint: "0.0.0.0:1234"
    metric_expiration: 180m
```

```
    enable_open_metrics: true        ◁         Enables exemplar
jaeger:                                         support in the
    endpoint: jaeger:14250                      Prometheus exporter
    tls:
        insecure: true
service:                         The metrics and
    pipelines:       ◁───┤       traces pipelines
        metrics:
            receivers: [ prometheus ]
            processors: [ batch ]
            exporters: [ logging, prometheus ]
        traces:
            receivers: [ otlp ]
            processors: [ batch ]
            exporters: [ logging, jaeger ]
```

If you want to see the raw exemplars, you could do the following on your machine (assuming Docker is running; http://127.0.0.1:8888/ is where the echo-svc is serving):

Sending this HTTP header   **The echo service endpoint,**
is key to get the exemplar   **serving the metrics in**
(asking for OpenMetrics).   **OpenMetrics format**

```
curl -H "Accept: application/openmetrics-text" \
        "http://127.0.0.1:8888/metrics"        ◁
```

When you execute the preceding curl command, you should see something akin to the following output:

A simple dimension,
represented via the
label for the HTTP
status code

```
# HELP echo Total invocations of the echo service endpoint.
# TYPE echo counter
echo_total 930.0 # {http_status_code="200",        ◁
                traceID="f2a9e19d5c34427cf2f50a430de9fa3c"}   ◁
                1.0 1.6801173123788908e+09
# EOF
```

The exemplar represented via
the Prometheus label traceID

With that, we have the setup in place to use signal correlation. Let's do that now.

11.2.2 Using metrics–traces correlation

It's time to correlate! Head over to your browser and enter localhost:3000, which opens up Grafana (no credentials required). Now, open the dashboard called Echo Service Dashboard With Exemplars, and wait a couple of minutes to gather enough data. You should then see something akin to figure 11.2. The first row contains the echo_total metric, with 200 and 500 status codes, and when you look closely, you will see some tiny dots toward the bottom of the graph. These allow the Grafana time series visualization to render exemplars. Hover over them, and you will see the span information; if you click on them, you will get to the Jaeger trace view depicted in figure 11.3.

The lower part of figure 11.2 shows error traces that you can also use to navigate to the Jaeger trace view.

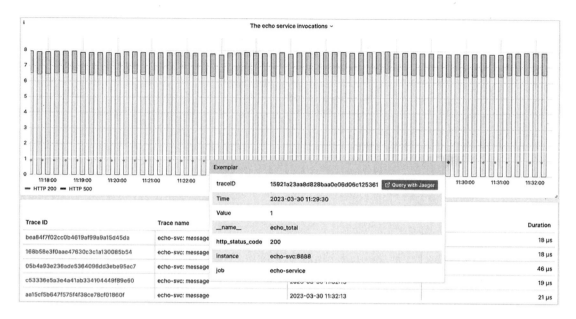

Figure 11.2   Screenshot of the Grafana dashboard with exemplars (the small dots at the bottom) for the `echo` service

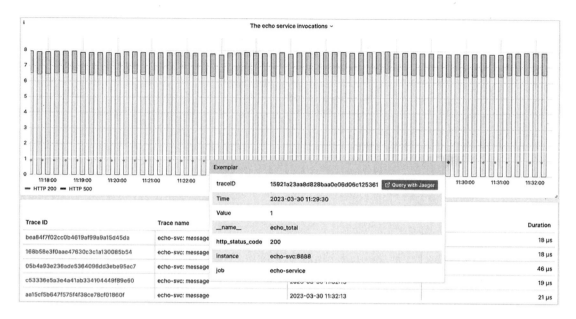

Figure 11.3   Screenshot of the Jaeger view for the `echo` service, focusing on the error span representing a 500 response

Take your time to explore the views and how to get from the metric, using exemplars, to the traces. It's a lot to take in, so this may take some time. Next up, we'll have a quick review of commercial offerings in the signal correlation space.

11.3   Signal correlation support in commercial offerings

While it's still early days and not all correlation paths are supported by every provider, there is already core support for a number of correlations available in the commercial space. Oftentimes, these are related to traces–logs and metrics–traces support.

Lets first have a look at cloud providers and their native monitoring and observability solutions:

- AWS has a comprehensive correlation strategy based on OpenTelemetry (http://mng.bz/jPqV), with traces–logs correlation supported via AWS X-Ray and Amazon CloudWatch (http://mng.bz/WzWd).
- Like AWS, Azure is standardizing on OpenTelemetry. For example, see the Application Insights—based correlation support (http://mng.bz/8rAW).
- Google Cloud offers support for correlating log entries (https://cloud.google .com/logging/docs/view/correlate-logs) in its operations suite.

Now, we will move on to commercial offerings from observability ISVs. In the observability space, almost all vendors offer one or another form of correlation support in their solutions:

- AppDynamics has support for custom correlation in languages such as Java (http://mng.bz/EQvD) and .NET (http://mng.bz/N2px) for metrics to events.
- In Datadog, you can correlate metrics (https://docs.datadoghq.com/dashboards/ correlations/), and they offer traces–logs correlation (https://www.datadoghq .com/blog/request-log-correlation/).
- With Dynatrace, you get a rich set of traces correlation (http://mng.bz/D4ng).
- Honeycomb provides a nice comparison (https://www.honeycomb.io/comparisons) of their approach to correlation to other APMs, pointing out things like their query speed and support for high-cardinality data analysis.
- Lightstep offers tracing-related (http://mng.bz/lWmR) correlation support.
- Logz.io offers traces–logs (http://mng.bz/Bm6l) correlation based on OpenSearch.
- In New Relic's offering, there is support for configuring correlation logic with decisions (http://mng.bz/d1R1), offering a blend of correlation paths.
- Splunk has an interesting approach, supporting the correlate command (http://mng.bz/rWXj) that lets you see an overview of the co-occurrence between fields in your telemetry data.
- Sumo Logic allows you to correlate signals in the context of security investigations via their Cloud SIEM (https://www.sumologic.com/blog/siem-investigation-correlation/) offering.

Now that you have an idea of both commercial offerings and open source tooling in the correlation space, let us move on to some general considerations on correlations and what to pay attention to when introducing them.

11.4   Considerations

By now, it should be clear that in the context of gaining actionable insights efficiently, signal correlation plays a pivotal role. I won't pretend it is easy to achieve complete and fully automated correlation, even in the best case, where you have a multisignal backend and a single pane of glass. There are, at the time of publication, still a large number of challenges associated with implementing correlation, representing the single largest risk category in the observability space. So on one hand, you shouldn't treat them as an afterthought, and on the other hand, you should be aware of the limitations and set your expectations appropriately. For example, if you're in a platform team (internal developer platform to streamline infra and app provisioning so that one can avoid TicketOps), you may want to prioritize correlation accordingly.

> **NOTE**   Here, *TicketOps* is not referring to the company but the slightly derogatory term that used to describe the process of developers creating tickets in, say, Jira, with operations roles (in the platform team) resolving them asynchronously. This may take some time (e.g., days or weeks) and is contrary to the automation mantra put forward by DevOps.

And now, without further ado, let's have a look at the concrete challenges of implementing signal correlation in your organization. I've grouped them into three buckets, and for some of the challenges, I suggest one or more remediations you could try out to mitigate the risk.

11.4.1   Early days

First off, let's review the main challenges associated with the state of observability, in general, and implementations, in particular.

LACK OF STANDARDS

APM and monitoring tools, open source and commercial alike, use different formats for the telemetry signals as well as various terminologies. This makes it challenging to correlate signals across systems.

The following is an appropriate remediation: if you want true interoperability and to avoid vendor lock-in, use OpenTelemetry.

LACK OF METADATA

To drive correlation, you need the connective tissue represented by metadata, including but not limited to EC2 metadata, Prometheus labels, Kubernetes labels, and OpenTelemetry resource and signal attributes. Few platforms and systems to date are "observability first" (designed with observability support), so it may be difficult to acquire said metadata or involve manual work.

The following are appropriate remediations:

- Evaluate (compute) platforms according to their metadata richness and degree of automation.
- Use OpenTelemetry-based systems.

11.4.2 Signals

Next, we will look at challenges related to the signals themselves.

TELEMETRY SIGNALS VOLUME

The overall volume of data generated from different sources makes it difficult to correlate signals efficiently. This is not just a cost issue but can have serious impact on performance and flow. For example, if you're indexing logs and your tooling is overwhelmed serving user lookup requests, operators may be slowed down, frustrated, and effectively blocked.

The following are appropriate remediations:

- Employ selective ingest, meaning you limit the volume up front. This can be quite tricky, since you don't know ahead of time what the "valuable" signals are that help getting to actionable insights. For logging, make sure you have a `priority` or `loglevel` attribute attached to your events. This lets you do things like *ingest all errors, 50% of all warnings, and 1% of informational log lines.*
- An a posteriori approach refers to employing machine learning (ML) to detect patterns. This can help you deal with the volume, in that it enables you to isolate and prioritize relevant events that could lead to the desired insights. Be aware, though, that with ML-driven anomaly detection, the cost is in the compute, not storage, so the ingestion costs are far higher than signal retention.

HIGH CARDINALITY

High-cardinality data, as discussed in chapter 5 (especially the cardinality explosion challenge), can make it difficult to correlate signals. This is because values may only occur a few times or, in the most extreme case, once.

The following are appropriate remediations:

- Limit cardinality. This entails enforcing hard limits, with the downside being that you don't know, in the general case, what the right cutoff point is, and you, again, may lose out on valuable signals.
- Make sure the observability offering of your choice supports high cardinality, which is especially important for Honeycomb and Lightstep.

SAMPLING

In the case of distributed tracing, sampling (see chapter 8, where we discussed this in detail) can be a challenge for correlation. Missing spans can cause holes in the correlation path, and with that, the overall usefulness decreases. There are a few vendors that can help you with that; for example, Honeycomb has a smart sampler, which uses a different sample rate for errors than the happy path. This is a variation on pretagging valuable signals.

DATA PRIVACY AND SECURITY

Many industries as well as geographies, such as Europe's General Data Protection Regulation (GDPR; https://commission.europa.eu/law/law-topic/data-protection_en), have policies requiring the de-identifying of data, such as removing personally identifiable information (PII). With that, it could be the case that, akin to sampling, parts of the information to drive correlation are deliberately not present. In addition, privacy legislation or industry compliance standards may demand that signals be handled strictly in-house and not sent to an SaaS provider or cloud provider outside a certain region.

11.4.3 *User experience*

Last, but most certainly not least, we will discuss challenges related to user experience (UX).

LACK OF ACTIONABLE INSIGHTS

Systems may implement some support for correlation, but I've found that it can be cumbersome or unintuitive to use. In that case, folks tend to not bother and, as a result, not use the feature.

The following is an appropriate remediation: besides (as a vendor) paying attention to UX, as an end user, you could evaluate offerings according to the value of insights they generate. Dynatrace and New Relic both provide (ML-generated) recommendations and insights, which may serve as a starting point for your evaluation.

END-TO-END SUPPORT

Sometimes, the UX challenges come from a lack of end-to-end support. This challenge may affect instrumentation, agents, backends, frontends, and so on.

The following are appropriate remediations:

- Use fully vertical integrated offerings, such as Datadog, New Relic, and Splunk, that own the entire stack.
- Bet on open standards, specifically, OpenTelemetry. At the time of writing, there is one area not yet covered by standards: querying backends. The community has identified this issue and is working on query standardization (http://mng.bz/V1jx) in the context of the CNCF Technical Advisory Group (TAG) on Observability.

11.5 *Conclusion*

With these considerations on implementing signal correlation in mind, we now conclude not only this chapter but the book itself. Stick around for the appendix, where we will get our hands dirty implementing observability in the context of an multisignal, multiprogramming languages app, using OpenTelemetry.

I would love to hear from you about your challenges and success stories regarding observability and anything else you'd like to share. Please reach out at mh9@olly .engineering. May the insights be with you!

Summary

- One signal type is usually not enough to gain actionable insights.
- Signal correlation is the metadata-driven process of connecting different signal types to gain actionable insights faster and more accurately.

- A correlation path can include more than one transition—for example, starting with a time series representing a metric to related spans to logs lines or profiles of a particular service.
- The metadata necessary to drive correlation can either be standardized after the fact (e.g., Prometheus relabeling) or up front (e.g., OpenTelemetry's semantic conventions).
- Not all correlation paths are equal. Some, like metrics–traces or traces–logs are widely used and supported, while others are not.
- Exemplars (in OpenMetrics and OpenTelemetry) allow you to do metrics–traces correlation by embedding a pointer to a trace in a metric.
- We're still in the early days of signal correlation; be aware of the limitations and set expectations accordingly.
- There are several challenges associated with implementing correlation, especially concerning UX and signals volume, cardinality, and sampling.
- Using OpenTelemetry is likely the most efficient and effective way to hedge against challenges in the correlation space.

appendix
A Kubernetes
end-to-end example

In this appendix, we will work through an end-to-end observability sample application in Kubernetes. Throughout the book, we've been using Docker Compose as our tool of choice. It has a number of advantages as an educational device; however, in reality, you will more likely use Kubernetes, Amazon ECS, or HashiCorp Nomad as an orchestrator. So this appendix will offer you a more native and consistent approach that covers all the tracing, metrics, and logging topics we discussed and allow you to play around with the setup.

> **TIP** You *could* use kompose (https://kompose.io/user-guide/) to turn any of the Docker Compose example files we've covered into Kubernetes resources (e.g., deployments and services) to get a feeling for how to work with the OSS tooling discussed in the book.

Luckily for us, there is already something available that fits the bill: the OpenTelemetry community demo (https://opentelemetry.io/docs/demo/). The demo covers several services written in different programming languages and features the tooling we've discussed. We will first discuss the demo and how it works, then cover the prerequisites to run it, and then walk through the demo together.

A.1 Overview

The OpenTelemetry demo is a microservices-based shopping app that uses 12 different programming languages, including Java, JavaScript, Python, and .NET, to implement services (https://opentelemetry.io/docs/demo/services/). The demo has all its services instrumented, emitting spans, metrics, and log lines. We won't be covering the details of the demo services and their interactions here, but if you're

interested in diving deeper, check out the OpenTelemetry docs that discuss the demo
architecture (https://opentelemetry.io/docs/demo/architecture/).

Figure A.1 shows the telemetry flow in the OpenTelemetry demo.

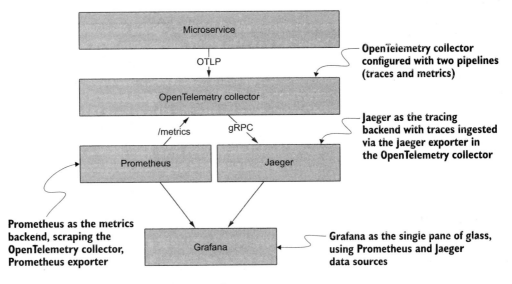

Figure A.1   OpenTelemetry demo telemetry flow

The relevant bits in the telemetry flow are

- *Microservices*—Instrumented to send telemetry data to the OpenTelemetry collector, using OTLP
- *The OpenTelemetry collector*—Has two pipelines configured (see listing A.1)
- *Prometheus*—The metrics backend
- *Jaeger*—The tracing backend
- *Grafana*—The single pane of glass, using Prometheus and Jaeger data sources

The OpenTelemetry collector configuration (http://mng.bz/x4p6) is shown in greater
detail in the following listing.

Listing A.1   OpenTelemetry collector configuration

```
receivers:
  otlp:                       We receive
    protocols:                signals via OTLP.
      grpc:
      http:
        cors:
          allowed_origins:
            - "http://*"
            - "https://*"
```

```
exporters:
  otlp:
    endpoint: "jaeger:4317"
    tls:
      insecure: true
  logging:
  prometheus:
    endpoint: "otelcol:9464"
    resource_to_telemetry_conversion:
      enabled: true
    enable_open_metrics: true

processors:
  batch:
  transform:
    metric_statements:
    - context: metric
      statements:
      - set(description, "Measures the duration of inbound HTTP requests")
        where name == "http.server.duration"
  filter:
    metrics:
      exclude:
        match_type: strict
        metric_names:
          - queueSize

connectors:
  spanmetrics:

service:
  pipelines:
    traces:
      receivers: [otlp]
      processors: [batch]
      exporters: [otlp, logging, spanmetrics]
    metrics:
      receivers: [otlp, spanmetrics]
      processors: [filter, transform, batch]
      exporters: [prometheus, logging]
    logs:
      receivers: [otlp]
      processors: [batch]
      exporters: [logging]
```

We have three exporters: Prometheus, Jaeger, and logging (to stdout).

We're using the spanmetrics connector to derive RED metrics from spans.

The pipelines are configured, with one for traces (connecting to metrics), one for metrics, and one for logs (to stdout only).

You can run the OpenTelemetry demo in several environments; we will be using the Kubernetes (http://mng.bz/Ao5Q) deployment in the following walk-through. But first, we need to make sure we have everything in place so that we can run the demo.

A.2 Prerequisites

To install the OpenTelemetry demo in Kubernetes, you will need a Kubernetes cluster:

- If you want to execute locally, some popular choices are
  - Docker Desktop (https://docs.docker.com/desktop/kubernetes/)
  - kind (https://kind.sigs.k8s.io/)
  - K3s (https://k3s.io/)
  - minikube (https://minikube.sigs.k8s.io/docs/)
  - Microk8s (https://microk8s.io/)
- Cloud providers have managed Kubernetes offerings, depending on where you typically work. Check out the following:
  - Amazon Elastic Kubernetes Service (EKS; https://aws.amazon.com/eks/)
  - Azure Kubernetes Service (AKS; https://learn.microsoft.com/en-us/azure/aks/)
  - Google Kubernetes Engine (GKE; https://cloud.google.com/kubernetes-engine)

You will also need the following CLI tools:

- kubectl—Install via the instructions in the Kubernetes docs (https://kubernetes.io/docs/tasks/tools/).
- eksctl—Install as described in the docs (https://github.com/eksctl-io/eksctl#installation).
- *Helm*—Install based on the docs (https://v3-1-0.helm.sh/docs/intro/install/).
- jq—Install via the docs (https://jqlang.github.io/jq/download/).
- curl *and* watch—Should be available on your system; otherwise, consult your Linux distro or Windows docs.

I recommend having at least two medium-sized nodes available in your data plane. For example, I'm using EKS with a three-node cluster that is using t2.large (https://instances.vantage.sh/aws/ec2/t2.large) EC2 instances (with two vCPUs and 8 GB of RAM per node).

To provision the EKS cluster, I'm using eksctl (https://eksctl.io/) with the config file otel-demo-cluster.yaml, shown in the following listing.

Listing A.2 EKS cluster configuration

```
apiVersion: eksctl.io/v1alpha5
kind: ClusterConfig
metadata:
  name: otel-demo
  region: eu-west-1
  version: "1.24"
iam:
  withOIDC: true
```

Make sure to set this to your region (here, in Dublin, Ireland, eu-west-1).

This will provision the OIDC provider so that you can attach IAM policies if you want to change the OpenTelemetry collector config, for example, to send metrics to Amazon Managed Service for Prometheus or traces to AWS X-Ray.

```
nodeGroups:
- name: default-mng
    instanceType: t2.large
    desiredCapacity: 3
cloudWatch:
    clusterLogging:
        enableTypes: ["*"]
```

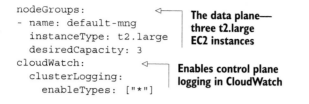

**The data plane—
three t2.large
EC2 instances**

**Enables control plane
logging in CloudWatch**

Then, provision and launch the EKS cluster as follows:

```
$ eksctl create cluster -f otel-demo-cluster.yaml
```

Wait 10 to 15 minutes, and then verify (you may see fewer nodes, depending on your settings):

```
$ kubectl get nodes
NAME                STATUS   ROLES    AGE      VERSION
ip-1..7.eu-west-1   Ready    <none>   2d23h    v1.24.10-eks-48e63af
ip-1..4.eu-west-1   Ready    <none>   3d14h    v1.24.10-eks-48e63af
ip-1..1.eu-west-1   Ready    <none>   2d23h    v1.24.10-eks-48e63af
```

Now, we're ready for the demo walk-through.

A.3   *Demo walk-through*

First off, we will install the OpenTelemetry demo. After installation, we'll be ready to use it!

A.3.1   *Installing the demo*

Use the following commands to install the demo. First off, we need to add the Helm repository of the demo, like so:

```
$ helm repo add open-telemetry \
       https://open-telemetry.github.io/opentelemetry-helm-charts
```

Now, we can install the demo:

```
$ helm install my-otel-demo \
      open-telemetry/opentelemetry-demo
```

Verify that everything has come up; this may take a few minutes. You should see something like the following (effectively, you want to make sure all pods are in the Running status; note that I have edited the output to fit):

```
$ kubectl -n default get pods
NAME                          READY  STATUS    RESTARTS      AGE
my-otel-demo-accountingse...  1/1    Running   4 (13d ago)   13d
my-otel-demo-adservice-86...  1/1    Running   0             13d
my-otel-demo-cartservice7...  1/1    Running   0             13d
my-otel-demo-checkoutserv...  1/1    Running   4 (13d ago)   13d
my-otel-demo-currencyserv...  1/1    Running   0             13d
my-otel-demo-emailservice...  1/1    Running   58 (83m ago)  13d
```

```
my-otel-demo-featureflags...  1/1   Running   1  (13d ago)     13d
my-otel-demo-ffspostgres-...  1/1   Running   0                13d
my-otel-demo-frauddetecti...  1/1   Running   0                13d
my-otel-demo-frontend-65d...  1/1   Running   0                13d
my-otel-demo-frontendprox...  1/1   Running   0                13d
my-otel-demo-grafana-8445...  1/1   Running   0                13d
my-otel-demo-jaeger-85484...  1/1   Running   2  (11d ago)     13d
my-otel-demo-kafka-77bfdc...  1/1   Running   0                13d
my-otel-demo-loadgenerato...  1/1   Running   7  (31h ago)     13d
my-otel-demo-otelcol-b75c...  1/1   Running   0                13d
my-otel-demo-paymentservi...  1/1   Running   0                13d
my-otel-demo-productcatal...  1/1   Running   0                13d
my-otel-demo-prometheus-s...  1/1   Running   0                11d
my-otel-demo-quoteservice...  1/1   Running   0                13d
my-otel-demo-recommendati...  1/1   Running   0                13d
my-otel-demo-redis-cf9dd8...  1/1   Running   8  (7h27m ago)   13d
my-otel-demo-shippingserv...  1/1   Running   0                13d
```

Now, we're ready to use the demo. Congrats!

A.3.2   Using the demo

To use the demo from your local machine (to access, for example, the Grafana UI), you first need to forward network traffic from the Kubernetes cluster to your machine.

First, we will expose the `frontendproxy` service. Use the following command to achieve this:

```
kubectl port-forward \
        svc/my-otel-demo-frontendproxy 8080:8080
```

For spans to be properly collected from your local browser, you will also need to expose the OpenTelemetry collector (`4318` is the OTLP port):

```
kubectl port-forward \
        svc/my-otel-demo-otelcol 4318:4318
```

If you now go to localhost:8080 (http://localhost:8080/), you should see something akin to figure A.2 (the OpenTelemetry demo shop front page).

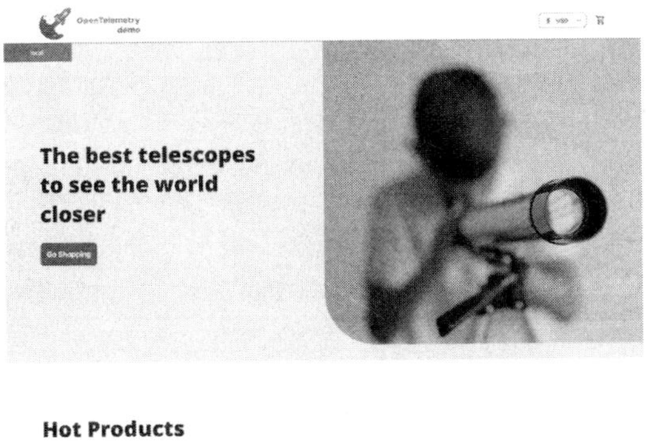

Hot Products

Figure A.2   Screenshot of the OpenTelemetry demo frontpage (shop)

Click Go Shopping, and start to add items to your shopping basket, and then check out with those items (don't worry—it's mocked, so you won't be using real money). While clicking around is a good way to get started, we don't want to wait too long to generate telemetry signals, right? That's why we're using a load generator (see figure A.3), which you can find at http://localhost:8080/loadgen/.

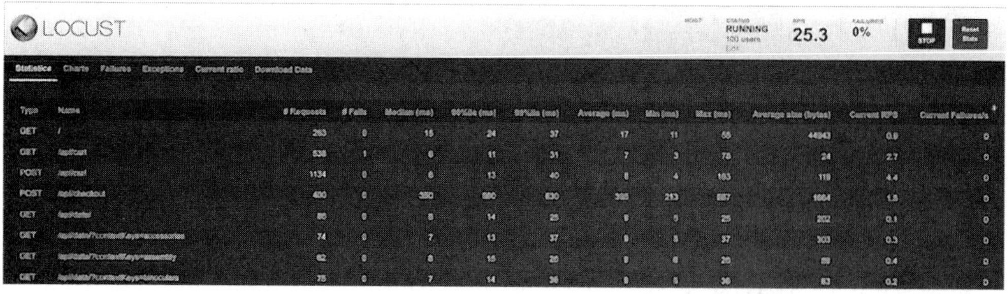

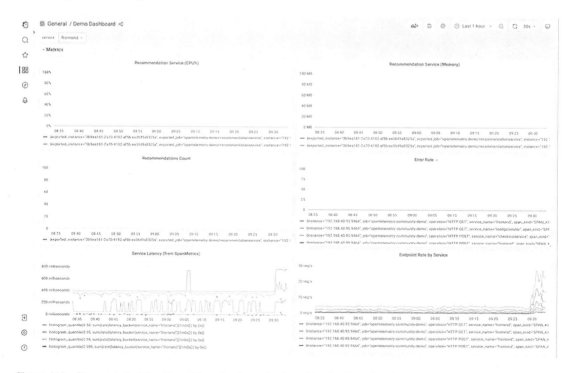

Figure A.3   Screenshot of the OpenTelemetry demo load generator

Figure A.4 shows Grafana as the single pane of glass. To be exact, that's the demo app dashboard showing you the `frontend` service metrics. Visit http://localhost:8080/grafana/ to get there.

Figure A.4   Screenshot of the OpenTelemetry demo Grafana (frontend service dashboard)

Figure A.5 shows the OpenTelemetry collector dashboard in Grafana.

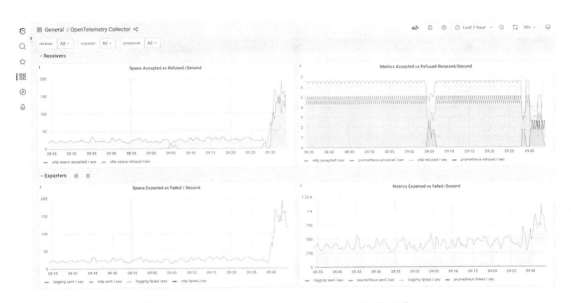

Figure A.5   Screenshot of the OpenTelemetry demo Grafana (collector dashboard)

Now, let's turn our attention to traces. Figure A.6 shows the Jaeger UI, accessible via http://localhost:8080/jaeger/ui/. What you see here is the span or trace view.

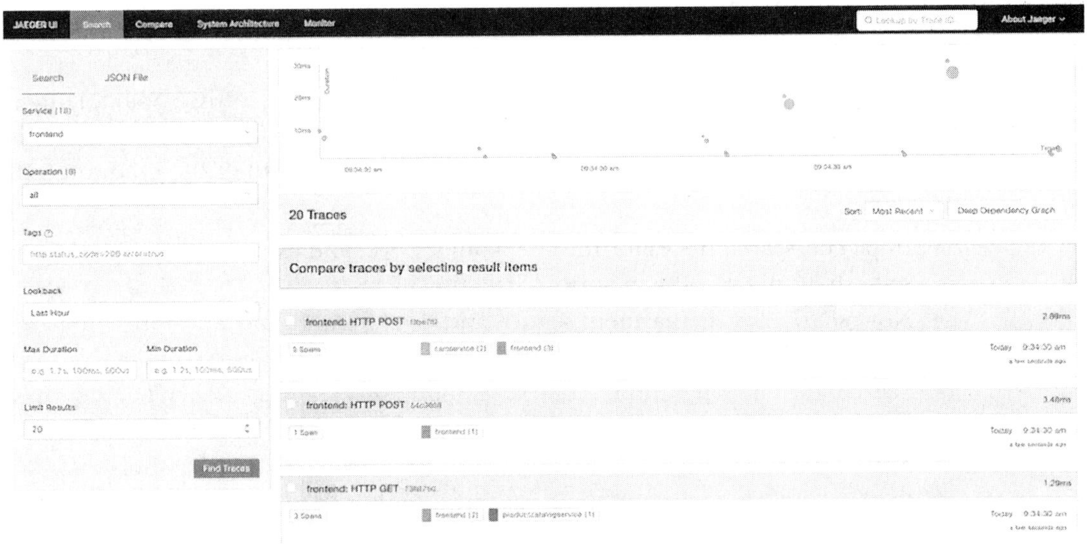

Figure A.6   Screenshot of the OpenTelemetry demo Jaeger (trace view)

Figure A.7 shows the Jaeger UI, showing the dynamic rendering of the OpenTelemetry demo app in the system architecture view.

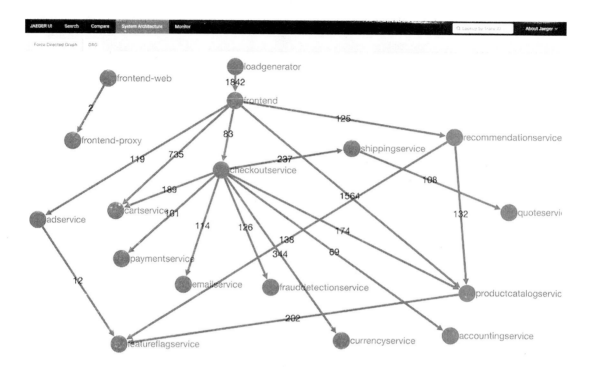

Figure A.7   Screenshot of the OpenTelemetry demo Jaeger (service map view)

There are even more screenshots available via the demo site (https://opentelemetry .io/docs/demo/screenshots/), if you don't want to set it up yourself.

To give you some ideas to explore, consider doing any or all of the following with the demo:

- In Jaeger, search traces for the checkout service, and examine a trace. Ask yourself, what call takes the majority of the time?
- Now, search for the payment service and do the same. Did you notice anything similar to the checkout service?
- Search for the operation `oteldemo.ShippingService/GetQuote`. What do these traces have in common?
- Search for `frontendproxy`. Why is the trace you see comparatively short?
- In the load-generator tab, increase the number of users to a larger number (10x, 50x, etc.). Now, how do the dashboards change, overall? How do the trace durations change?

In the context of the OpenTelemetry project, the community is also working on various demo scenarios; for example, check out the "Using Metrics and Traces to Diagnose a Memory Leak" scenario (http://mng.bz/ZqN9), which is already available online.

index